Work Left Undone

CHOICES & COMPROMISES
OF TALENTED FEMALES

Sally Morgan Reis

CREATIVE LEARNING PRESS, INC.,
PO Box 320
Mansfield Center, Connecticut 06250
Phone: 860-429-8118 • 860-429-1653
Fax: 860-429-7783
www.neca.com/~clp

Editor: Rachel A. Knox

ISBN: 0-936386-76-2

Cover Artwork: *The Pattern of Our Being*
by Brenda J. Bergen, Storrs, CT
© 1998, Brenda J. Bergen

Permissions

Ladder of Years by Anne Tyler. Published by Alfred Knopf. ©1995.
Paths of Power by Natasha Josefowitz. Published by Addison Wesley.
©1980 Natasha Josefowitz.

❧

Dedication

This book is dedicated to my lively and spirited daughters,
Sara and Liza,
and to my stepsons, Mark and Scott,
—all an important part of my life;
To my sisters and brothers,
Jane, Rick, John, Kris, and 'Beth,
who have shared so much;
To my mother, Letitia,
who provided unequivocal love and affection;
To my father, Dick, who enjoyed having a smart
daughter and encouraging her aspirations,
And especially to Joe,
who has always believed in me and supported
my dreams and hopes.

❧

ACKNOWLEDGMENTS

Many people have helped me explore and develop my interests and research about gifted and talented females. My husband, Joseph Renzulli, has provided unwavering support and constant belief in me. His sense of joy in any success I have had in my life has provided a basis for my journey to find my own voice and explore my talents. Our children have also encouraged me and taken on additional responsibilities to provide me with time for my work. Sara and Liza have taught me about what smart girls experience in today's world in addition to providing me with a better reason to finish this book. My parents and brothers and sisters have also been an ongoing source of humor and love throughout my life. I am grateful to my entire family.

Carolyn Callahan first exposed me to her work in the area of gifted females in the late 1970s and has been a role model, colleague, and friend for a very long time. Other friends have also encouraged me in my work including Sandra Kaplan, Karen Case, Peg Beecher, and all of my friends at the Neag Center for Gifted Education and Talent Development at the University of Connecticut—Jean Gubbins, Deb Burns, and Karen Westberg. I thank them all. A valued colleague and friend in the School of Education, Miriam Cherkes-Julkowski, provided me with the title of this book during a special conversation, and I thank her.

I have had the privilege of working with other talented women who have helped me in numerous ways during the last ten years—Dee Korner, Ann Marie Fortier, Dawn Guenther, Judith Matthews, Cathy Suroviak, and especially Joann Easton, who has provide me with great personal and professional encouragement. Several of my graduate students read drafts of this book and I thank them. I especially acknowledge the help of Nancy Bickley, Robin Schader, Melissa Small, Alex Guenther, and Tara Brinckerhoff whose comments and insights were particularly meaningful to me. I also thank Rachel Knox, Deb

Briatico, Kris Morgan, and Lori Frazier of Creative Learning Press for their editorial help and suggestions.

I also acknowledge the contributions of my colleagues who worked with me on many of the studies cited and discussed in depth in this book. All studied gifted females with me and provided ideas, feedback, and ample time for discussion as we completed our studies. They are Alane Starko, Katherine Gavin, Bob Kirschenbaum, Leticia Hernandez, Mary Rizza, Nancy Lashaway-Bokina, Jann Leppien, Del Siegle, Stuart Omdal, Sunghee Park, Marcia Gentry, Laurie Shute, Caroline Cohen, and Patricia Schuler. I have been blessed with the opportunity to work with motivated and committed doctoral students who are now friends and colleagues, and I thank them all.

Finally, I acknowledge the contributions of the girls and women involved in my research. I learned from all of them, was inspired and motivated to work harder by what these girls and women had taught me, and thank them all for their time, wisdom, and patience.

The intricate challenge of trying to define and write about talented women and the difficult choices they face caused me to spend the last twenty years involved in this area of research. I have researched thousands and interviewed hundreds of young girls, teenagers, and women who are now between the ages of 6 and 93. This work has helped me understand the labyrinth of choices faced by talented females and realize that the outcomes of their choices will have an impact on many lives. In the midst of this research, I became a mother of two daughters and came to understand, with humility, how much more complex the issues are than I had previously imagined. Each time a baby cried and I put away my work to go to her, or stayed home from work to take care of a sick child, or made a choice that was good for my daughters but not for my career, I reflected on the choices made by women. As I watch my daughters grow, I continue to learn more, especially about the convoluted stereotypes they encounter in their world outside of my home.

This book describes the current network of choices and options facing gifted and talented girls and women today and how the personal choices and decisions they make influence the ways in which they develop and use their talents. I began this book in 1984, and over the next fourteen years I struggled with bouts of frustration as I tried to find blocks of time to work on it. However, I also continued to learn—from the research I was conducting, my daughters and friends, and the many talented women who entered and completed the graduate program in gifted education at the University of Connecticut. Although I was often disappointed that I was not able to finish this book earlier, I realize now that I am fortunate to have had the opportunities provided by the discontinuities in my life. These periods enabled me to learn about the additional challenges of understanding gifted females, both those that come from the changes in my life (especially those changes brought about by the birth of my daughters, Sara and Liza) and those that come with maturation and aging. I have had the time to reflect upon the ways our society defines accomplishment, a definition which often omits the multiple ways in which talented girls and women achieve. I hope this book causes readers to devote more thought to the ways in which we all regard accomplishment in individuals and more respect to the variety of ways in which individuals develop their talents.

TABLE OF CONTENTS

~:~

❦

Part Two: Case Studies of Gifted & Talented Females Throughout the Lifespan

List of Figures

Part One

~:~

Issues & Barriers Facing
Gifted & Talented Women

CHAPTER ONE

~:~

THE ISSUES & CHALLENGES FACING TALENTED WOMEN

Life is a verb, not a noun.
—*Charlotte Perkins Gilman*

*Tremendous amounts of talent are being lost to our society
just because that talent wears a skirt.*
—*Shirley Chisolm*

Little has been written in history books or otherwise about talented women, the choices they faced throughout their lives, and the decisions they made. Some philosophers and feminists believe that the lack of continuity in women's history results in the need for each generation of women to reinvent both ideas and a feminist consciousness—ideas already invented, but forgotten, by previous generations. According to Gerda Lerner (1993), women throughout history have always recognized that they had talent, enabling them to disregard patriarchal constraints, gender-defined roles, and a constant barrage of discouragement. Lerner also believes that the inner assurance and serenity that come with form-giving talent allowed such women to make their own place in the world and stand by their talent, often in isolation, in loneliness, and under the derision of contemporaries. For a woman to realize her talents requires effort, conscientious decision-making, and an understanding that the full range of talents and gifts of many women go unrealized. Many people never fully understand the opportunities denied to girls and women because realities and experiences in today's world reinforce certain roles and obligations for women.

Our first responsibility as a society is to notice the stereo-typing which affects all of us and, in turn, influences our perceptions about our own abilities and choices. Our second responsibility is to understand how difficult it is to help gifted girls unless we learn from the lives of gifted women. Learning about the obstacles faced by many talented women will help us to enable gifted girls to learn how to plan and overcome difficulties which have hindered their mothers' and grandmothers' journeys toward their dreams and aspirations. When we help young girls overcome these issues, each succeeding generation of talented women will have taken one more step toward equity and resolving the problems discussed in this book.

An explanation about terminology may be needed to frame the discussion about the terms gifted and talented. For decades, researchers and authors have argued over these terms, and there is not one universally accepted definition for either. Some use the terms interchangeably, while others argue incessantly over which term applies to certain groups of children and adults. In this book, I use gifted to apply to those with high abilities or potentials in several areas or in general, and talented to indicate individuals with distinct abilities in one or two areas, such as science, math, and art.

You Just Didn't Notice

In 1976, Heather, my sixth grade student who had spent seven months studying robotics, and then designing and building a life-sized robot as a part of her work in a program for gifted and talented students, approached me with a disturbing observation. Several people had visited our school to see Heather's robot after a story had appeared about it in our local newspaper. It seemed, she said, that the male and female visitors asked different kinds of questions about her robot. Heather noticed that the women who came to see the robot asked her about how she designed it, what kind of motor she had used, how she had got-

4

ten the idea, and other questions about the process of building the robot. The men who visited, however, all asked variations of a single question in a rather teasing and playful way: they wanted to know if Heather had built the robot to do housework.

At the time, I was surprised by Heather's observation and insisted that she was mistaken in her conclusions. Heather looked at me quietly and said, "You just didn't notice." In the weeks that followed our conversation, I listened to the comments of those who visited our school and discovered that Heather had been right: I had not noticed. The first or second question that most male visitors, regardless of their ages, asked about the robot concerned whether it had been built to do housework. This experience caused me to consciously "notice" more and assume less. Some might deny it, but gender stereotyping and prejudices are pervasive in our society. In the years that followed, I have repeatedly watched stereotyping affect smart young girls in their formative years and influence their ability to fulfill their potential in their adult lives.

Few questions can be raised about whether or not the underachievement of talented women exists. The fact remains that in most professional fields and occupations, men surpass women in both the professional accomplishments they achieve and the financial benefits they reap. Today statistics show that women continue to earn less than men and receive only a small fraction of the patents granted. In comparison to men, they write fewer books and research articles and compose and paint only a fraction of the world's art. Some may argue that these facts alone do not represent an adequate measurement of female underachievement. However, it is important to recognize that many talented women perceive that they missed opportunities and either abandoned aspirations or were forced to choose lower goals during their lives. We can measure the extent of female underachievement by listening to the many older women in our society who look back on their lives with feelings of regret, saying, "I might have but . . ." or "I could have if . . ." or "I never had time to

. . ." It is our responsibility to help young women carefully consider their decisions and choices and to help older women realize that it is seldom "too late." It is also essential that we realize how difficult it is to discuss gifted girls without discussing gifted women because most young women believe that they can "do it all" or "have it all," while most older women understand that they cannot and that they must make "either/or" decisions.

DEFINING UNDERACHIEVEMENT IN TALENTED FEMALES

What do I mean by underachievement in relation to talented females and at what age does it surface? The answers to these questions are important if we are to understand the disparity between male and female achievement and if we are to succeed in our efforts to improve the situation. Definitions of underachievement, always problematic, vary with the age of the person under consideration and seldom apply in the same way to males and females. Researchers often define underachievement in young girls as "failing to do as well as might be expected in school." However, since females receive higher grades than males throughout elementary school, secondary school, and college, but their professional productivity is lower, I have argued that grades in school should not be equated with underachievement, but rather what a person believes can be attained or accomplished in life (Reis, 1987). A university honors student in one of my classes a few years ago put it succinctly, "My parents expected me to get good grades, but they expected my brother to be a doctor."

Another difficulty in trying to discuss underachievement in girls is related to stages of life. A teenage girl who achieves at extraordinary levels in high school has less of a chance of realizing her potential than a male peer because so many talented young women defer their dreams during college when they become involved in a relationship or interact with female peers who are less ambitious.

Underachievement in adult women is a totally different concept than underachievement in younger women because it defies measurement by the grades achieved in school. Adult standards for achievement might be centered on profession, status, career-related accomplishments, satisfaction, or productivity. But to what extent are these standards defined by the work of males? Perhaps we should reexamine the concept that underachievement in talented women is based on the same professional accomplishments as their male counterparts. The realization of women's talents may need to be redefined to include the joy of accomplishment as they pursue a career that still allows time for a satisfying personal life, nurturing children and family, or the success of being outstanding in an area outside of professional work.

A Case in Point

One of my closest childhood friends was a superb student, brilliant in math and science. We were in the same accelerated program in junior and senior high school and spent a great deal of time together. She lived with her parents and several siblings in a rather shabby, second floor apartment in the middle of the small city where we grew up. Her father was a salesman and her mother stayed at home to raise the family, as did most of our mothers in the 1950s. My friend's mother fascinated me and I looked for excuses to spend time with her. She was a highly intelligent graduate of one of the finest women's colleges on the east coast. She read at least five or six books weekly and always had books that she wanted to discuss with me or any of our other friends who would listen. She read philosophy, science, history, poetry, and fiction of the type that I had never seen. I don't think I have ever met anyone who was as hungry to learn and to think as my friend's mother. I often wondered about my friend's mother. Why didn't she do something to improve her life, find another outlet that would enable her to use her considerable intellect, and apply some of her many talents to find challenging work outside of the home?

After college, when I returned to my home town as an English teacher, I saw my friend's mother often. She checked out seven or eight books each week from the city library where I often went to prepare lessons or look for books myself. We talked regularly and I came to understand that she was a very contented woman who loved to learn, loved her children, and led one of the happier lives I knew. My friend grew up to be a scientist, one of the few women in her college class to earn a Ph.D. in science. She later told me that her mother was her greatest support system and the one person with whom she could discuss ideas. Were her mother's talents wasted? Or were they, instead, focused on the pursuit and love of learning that she was able to pass on to her children, all of whom grew up to be talented, productive adults? My friend's mother clearly displayed maternal giftedness and unconditional support for her children's interests and talents. In discussing female accomplishments, how do we frame a discussion about women like her?

CREATIVE PRODUCTIVITY OF FEMALES

Some researchers have found that male professors produce more creative work in the form of research publications than female professors (Axelrod, 1988; Ajzenberg-Selove, 1994; Bateson, 1989). Other researchers have observed that men write more books, earn more degrees, produce more works of art, and make more contributions in all professional fields (Callahan, 1979; Reis, 1987, 1995). Research about gifted women consistently cites the lower adult creative productivity of women (Ochse, 1991; Pirto, 1991; Kirschenbaum & Reis, 1997). Even in areas such as literature, in which both men and women believe that females excel, men are more productive in professional accomplishments. For many years, more men than women have been recipients of grants from the National Endowment for the Arts Fellowships in Literature.

One of the major reasons that males consistently demonstrate more creative productivity in their professional lives is that they have more time for their work and fewer home-related duties. Many talented women who assume the primary responsibility for domestic chores or who are single parents demonstrate creativity in different ways. Their creativity is seldom applied directly to one aspect of their life; rather it is diffused into many directions within their family and home—in the Halloween costumes they design for their children, the way they decorate their homes, the meals they prepare, the complicated schedules they plan for their families, the creative ways they stretch the family budget, and even the clothes they purchase or sometimes design and sew. Because women still assume the primary responsibility of family nurturer and caretaker, many creative energies are directly channeled into their family and home, while their spouse's creative energy is free to be directly applied to his work. While this caregiving has in the past been directed primarily to childcare, people are living longer and elderly parents often need to be cared for as well. In the early 1970s, only 25% of people in their late 50s had a surviving parent, but by 1980, 40% did, as did 20% of those in their early 60s, and 3% of those in their 70s. The need for care has become most necessary for the oldest people in our society, those over the age of 85, a group that has grown from fewer than 300,000 in 1930 to over 3 million today. Those caring for these elderly parents are women, and thus, the responsibilities for caregiving increases.

Completing creative work requires long periods of concentration, time which is clearly not available to many women in their peak work and childbearing years and perhaps not even in their older years. Wahlberg and Stariha (1992) suggest that achieving eminence in a given field may require as many as 70 hours of work per week for over a decade. Younger women who have families simply do not have that kind of time available for their professional work. Because of the way women have been raised and the messages they may have received from our culture, even single women without families may not possess the confidence required for this type of commitment to work. Instead, they may be content to work in the background in a less "center stage" position. Female creative work, therefore, may be directed at lower-profile products. While their male counterparts produce plays, write articles or books, undertake large deals, and are viewed as high creative achievers, many women make conscious or unconscious decisions to work in a more facilitating role, implementing the creative ideas of others.

In addition, fewer women fulfill their potential to complete professional and creative endeavors simply because they have different priorities. Most women face a multitude of important issues that need and deserve their time and attention. People they love more than their work, a sick child or elderly parents who need care, a friend who is in trouble, and many other personal issues force talented women to make decisions about what is most important to them. A dear friend who died of cancer at the age of 33 told me that the only comfort she had about her imminent death was that during the previous eight years, her three sons, ages 8, 6, and 3, had been her major priority in life. Because she had delayed her career after having her first son and had taken care of her children full-time, she felt no guilt about having spent enough time with her children. For many women, having to split time between those they love and their work is a difficult and often wrenching choice.

A third reason that women may not pursue creative productive work is that they may possess certain personality traits which often conflict with high-profile creative endeavors. These traits occur in many women, whether they work within or outside of the home, are married or single, and whether or not they have children. One of the most common traits is perfectionism, which causes some girls and women to expend maximum energy at all times, attempting to do everything and do it well. Often, it is not enough to try to be outstanding in the work they do. Perfectionistic women also feel they must strive for a flawless body, a house that could be on the cover of *Better Homes and Gardens*, and perfect children. These talented women wear themselves out trying to do everything well, often with minimal help from their spouses. Despite these accomplishments, they still feel plagued by the guilt that they may not have given enough to their husbands, children, home, and career.

Factors Contributing to Underachievement in Talented Females

While difficulties exist in defining and measuring underachievement with certainty, I have been able to reach some conclusions about this elusive subject after almost two decades of work. Rather than reviewing the increasing body of research that concentrates on biological differences between men and women across the lifespan, I have concentrated my efforts in both my research and in this book on the sociocultural issues facing talented and gifted women. Sex differences which are biologically determined can certainly be viewed as contributing to differences in achievement between men and women. I believe, however, that it may not be possible to truly understand the biological differences until we are able to reduce differences caused by sociocultural issues. My research has demonstrated that specific sociocultural issues and messages contribute to underachievement and lower expectations in girls and women.

Cultural Stereotyping, Sex Roles, and Different Messages

Sexual stereotyping regarding females exists at every level of our society. We need only glance at a magazine, turn on a television, examine the differences between girls' and boys' toys, or read current popular children's magazines or books to be reminded of the differences in cultural expectations for males and females. Many years ago, I remember being startled by an advertisement on the back cover of a popular psychology journal, depicting a man using a telescope (caption: "he likes the planets") and a woman reading a book about Hollywood (caption: "she likes the stars"). Recently, *Newsweek* displayed a matrix of six popular teen magazines, giving examples of teen jargon, stories on role models, boy-crazy headlines, and serious issues. Newsweek's editorial summary is an apt descriptor of stereotyping: "Do editors think girls are psyched for anything besides boys, celebs and zits?" (Media, 1998, p. 6). This stereotyping delivers powerful messages to females about their role in life, their own importance, and their worth.

Bright young girls are often caught in a bind between their intelligence and their gender. An eager, questioning mind may cause a student to call out in class, to debate, to argue, to ask questions. A boy who acts in this way may be labeled precocious, while a smart verbal girl who asks too many questions may be labeled obnoxious, aggressive, or even unfeminine. These stereotypes often continue through adult life, as demonstrated by case studies in later chapters of this book.

In research about schools and stereotyping, Myra and David Sadker (1994) found that boys vocally dominate the classroom. In more than one hundred fourth-, fifth-, and sixth-grade classes in four states and the District of Columbia, they found that boys got more attention and encouragement than girls and that in all subject areas boys dominated classroom communication. The Sadkers' research also demonstrated that teachers behaved differently when boys or girls called out in class without raising their hands. When boys answered without being called on, teachers accepted their answers; the same behavior from girls, however, resulted in negative responses toward not raising their hands. This research illustrates a subtle but powerful message for girls: boys should be academically assertive and demand teacher attention, and girls should act like ladies and keep quiet. Being eager and assertive in asking questions in school may also contrast sharply with the polite manners most parents demand of their daughters. This confusion about appropriate behavior and the mixed messages intelligent girls receive from parents and peers is best described in a letter I received from a nineteen-year-old female:

Caught in the double-bind of being labeled talented, being told I can do anything, being treasured as a bright young person, and at the same time being told not to compete, not to try to "run with the guys and not to show off," to "be a lady," I spent many years and much invaluable energy in the psychic bind of the talented girl. Even now, although the circumstances have changed (after all, I am in college!), I still fight the same old battles of outside expectations, awkward roles, and self-sabotage.

Current research (discussed later in this book) indicates that girls are treated differently in elementary and secondary classrooms as well as college classrooms. Talented females with many questions and ideas may suffer more than any other group from the mixed messages they receive from their parents, teachers, and peers. Parents who demand high grades in every subject on report cards might also urge their daughters to act like young ladies and refrain from arguing a point or questioning authority, thereby hindering the development of certain skills which are necessary for a rigorous academic education.

CONCERNS ABOUT RELATIONSHIPS

Another issue related to bright women is the kind of advice and counseling used to encourage them to pursue advanced course work, graduate school, and fulfilling professional lives. Without making any value judgments, women must realize that a demanding professional career will undoubtedly result in some difficult choices. As Carol Gilligan (1982) sensitively pointed out in her book, *In a Different Voice*, the value systems of women are different from those of men. If, as Gilligan believes, women view moral concerns in terms of interpersonal relationships and responsibilities to others, they may have a difficult, if not impossible, time putting their own needs in front of the needs of those they love. The "different voice" that Gilligan discusses lies in an ethic of caring and a close tie between relationship and responsibility. This voice may be the reason that many women choose to remain in lower-paying or lower-status jobs. The personal relationships they have developed in their work or the flexibility these types of jobs offer, enabling them to have more time with their families, are often more attractive to women than jobs of a higher caliber.

SPECIAL POPULATIONS OF TALENTED GIRLS AND WOMEN

Underlying the problem of underachievement in talented girls and women are certain cultural and environmental factors that become overwhelming influences in their lives. We know that women who receive doctorates are more likely to come from higher socioeconomic homes and have parents who are professional and successful. Higher socioeconomic status may not only result in the financial ability to send a daughter to college and graduate school, but also in the encouragement, expectations, and advice that parents provide to help their daughters gain the independence and self-confidence necessary to leave home and attend college. This encouragement and specific advice may be less prevalent in lower socioeconomic families in which some parents do not have the experience of having attended college themselves or the knowledge to help their daughters find scholarship opportunities or loan applications.

We cannot measure the lost potential of some talented females without calling special attention to the problems of economically disadvantaged females as well as young women and girls from culturally and linguistically diverse backgrounds. How many African American, Native American, or Hispanic girls have the potential to become scientists, writers, artists, or musicians, but will not because they do not believe these goals to be within their reach? Not only do these young women believe that most scientists are male, they also have come to understand that most are not from their culture.

We must acknowledge that escaping poverty to meet one's

potential is difficult enough for males who expect to have a life-time of work outside of the home. Females who are expected to care for brothers and sisters, cook the family's meals, keep the house clean, marry young, and have children of their own, often lose the opportunity for a different future. The brilliant young Hispanic females profiled in this book had to push the limits of their culture to enable themselves to leave home to attend college.

Defining Gifts and Talents in Women

Perhaps one of the best ways to learn how to overcome the challenges and choices faced by talented females is to study the qualities exhibited by those who have been successful, as well as those who have not realized their potential. My research with talented women has enabled me to identify common traits and influences that they share. Figure 1 summarizes these similarities in women's self-perception, personality, and experiences. Many of the women who participated in my research made a conscious decision to actively nurture and develop their talents. The following four factors defined the realization of their talents: (a) above average ability and/or special talents, (b) personality traits, (c) environmental issues, and (d) the perceived social importance of the use or manifestation of the talent. Each of these factors helped these women believe in themselves and promoted their desire to contribute, thus enabling each woman to actively develop her talents.

Above Average Ability and Special Talents

Most of the women I studied were good, but not always superior, students in school. However, they each had special talents such as musical ability, superior writing skills, or dramatic talent. Joseph Renzulli (1978, 1986) has distinguished between schoolhouse giftedness and creative-productive giftedness, believing that while both are important, individuals who make contributions recognized by history or within particular

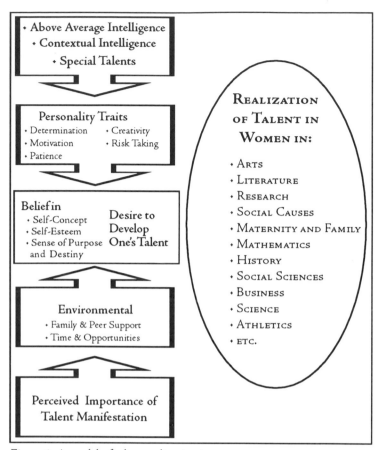

Figure 1. A model of talent realization in women

domains of human performance are often those who display creative productive giftedness. The women who realized their talents as adults were not always superlative students, but they certainly displayed creative and productive behaviors in their areas of talent and ability. In almost every case, their interests and motivations merged to enable them to develop their talents. In addition, what Robert Sternberg (1986) has described as contextual intelligence was also displayed by the participants, as most had to adapt or change their environment in order for their talents to be realized and developed.

Personality Traits

Most of the talented women I studied exhibited specific personality traits including determination, motivation, creativity, patience, and the ability to take and, in some cases, thrive on risks. The one trait clearly exhibited by every woman was determination. The ability to strive for success and continue to work hard, often under adverse conditions and sometimes without the love and support of her family and/or partner, was evident in all.

Each explained her source of determination and motivation differently. Some were certain it had developed from the positive role modeling of their parents in teaching them how to work. Others believed they developed their motivation because of a strong purpose in their lives such as preserving the environment, being a successful composer, or bringing theater to disadvantaged urban youth. Still others believed that their motivation came from a desire to produce, to leave a mark upon the world, and from the sheer joy of the creative act.

They each displayed creativity, which was evident in their talent areas as well as in the way they found time for family and relationships. The sheer volume of their work and their persistent evolution into higher talent forms resulted both from their own creativity as well as the intense love for their work. These talented women also displayed patience. Some waited years to have the opportunity to invest considerable blocks of time to develop their own talent, and some worked steadily over the years only to be acknowledged for their specific talents later in life. A congresswoman who waited until her youngest daughter was ready for college before running for office, a composer who worked year after year to improve her art form, and a forester who pursued work in her own field decade after decade all displayed this patience in the development of their talents. In addition, these talented women also displayed a willingness to take risks and attempt tasks that others did not have the courage to pursue.

The last trait is more difficult to define, but can be described as energy and interest. All of the successful women emanated a different style of energy and an enjoyment of life. Some were enthusiastic, while others were intensely quiet. Some laughed frequently and moved constantly, while others were very calm and almost reserved. However, each woman exuded an intensity about her life and work that seemed to give her the vitality she needed to pursue her talents.

Environmental Issues

Possibly the most diverse area that emerged as a factor in the talent development of women in my studies were the environmental issues that contributed to their success. Some came from upper-middle-class families; some were born into poor families. Some had parents who were highly educated; some had parents who had little or no education. Some attended prestigious women's colleges, some went to large state universities, and still others did not graduate from college. What environmental factors did they have in common? Most had nurturing families, but a few had families who were distant or abusive. Almost all had siblings. Those who had brothers usually agreed that their parents paid more attention and provided much more encouragement to their brothers. Most of the women were married or had long-term relationships and almost all of those who married had children. Many also divorced after finding that their partner was not very supportive of their talent development. Some delayed placing a primary emphasis on their career until they were able to do so because their children needed them, and some labored constantly on their journey to accomplishment. Most found ways to do both, and continued to actively seek support, help, further education, more knowledge, and increasing levels of sophistication in their work.

Perceived Social Importance of Their Work and a Sense of Purpose to Life

The gifted women in my study who achieved eminence had a strong desire to use their talents in ways that were personally satisfying to them and would benefit society. They each had a sense of purpose about life. They enjoyed life, but were not content with raising their families and having good relationships. Their work was critical to them, and they believed they could make a difference in the world because of their work. For these women, there was no choice about this contribution. They were simply not satisfied with their lives unless they could actively develop their talents. Most had friends and siblings who were just as smart or even smarter (if academic performance in school is the basis for assessment), but who were content to lead lives that did not involve the work or energy needed to develop her talent.

Why did these talented women work so hard when their friends and colleagues lived such different lives? My research found that these women had no choice; they wanted to contribute in some way, and they believed in themselves in a way that made it necessary to do what they did. "Something inside of me had to come out," several explained eloquently.

In addition to this drive to succeed, these women defined success in their own unique way. Most women wanted to take a different path in combining work and family. The women I studied were not content to be like other women who had successfully raised their children and then enjoyed their middle or later years by working in a career or job they enjoyed, pursuing hobbies or spending time with friends or family. Their work was critical and to accomplish their work, some women shifted career goals, trying different tasks each decade until they finally achieved their own goals. Others quietly worked to produce products such as books or art that were personally fulfilling and would bring joy to others.

Belief in Self and Desire to Contribute

Each of these talented women developed, from a combination of the factors already discussed (personality, environmental, etc.), a belief in themselves and a desire to translate their sense of purpose in life into some action which either made a difference or resulted in a creative contribution. They all had high self-esteem, a trait that has been found to characterize other successful women. Most of the women believed that their self-concept and self esteem were created from their own successes and from the love and support they received from family and friends.

Difficult Choices

A crucial point in the discussion of talented females is the knowledge that there is not one right or wrong way to use one's talents in life. My college roommate, Chris, recently sent me a Christmas card in which she told me that she had gone back to work in her husband's very successful plumbing business after the untimely death of one of his most reliable employees. She explained, "You'll be angry with me when you hear this, but I don't want to keep working, and I definitely don't want to become more computer literate. I want to go back to being a full-time Mom and having time for what I love—my family and my needlework and embroidery." My friend was an honors student in college, excelled in English and in creative writing, and became a terrific mother. Her children are happy and successful; her daughter is in her first year of college and plans to attend law school. My friend's needlework is beautiful, and she loves spending time on it. She continues with her creative writing and although she has not published her work, she still loves the writing process. Chris uses her talents in the way she chooses; she creates beauty in her life—by raising two successful and well-adjusted children and through her needlework.

According to the 1996 Statistical Abstract of the United States, fewer than half of mothers with children under the age of six are currently employed, and only about a third of mothers with young children work as much as 35 hours per week. When mothers do work full-time (40 hours a week or more), 33% have their children cared for by a relative as opposed to day care personnel. Choosing to care for children at home or choosing to work less than full-time are two important issues facing American women. As there is not one right path for any talented woman, the lives of all of the women that I have studied include complex decisions, compromises, conflicts, and contradictions. However, one finding is obvious—as long as women continue to feel frustrated about opportunities denied because of their gender, or the absence of time for female talent development, we must continue to discuss these issues and society must respond. We must begin to listen more carefully to the lessons learned by older talented women and pass along their wisdom to a younger generation, or we will continue reinventing a feminist consciousness each generation.

No doubt exists that research on the abilities of females has progressed since the Victorian Age when scientists argued that if women used their brains or exercised excessively, they would impair their fertility by draining off blood cells needed to support their menstrual cycle. However, until talented girls and women have the opportunities to grow, flourish, and achieve without the stereotypes and negative influences in our world, their talents may never be realized. To provide these opportunities, parents and teachers must work to make schools, homes, and society more sympathetic to, and supportive of, the special challenges and special needs of talented girls and women.

CHAPTER TWO

~:~

CONFLICTS ABOUT ACCOMPLISHMENT IN TALENTED GIRLS & WOMEN

I want my daughters to be beautiful, accomplished and good; to be admired, loved and respected; to have a happy youth, to be well and wisely married, and to lead useful, pleasant lives, with as little care and sorrow to try them as God sees fit to send. To be loved and chosen by a good man is the best and sweetest thing which can happen to a woman, and I sincerely hope my girls may know this beautiful experience.
—*Louisa May Alcott, Little Women*

That's the way the system works. Sometimes you get the bear, and sometimes the bear gets you.
—*Sue Grafton*

Gifted females face conflicts between their own abilities and the social structure of their world. They face both external barriers (lack of support from families, stereotyping, and acculturation in home, school, and the rest of society) and internal barriers (self-doubt, self-criticism, lowered expectations, and the attribution of success to effort rather than ability). While women must shoulder partial responsibility for the conflicts and barriers they face, greater blame for the role confusion lies in the ambivalence our society displays toward talented females and the barrage of often harmful messages which influence females throughout their lives. In August of 1997, a Baptist church in Little Rock Arkansas closed its day care center. A letter sent out by the church explained that working mothers neglect their children, damage their marriages, and set a bad example. The letter further stated that "God intended for the home to be the center of a mother's world. In Titus 2:5, women are instructed to be discreet, chaste, keepers at home, good and obedient to their own husbands" ("Saying Day Care . . .," April 4, 1997). In 1949 when Pearl S. Buck originally published the novel, *The Long*

Love, she used the pseudonym of John Sedges, explaining, "I chose the name of John Sedges, a simple one, and masculine because men have fewer handicaps in our society than women have, in writing as well as in other professions."

The conflicts and barriers that gifted females face involving their own abilities and the external pressures of their world have a direct impact on some of their most difficult decisions. These conflicts include the effects that challenging careers have on women's personal lives, those which occur because talented women's multipotentiality often prohibits appropriate career counseling and decision making, and the absence of helpful encouragement needed to succeed. Useful strategies for success are often obscured in a variety of mixed messages from women's families, friends, and society. One of the most frequently cited messages is that women should not boast, brag, or even be too proud of their accomplishments. Deborah Tannen (1990), in her thoughtful book, *You Just Don't Understand*, explained the dilemma well: "The different lenses of status and connection may once more work against women. Women are reluctant to display their achievements in public in order to be likable, but regarded through the lens of status, they are systematically underestimated, and thought self-deprecating and insecure" (p. 224). These external barriers often result in internal barriers such as lowering expectations and career achievement, poor planning, lack of confidence in one's ability and the attribution of success to effort rather than ability.

Current Statistics about Women, Work, and Accomplishments

Recent statistics highlight some of the problems facing talented women. These statistics, of course, tell only part of the story and the story changes frequently. Since 1993, women have been losing ground to men in salary (Epstein, 1997). In 1979, women earned just 62.5 cents for every dollar earned by men. The difference between male and female earnings had been hovering at that level for a generation or so, Epstein reported. A large number of antidiscrimination suits and an influx of women into the work force caused women to gain in salary benefits during the eighties and early nineties. By 1993, women were earning 77 cents for every dollar earned by men. Epstein reported that since then, equity in salaries has been in a downhill spiral. By 1996, women were earning only 75 cents for every dollar earned by men and the figure has declined since then to 74 cents. Epstein believes that "because women as a group are lower on the company totem pole, they lose out on the prerogative to bestow bonuses, to distribute raises, and to hire, fire, transfer and promote. Such power remains the preserve of men" (p. 35).

Epstein (1997) also reported that among the Fortune 500 companies, there are only two female CEOs; among the next 500 companies, there are only five female CEOs. Golden West Financial Chief Executive Marion Sandler explained, "The people who are in a position of authority promote after their own image" (p. 35). Carolyn Rogers, a vice president of J & W Seligman, agreed, indicating that the top echelons of business are ". . . a men's club." Rogers explained that men prefer to work with other men:

> It's not that they are intentionally overlooking women, it's just that's who they've hung with, who they feel comfortable with, who they can communicate with, and who they trust are other men. And this kind of thing can often be a lot more important than sheer ability in determining the jobs women get. (p. 35)

In "Women at Thirtysomething," a study released by the Office of Education, the educational careers and job market experiences of women who graduated from high school in 1972 were studied. Six surveys were conducted between 1972 and 1986 on a sample of over 22,000 women. The study found that as a group, women outperformed men academically at every level, had higher grade point averages, completed degrees faster, and developed more positive attitudes toward learning. At the same time, a much higher percentage of women experienced genuine unemployment than men, regardless of what degree they earned. In only 7 of 33 occupations did women achieve pay equity with men.

Catalyst, a nonprofit group, recently published a study, "Women and Corporate Leadership," that indicated that half of the female executives interviewed about leadership reported that the major obstacles holding women back from top management positions were "male stereotyping and preconceptions of women" and "exclusion from informal networks of communication." Those who work in business continue to cite issues dealing with double standards and misperceptions of women. Figure 2 presents examples of the unfortunate stereotypes that many women believe continue in business offices today.

Another area in which statistics have not greatly changed for talented women is academe. According to the Digest of Education Statistics, in the 1980-1981 academic year, 70% of full-time male faculty positions were tenured, as compared to 49.7% of female faculty positions. In 1994-1995, the tenure gap was virtually unchanged, at 71.3% for men and 50.3% for women. At many of our most prestigious universities and colleges, the percentage of women who reach the rank of full professor is still surprisingly low. The figures for 1997-98 indicate that at Category 1 (doctoral granting) universities, the percentages of men who reach the level of full professor is 35.6% as compared to 5.7% for women. At the associate professor level, a discrepancy still exists with 20.3% of men reaching that level as compared to 8.7% of women. Likewise, 12.3% of men reach the assistant professor level as compared to 9.3.% of women (Schrecker, 1998, p. 34). Differences in salary also exist as male full professors at Category 1 universities earn $80,391 as compared to female full professors who earn $72,839. At every rank and in every category male professors earn more than female professors, even at the instructor and the lecturer levels (Schrecker, 1998, p. 27).

HE WORKS, SHE WORKS
But What Different Impressions They Make

The family picture is on **HIS** desk:
Ah, a solid, responsible family man.

The family picture is on **HER** desk:
Hmm, her family will come before her career.

HIS desk is cluttered:
He's obviously a hard worker and a busy man.

HER desk is cluttered:
She's obviously a disorganized scatterbrain.

HE'S talking with co-workers:
He must be discussing the latest deal.

SHE'S talking with co-workers:
She must be gossiping.

HE'S not at his desk:
He must be at a meeting.

SHE'S not at her desk:
She must be in the ladies' room.

HE'S not in the office.
He's meeting with customers.

SHE'S not at the office:
She must be out shopping.

HE'S having lunch with the boss:
He's on his way up.

SHE'S having lunch with the boss:
The must be having an affair.

The boss criticized **HIM**:
He'll improve his performance.

The boss criticized **HER**:
She'll be very upset.

HE got an unfair deal:
Did he get angry?

SHE got an unfair deal:
Did she cry?

HE'S getting married:
He'll get more settled.

SHE'S getting married:
She'll get pregnant and leave.

HE'S having a baby:
He'll need a raise.

SHE'S having a baby.
She'll cost the company money in maternity benefits.

HE'S going on a business trip:
It's good for his career.

SHE'S going on a business trip:
What does her husband say?

HE'S leaving for a better job:
He recognizes a good opportunity.

SHE'S leaving for a better job:
Women are undependable.

<u>Note.</u> From *Paths to Power* by Natasha Josefowitz, 1980, New York: Addison-Wesley. Copyright 1994 by Natasha Josefowitz. Reprinted with permission.

<u>Figure 2.</u> Examples of double standards in the office.

Other statistics highlight issues which suggest that barriers continue to exist which threaten accomplishment by women in general and talented women in particular:

- Women comprise three-quarters of all older Americans living in poverty. In fact, older women are almost twice as likely as older men to be poor.

- Women over 65 are three times as likely as men to be widowed.

- Women provide three-quarters of the family caregiving in this country. For 12% of caregivers who also live outside the home, the demands become so intense that they must leave paid employment, losing or compromising retirement benefits which hurts their own long-term security and independence.

- An ad hoc newsroom committee from the *Hartford Courant* counted the photo and story subjects on their section fronts in a three-week period in the spring of 1997, and they found that approximately 80% were male while only 20% were female. Since newspapers record history and reporters and photographers are eyewitnesses to the events, experiences, and personalities that define our world, feature columnist and reporter Barbara Roessner explained, "we like to think we seek truth, without fear or favor, and then follow wherever it leads us. But do we? Why, on some days, was there not a single female voice or image on the cover of our Sports section? Why, most days, were so few women seen or heard on . . . the Business cover; the Town News front?" (Roessner, 1998).

- Of the world's 1.3 billion illiterate adults, two-thirds are women.

- In the 100 year history of the Nobel Prize, only 11 prizes have been awarded to 10 women scientists. (Marie Curie won the prize twice.)

- Since 1809, only one out of approximately every 1,000 patents has been issued to a woman inventor. Approximately 8% of patents granted to Americans in 1993 included the name of a woman, and of these, 50% were in the high technology fields.

- Less than 5% of the National Academy of Sciences members are women.

- In 1978, two women headed Fortune 1000 companies. In 1996, there were four women who headed Fortune 1000 companies. A 1996 review of the 1,000 largest firms in the United States showed that only 1% of the top five jobs in those corporations, 60 out of 5,000 positions, were filled by women.

- Women make up less than 12% of the world's parliaments, and less than 11% of political party leaders.

- Female musicians are drastically underrepresented in major orchestras in the world. Women often work in an atmosphere of exclusion and intimidation even after they have obtained an orchestra position. Within the 21 highest budgeted orchestras in the United States, there are no female musical directors or conductors in permanent positions. (Of the total 1530 pieces programmed in concerts for these orchestras, only three pieces were composed by a woman.)

- Only 24 women have been elected heads of state or government in this century.

- Of the 185 highest-ranking diplomats to the United Nations, only 7 are women.

- Of the doctorates granted in mathematics in the mid-1990s, 78% were awarded to men while 22% went to women.

♦ Of the doctorates granted in physical sciences in the mid-1990s, the same percentages held as 78% were granted to men and 22% to women. Doctorates in engineering in the same time period reflected lower levels for women as 88% went to men and 11% to females.

♦ Women on the Ladies Pro Golf Tour earn 28 cents for every dollar earned by a man on the Pro Golf Tour.

♦ In the House of Representatives, women hold just 10.9% of the seats. In the U. S. Senate, women hold only 10% of the seats. Compare these to the percentage of women in the legislatures of the following countries: Sweden-40.4%, Norway-39.4%, Finland-33.5%, Germany-26.2%, South Africa-25%.

♦ Women currently make up 44% of students registered in ABA-approved law schools in 1995, but women represent only 8% of the deans of law schools and 17% of the professors. Although 30% of all lawyers are now women, female attorneys earn 22% less than male attorneys.

♦ The participation of women in the area of biotechnology is also lacking. Of 122 companies recently responding to a survey in *Biopeople*, only 5% had a woman as a CEO. Only 3% had women as Heads of Product Development or Sales and Marketing. And 77% had no women directors who were currently on their Board of Directors.

♦ Males continue to outperform females in math and science around the world in the Third International Math and Science Study (TIMSS), regarded as the most comprehensive international comparison to date with half a million students participating. The TIMSS examined how advanced 12th graders in the US compared to advanced students in 15 other countries. Males outperformed females in all but one of the 21 countries testing how students use their knowledge to address real world problems. Males had significantly higher physics achievement than females in all but one country, Latvia. In advanced math achievement (equations and functions, calculus, and geometry), significant differences were found favoring males in all countries except Greece, Cyprus, Australia, Italy, and Slovenia.

Clearly, while women have made inroads into many different occupations and areas, they have a long way to go in other occupations as indicated by the statistics above and those in Figure 3.

FINANCIAL PROSPECTS IN OLD AGE

Not only are women's occupational patterns quite different from men's, so are their financial prospects in old age. After children, the single largest poverty group in our country is women over the age of 60. While the gap between earnings for women and men has decreased in recent years, the picture is much bleaker for older women, whose pensions are often a fraction of men's. The median annual pension benefit for newly retired women is $4,800 or half that of men's at $9,600. Many factors appear to be detrimental to women in their retirement: their concentration in lower paid and part-time jobs with no retirement benefits, career interruptions to take care of family, and a tendency to avoid risky investments which may have big payoffs. As with other societal issues, "retirement today is based on the male pattern of life, not the female," according to Deborah Briceland-Betts, director of the Older Women's League, a national advocacy group (Zaldivar, 1997, p. 10).

Women's patterns of education differ as well, as they more often pursue high school and associate's (two years of college) degrees. More men than women complete degrees at the bachelors and graduate levels (see Figure 4). A decreasing number of

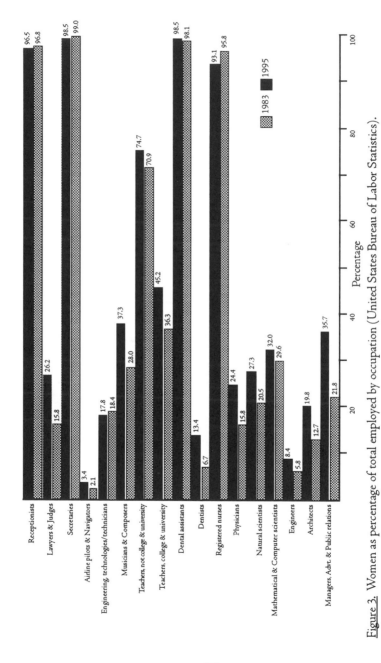

Figure 3. Women as percentage of total employed by occupation (United States Bureau of Labor Statistics).

women are pursuing formal education for a number of reasons. My research indicates that in most cases fewer women pursue higher education because time- and energy-consuming relationships develop or because parents provided more emotional and financial support for their sons to complete degrees than for their daughters.

Recent Surveys About Women and Girls

In a national survey conducted between December 1996 and June 1997 by Louis Harris and Associates, Inc. (Portner, 1997), 6,748 girls and boys in grades 5-12 in the United States completed in-class questionnaires on a range of topics, including violence, risky behaviors, mental health, and eating disorders. Twenty percent of high school girls said they had been sexually or physically abused, and 8% of the responding teenage girls said they had been forced by a date to have sex against their will. According to the study, teenage girls who have experienced abuse are far more likely than their peers to become depressed, have suicidal thoughts, use drugs or alcohol, and suffer from eating disorders (p. 12).

In another 1997 study ("American Women"), a random sample of 1,000 American women aged 18 and older was surveyed by a professional social science research firm for *Ladies Home Journal* (*LHJ*). In the *LHJ* survey, 76% of the women said they do most of the laundry, 73% do most of the cooking, 70% do most of the housecleaning, 67% do most of the grocery shopping, and 56% pay most of the bills. The task most men handle is car maintenance. In a study I conducted, women reported having an average of thirty minutes each day of free time and did most of the household chores despite full-time work for both spouses.

An interesting paradox emerged in the *LHJ* survey ("American Women," 1997). While large percentages of women believed they have more opportunities for self-expression (86%), increased opportunities in the workplace (78%), and more political power

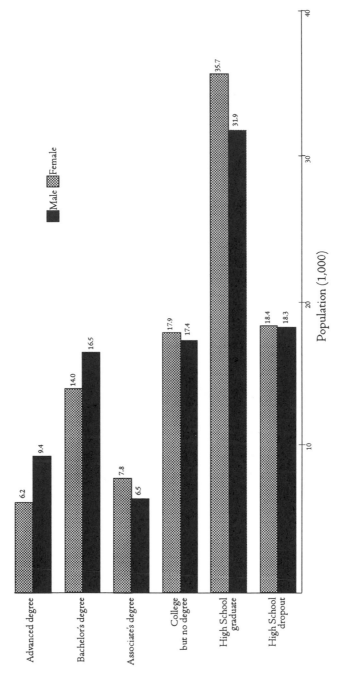

Figure 4. Educational attainment for men and women over the age of 25 (U.S. Bureau of the Census, *Current Population Reports*, 1995).

(68%), the majority (80%) feel increased levels of stress due to increasing responsibilities caused by balancing work and family. Of this group, a 25% describe themselves as "stressed to the max." One woman explained, "Women in the workplace try to be equal with men; then they have to go home and give some more. I'm taking care of everyone. Who's taking care of me?" (p. 132).

The paradox faced by women also emerged in other statistics from the same study ("American Women," 1997). Sixty-seven percent of respondents believed that although their lives are better than their mothers' lives, they worry about the impact of changes in their current lives on their family. Children have lost the most, according to 59% of respondents, while 80% believed that the biggest unintended consequence of the changing role of women is the "declining moral values of today's children, and the breakdown of the traditional family" (p. 132). These paradoxes, perhaps, point out the most striking challenges facing women today. Those challenges involve reconciling the gains that working women have made, the happiness found through careers and the freedom to work, with the losses, the guilt and sadness that their children aren't getting the full attention of a stay-at-home mother.

Even if women today recognize that their mother might not have been happy staying at home, they nevertheless feel guilt because their own children are growing up very differently than they did. Central to overcoming these feelings of guilt is understanding that a childhood which differs from one in the 1950s or 1960s is not necessarily negative. My research has indicated that many talented women perceive that their children have developed greater independence, greater creativity, and greater self-sufficiency.

Another interesting statistic that emerged in the *LHJ* survey is the dissatisfaction with life reported by older women ("American Women," 1997), which is in marked contrast to the reports of older women I studied who pursued their dreams and talents at a later age. Women aged 52-67 in the *LHJ* survey reported some major dissatisfactions with their life, saying that as they age, they become increasingly lonely and worried about managing on their own. They are also more likely to be disappointed about the way their lives evolved. The older gifted women I studied described themselves as happy, confident, and glowing with satisfaction. This certainly seems to indicate that differences exist between some older gifted women and the majority of older women who responded to this survey.

External Barriers

The importance of environmental variables on the development of gifted and talented females cannot be overstated. Almost from birth, females find themselves in a world of limiting stereotypes and barriers to achievement. Research, my own as well as that of others, has identified external barriers which seem to negatively influence the development of talents and gifts in some gifted girls and women. These barriers include the role of parents, school, and the environment in general.

Parental Influences

The first set of external barriers gifted women face deals with childhood family issues and statistics, such as number and sex of siblings, birth order of siblings, and presence or absence of one or both parents. Other childhood issues include the parental attitudes toward having and raising girls as opposed to boys. Children usually learn the behaviors of their sex at an early age and display particular behavior patterns and play preferences even during preschool years (Blaubergs, 1980; Kirschenbaum, 1980; Paley, 1984). Research in the 1970s indicated that parents usually wanted a male child (Peterson & Peterson, 1973) and this trend may continue. Once a child is born, various studies have reported that parents held their children differently depending on whether they were girls or boys and purchased different toys which were stereotypical for each gender (Kuebli & Fivush, 1994; Schwartz & Markham, 1985). The contents and furnishings of girls' and boys' rooms have been found to be drastically different, with girls' rooms having more dolls and doll houses and boys' rooms having more vehicles, educational and art materials, and machines (Rheingold & Cook, 1975; Pomerleau, Bolduc, & Malcuit, 1990). Many studies have suggested that gender stereotyping in toys contributes to lower math and science scores for adolescent girls on achievement tests (Yee & Eccles, 1988; Lummis & Stevenson, 1990; Olszewski-Kubilius, Kulieke, Shaw, Willis, & Krasney, 1990). Patricia Casserly (1975), an early researcher in the area of gifted females, indicated that gifted girls were often frustrated because their parents would not buy them chemistry sets or construction sets as toys. However, many of the women I studied who were the oldest child in the family reported that their fathers bought them toys which were traditionally marketed for boys rather than girls, such as rockets or tool kits.

Parental influences have also been shown to have an impact on the lives of talented females, including the educational levels and occupations of both father and mother, as well as the type and level of parental aspirations for children's educational and occupational goals. "Shortchanging Girls, Shortchanging America," a recent study conducted by the American Association of University Women (AAUW, 1991), included a poll of 3,000 students in grades 4 through 10 in twelve locations across the United States. The study found that as girls get older, their self-esteem drops dramatically. Enthusiastic and assertive at age 8 and 9, they begin to lose confidence in their abilities at age 13 and 14 and emerge from high school with measurably lowered goals and future expectations. While 60% of the girls said they were happy with themselves in elementary school, 37% were still happy with themselves in middle school, and only 29% were still happy with themselves in high school. The reasons for the decline in self-esteem are very interesting—students' families and their school experiences had the greatest impact on adolescents' self-esteem.

Parents often send contradictory messages that they want their daughters to get good grades in all subjects, but also to exhibit "appropriate" polite and even demure behavior for a female, a clear finding derived from many case studies discussed in this book. The stereotypical behaviors often conflict with the personal attributes a gifted female needs to succeed. Some parents require, or at a minimum, expect their daughters to be polite, well-mannered, and consistently congenial. According to the stereotype, girls are not supposed to be too independent. The same parents who demand top grades in all subjects may be overprotective and make all of the decisions for their daughters at home.

Mothers seem to have a particular influence on their gifted daughters. My interviews have found that talented girls with career-oriented mothers tended to develop a variety of talents and interests early in life and feel less conflict about growing up and becoming independent, autonomous women. Girls in my study whose mothers had been at home, however, struggled with ambition and conflicts about work and home. Lashaway-Bokina (1996) found similar results in her study of Latina American gifted females who had dropped out of high school. Many of the young women she studied were initially content to stay at home with their mothers and watch soap operas in the afternoon. These gifted females received confusing messages about their own future and their relationship with their mothers and regarded their own abilities and talent development with ambivalence and questions. Their love for their mothers caused them to feel unsure about the development of their own talents. Their academic abilities, if developed, would lead to an unequivocally different life from the one in which they currently lived and their mothers would always live. Being different from their mothers and separating themselves, in a number of ways, from their families caused fear and tension in these young women.

Change is very difficult for many talented girls who are the first in their family to go to college or to pursue a challenging career. A popular bumper sticker appropriately reads, "Change is good, you go first." With time, however, some of the young women interviewed by Lashaway-Bokina (1996) managed to reconcile some of their problems and return to high school. Few at this time, however, have realized their potential and gone on to pursue postsecondary education.

EXTERNAL EVENTS INFLUENCING CREATIVE DEVELOPMENT

The availability (or absence) of role models who can help gifted girls realize their potential has been a key issue with some of the women I have studied. If women have knowledge of or personal contact with someone who acts as a positive role model, especially in their area of career interest, attaining that career can seem like a much more reasonable goal. A family's financial resources may also be a contributing factor in a woman's ability to realize her educational dreams. In some cases, financial security can make pursuing one's dream much easier. However, my research has indicated that the absence of financial security did not hinder many women's pursuits of career or talent goals.

Dean Simonton (1978) suggested various external events that may influence creative development including the two issues mentioned above, formal education and role-model availability. Simonton, whose work has mainly focused on men, also indicated that zeitgeist, political fragmentation, war, civil disturbances, and political instability can all influence creative development. Simonton distinguished between two phases of a creator's life arguing that sociocultural events may influence either the developmental or the productive period of a creator's life. He speculates that a special set of political, social, and cultural events is most conducive to the development of creative potential and concludes that three sociopsychological processes are central to creative development: role model availability, exposure to cultural diversity, and the generation of a set of philosophical beliefs essential to the development of creative potential.

Although Simonton's theory, like those of others, is primarily derived from male models of creative development, an examination of two of the sociopsychological processes he discussed provides insight into why many gifted females underachieve. First, many highly able women do not have role models who can exemplify what they hope to accomplish in life, and even if they do, their availability may not be enough to overcome social forces. Consider the explanation of this phenomenon by Mary Catherine Bateson (1989), whose parents were Margaret Mead and Gregory Bateson. She discussed the negative influences of social factors she experienced in her life:

> I believe the issue of female inferiority still arises
> for virtually every woman growing up in this
> society. I grew up in an environment where no
> one told me females were inferior or that significant
> achievement would necessarily be beyond my reach, but the belief was all around
> me. (p. 40)

Another process discussed by Simonton seems to be particularly cogent for gifted females: the development of a set of philosophical beliefs essential to the development and continued growth of creative potential. In a society in which the majority of our leaders, politicians, artists, musicians, and inventors are male, how does a young female develop a philosophical belief about her own creative potential? How might she overcome her upbringing, her parents' and teachers' advice, and the knowledge that creative contributions take great amounts of time?

When Maria Goeppart-Mayer made the discovery that later earned her a Nobel prize in physics, she delayed publishing her results for months. Her biographer concluded that modesty caused this delay (Dash, 1988, p. 322). However, her hesitation may also reflect the intrinsic belief imposed upon highly able women by our society—that discoveries, inventions, and creations are usually the work of men. Until many more women are visible as discoverers, inventors, or creators, they may be relegated to the traditional roles they have generally held in the past—implementers of others' ideas, organizers, service providers, and the painters of the backdrop of creation. Again, these remarks are not made in a pejorative manner, for it is the quiet service of women that runs many of the organizations in our country. This service of women runs many of our schools, hospitals, volunteer organizations, and businesses. We must, however, recognize as a society that if women are capable of and want to pursue the creation of ideas and experience the joy emanating from the discovery of new products and the creative act of production, we must support them in these endeavors. We must develop a society in which time and resources are devoted to nurturing and developing talent in women, and we must find new ways of structuring work and home responsibilities to enable this productivity to occur.

CLICK, CLICK, CLICK: THE FORMATION OF ATTITUDES AND OPINIONS

Like a camera in the brain, each time a child has an experience, a snapshot is embedded in her experiential base. Millions of snapshots produce attitudes, which, in turn, affect actions. Stereotypes abound in our society, from shampoo commercials and newspaper ads to the teen magazines our daughters read. Newspapers and news shows on television regularly feature photographs and feature stories about men in positions of authority. Children's books, television shows, and textbooks all present more men than women, and when women are presented, their appearances are usually stressed.

Recent examples abound: a flyer from a cancer research group asking for donations for breast cancer research depicts a bra with a large sign under it—"*Save the contents.*" An article in the *Wall Street Journal* ("Kindergarten Awards," 1994) discusses a kindergarten awards assembly in which a male executive had observed a marked difference between the awards given to boys

41

and to girls:

>**Boys' Awards:** Very Best Thinker, Most Eager Learner, Most Imaginative, Most Enthusiastic, Most Scientific, Best Friend, Mr. Personality, Hardest Worker, Best Sense of Humor

>**Girls' Awards:** All-around Sweetheart, Sweetest Personality, Cutest Personality, Best Sharer, Best Artist, Biggest Heart, Best Manners, Best Helper, Most Creative

When the executive and his wife discussed the differences with their child's teacher, they learned that the awards had been given for years and no other parent had ever voiced a concern. The teacher had not realized that she was participating in stereotyping; she "just didn't notice."

Women are also bombarded with unrealistic and superficial images of what they should look like, and little girls continue to think that a Barbie Doll's dimensions are ideal. The average height of an American women is 5' 4" and the average weight is 142 pounds, while the average height of a model is 5' 10" with an average weight of 110 pounds. Stereotyping about weight and ideal proportions of females is a constant reminder to real women that they look less than ideal. Young women are encouraged to try to change themselves physically in order to gain happiness—to see supermodels as role models. Many talented girls are affected by the pressure to look like a model. Despite their academic success, they have consistently told me in interviews that they seek and need approval from the males they either like or date: "Males expect ideal body images, the impossible image. Many of us feel we will never measure up and many guys make comments if we don't."

Each time a young girl turns on the television, reaches for a magazine, participates in or overhears a conversation between friends, she is in the process of experiencing and being influenced by her social surroundings. The process begins at birth and continues throughout life, and the effects of environmental socialization are pervasive and overwhelming. Attitudes and opinions about what girls should look and act like come from family and friends, from observations throughout life, television, and other media, and print materials including books, magazines, and textbooks. Suggestions for ways to eliminate or, at the very least, reduce gender stereotypes that currently impede gifted females from realizing their potential have been made by researchers and educators for the last decade or two. However, we seldom witness the implementation of the widespread, comprehensive efforts necessary to ameliorate the effects of all of the "clicks" and social pressures that affect talent development in girls.

Imagine an American teenager waking up in the morning and turning on the news. She watches as the president of the United States answers a question about foreign policy asked by a male reporter. She sees a shot of the Senate, an overwhelmingly male dominated body, followed by a story on the Supreme Court (seven men and two women), and then a story on problems in the United Nations Security Council, another male dominant group. If she watches sports, she will usually listen to scores reported by male sportscasters about primarily male teams.

Television shows and children's programs (e.g. Saturday morning cartoons), fiction and nonfiction books, textbooks, and even classic movies such as *Sleeping Beauty* and *Cinderella* may impart a negative message to both young girls and boys. Many researchers, educators, and parents believe that television plays an especially important part in the erosion of self confidence and self worth in young girls. Many cartoon shows, situation comedies, and other programs aimed specifically at children depict women as victims or as dominated by men. In addition to television, some books that children are regularly exposed to help to stereotype experiences for girls and boys. A closer look at several popular children's writers such as Richard Scary reveals examples of gender stereotyping of careers, roles, and expectations.

Many older library books on shelves across the country are replete with examples of stereotypes. These books contain photographs depicting men as doctors, lawyers, veterinarians, and women as secretaries and receptionists and influence young girls negatively. Those most at risk are the girls with the potential to be doctors, lawyers, and veterinarians.

Aware of all of the socializing incidents that affect young girls, my husband and I made a conscious attempt from the day both of our daughters were born to provide an equitable and fair environment for them. We tried to expose them to female role models, both in life and through nonfiction and fiction literature. We drove a fair distance to take them to a female dentist. They had medical visits with females. My friends sometimes teased me about my mission to have my daughters know the names of Rosa Parks, Rachel Carson, Marie Curie, Hypatia, and other accomplished women. We bought books about female doctors, scientists, and lawyers, and I was satisfied with my efforts. My husband and I share household tasks and participate equally in caring for our daughters. One afternoon when we picked up our six-year-old daughter from day care after school, she sat in the back of the car and sighed loudly—a signal we had come to understand as her way of telling us something was bothering her. As I was driving, my husband turned around and asked, "What's the matter, Sara?"

She paused and said, "I wish I was a boy."

My husband's face became incredulous as he turned to her, "Why on earth would you want to be a boy, Sara?"

She responded, "They just get to do more!" She told us about a number of specific incidents in her classroom which had led her to this conclusion. It became clear that she was reacting to the environment in her school and classroom, and a long conversation with her classroom teacher indicated that Sara's observations were on target. Her teacher explained to us that the boys tried to monopolize the computer in the classroom, spoke

44

out more in class, and constantly competed for more of her time and attention. Despite her efforts, Sara's teacher reported to me, she had begun to notice that some of the girls were becoming quieter. Even when she had tried to establish "girl only time" on the computer and some of the other equipment in the classroom, she found the girls were giving up their computer time to their male friends who seemed to cajole the girls into additional time. Despite our efforts to provide role models and equity for our daughters at home and to limit television time and exposure to negative print materials, we were struck head-on with their encounters in the world outside of our home. Although that incident occurred almost six years ago, daily reminders of stereotyping continue to occur in our lives. Recently, while standing in line to pay for purchases in a large store, Sara, now twelve, asked if she could buy a copy of the new teen magazine, YM (*Young and Modern*). She picked it up and handed it to me with a pleading look. "Please Mom," she said, "all of my friends are reading this magazine. Can I get a copy?" On the cover of the November 1997 magazine was the photograph of a very slim, beautiful, young teenage girl, and I read with amazement the bullets of some of the stories inside: "Total Love Guide: 100 Guys Dish the New Rules,""Kiss and Be Kissed: 26 Pucker-up Pointers,""Dazzle Him: Hottest Date Clothes Ever,""31 Signs the Boy's Sweatin' You Bad,""Buff your Bod: The Rock Goddess Way," and "12-page Beauty Blitz and Major Makeovers: 10 Hot New Looks—Find the One For You." The table of contents listed the following departments: "Reads" (including gems about romance and kissing), "Guys" (including stories about guy watching and the guys love guide), "Fashion" ("Be a Date Diva"), "Beauty/Fitness; The Inner You" (with a quiz entitled "Is He Whipped for You?"), and "Stars" ("Stories on Babe Watch," entertainment, etc.). We did buy the magazine, primarily as a way of discussing gender stereotyping, and we later wrote a letter to the editor about the content of the articles.

STEREOTYPING IN SCHOOL

These issues have concerned me for over twenty years, since Heather reminded me that "I hadn't noticed." Stereotyping has been repeatedly mentioned by the talented women I have interviewed or with whom I have spoken. Ellen Strickland, a talented teacher who had wanted to become a scientist at an earlier age, told me that in 1972, she was the recipient of the Rensaeller Award at an academic awards assembly in her high school. This award was given to the senior with the highest average in math or science, and it was a tie tack. At the same assembly, she received an award for the highest math average in the senior class. The award was a book entitled *Men and Mathematics*. We've come a long way from that time period and an even longer way from the time period during which some of us read textbooks such as the one in Figure 5, but gender equity has still not been achieved in school textbooks and messages young people experience in their world.

In the past ten years, a number of national reports and books have examined the impact of stereotyping on girls. One comprehensive book written in 1994 by Myra and David Sadker, *Failing at Fairness: How America's Schools Cheat Girls*, details differences in test scores, grades, classroom interaction, and numerous other areas such as textbook inclusion of females. They cite as an example *A History of the United States*, a textbook in which fewer than 3% of the more than 1000 pages focused on women.

Judy Mann's book, *The Difference: Growing up Female in America* (1994), is another publication in a series of books examining the loss of confidence and self-esteem in young girls. The culture of girls' silence reported in both of these books should be clear to anyone who has entered a middle school in the last few years. I recently gave a career talk to a group of seventh-grade gifted students which included 13 boys and 12 girls. After a half-hour discussion about the ways researchers work and carry out data based studies, I pointed out that I had posed about a dozen questions during my talk and asked the

HOW TO BE A GOOD WIFE

Have dinner ready.
Plan ahead, even the night before, to have a delicious meal—on time. This is a way of letting him know that you have been thinking about him and are concerned about his needs. Most men are hungry when they come home and the prospect of a good meal is part of the warm welcome needed.

Prepare yourself.
Take fifteen minutes to rest so that you will be refreshed when he arrives. Touch up your make-up, put a ribbon in your hair and be fresh looking. He has just been with a lot of work-weary people. Be a little gay and a little more interesting. His boring day may need a lift.

Clear away the clutter.
Make one last trip through the main part of the house just before your husband arrives, gathering up school books, toys, papers, etc. Then run a dust cloth over the tables. Your husband will feel he has reached a haven of rest and order, and it will give you a lift, too.

Prepare the children.
Take a few minutes to wash the children's hands and faces (if they are small), comb their hair, and if necessary, change their clothes. They are little treasures and he would like to see them playing the part.

Minimize the noise.
At the time of his arrival, eliminate all noise of the washer, dryer, dishwasher or vacuum. Try to encourage the children to be quiet. Greet him with a warm smile and be glad to see him.

continued on page 48

Figure 5. Common advice from high school home economics books in the 1950s.

How to Be a Good Wife (conintued)

Some don'ts: Don't greet him with problems and complaints. Don't complain if he is late for dinner. Count this as minor to what he might have gone through that day. Make him comfortable. Have him lean back in a comfortable chair or suggest that he lie down in the bedroom. Have a cool drink ready for him. Arrange his pillow and offer to take off his shoes. Speak in a low, soft, soothing and pleasant voice. Allow him to relax and unwind.

Listen to him. You may have a dozen things to tell him, but the moment of his arrival is not the time. Let him talk first.

Make the evening his. Never complain if he does not take you out for dinner or to other pleasant entertainment. Instead, try to understand his world of strain and pressure, his need to unwind and relax.

The goal: Try to make your home a place of peace and order where your husband can relax in body and spirit.

Figure 5. Common advice from high school home economics books in the 1950s (continued).

students who had responded to these questions to raise their hands. Not one girl had tried to answer during the entire half hour. The girls had spoken only when I had called on them directly, and even then, some blushed, looked away, and/or chose not to respond. The entire classroom of students seemed surprised that the girls had not contributed. When I later asked the girls directly why they had not raised their hands during my talk, they offered interesting responses such as "it's a lot more important to the boys to call out answers," "they need to be right," and "we don't have to talk to learn." The explanations the girls in this group gave for their silence demonstrate the insight which some of them are already beginning to gain about their role in school and, perhaps, in life.

The climates of elementary, middle, and high school as well

as college have all been discussed as being responsible for changes in the attitudes of girls and women relative to achievement in school. Research in the past 10 or 15 years has indicated that boys actively participate in school more and receive more attention from teachers (Hall & Sandler, 1982; Jones, 1989; Krupnick, 1984, 1992; Sadker & Sadker, 1985, 1994). Some research indicates that a few male students receive more attention than all other students in math classes. Some evidence exists that the amount of teacher attention given to girls is lowest in science classes (Jones & Wheatley, 1990; Handley & Morse, 1985; Shepardson & Pizzini, 1992). In a study I conducted with my colleague, Karen Kettle, (Reis & Kettle, 1995) of science groups at a Connecticut Science Center, we found that having mixed gender groups usually resulted in the boys dominating and conducting the hands-on science experiments. In groups of all females, however, the problem was eliminated and girls were able to fully participate.

Science and math classes, in particular, seem to include multiple examples of stereotyping. In a recent study, Lee & Marks (1992) reported that they discovered the most blatant examples of stereotyping in chemistry. In another study, Tobin and Garnett (1987) found that 79% of the science classroom demonstrations were conducted by boys. These findings should raise some doubts about some of the suggestions made in the research literature about how females may benefit from cooperative learning groups (Eccles, 1985; Peterson & Fennema, 1985; Fennema & Leder, 1990).

A recent study (Hernandez Garduño, 1997) on gifted females who learned math in problem-solving situations indicated that females' attitudes toward math did not improve in class instruction scored higher in achievement tests than those in the cooperative learning groups. Qualitative data collected in the same study indicated that the talented girls who scored highest in math enjoyed competing with boys and liked trying to be the best. The mathematically talented girls studied by Leticia

Hernandez Garduño were sometimes frustrated by the lack of challenge in some of the mixed gender and single sex cooperative learning groups. One participant explained, "It is interesting to work with others, but you get bored when you have to explain the same thing over and over and you want to go to the next problem. Sometimes it is better to be alone when you are solving problems." Another commented, "I think we should always be able to choose who we want to work with. I would always choose those who understand things fast and who can also explain things to you. Otherwise, you don't feel so motivated to work anymore." More research needs to be conducted to examine whether talented females benefit from various types of cooperative learning.

Katherine Gavin (1996) obtained similar results studying gifted female college students who enjoyed academic competition and liked trying to be the best. Gavin cited two representative comments from gifted female math students she interviewed. "I enjoy competition and I enjoy being tested," explained one student. Another comment provides other insights, "I like to be at the top. . . I like to be the best." In another recent research study on gifted females who scored at the very highest level on the math section of the SAT, O'Shea (1998) found similar results, confirming the research of both Gavin (1996) and Hernandez Garduño (1997). The gifted young women O'Shea studied enjoyed both competition in math and competitive fast-paced math classes. Therefore, it would be a mistake to confuse what may be appropriate for the majority of female students with what may be instructionally appropriate for talented females.

In another recent study of high ability female students, my colleague, Mary Rizza, (1997) found support for the research conducted by Hernandez Garduño regarding the need for talented females to work alone. Rizza's research found that "solitary learning" was necessary when challenging academic work was pursued by gifted female high school students she investigated. Although these young women liked their friends a great deal and enjoyed socializing with them, most participants in Rizza's study wanted and needed to work alone when they had difficult academic work to complete.

SEXISM IN COLLEGES AND UNIVERSITIES

Researchers have also found that college classrooms have numerous instances of silent sexism (Hall & Sandler, 1982; Chamberlain, 1988; Glaser & Thorpe, 1986; Rubin & Borgers, 1990; Grant, 1988). It would appear from reports and research articles to be commonly acknowledged that an atmosphere of inequality exists in many university and college classrooms. Fay Ajzenberg-Selove (1994), a noted physicist, discussed this issue frankly in her autobiography:

> Are young women and young men treated equally in college? No, they are not. Overwhelmingly their science professors, particularly at the more prestigious universities, are males of an earlier era, an artifact of discrimination. Many of them, though consciously unaware of it, are uncomfortable with the women students in their classes. They are less likely to include women in class discussions and more likely to underestimate them. They can be intimidating and unpleasant. I believe that it is necessary that women faculty, as well as enlightened male faculty, discuss the importance of this problem with their other colleagues. It is very often the college which is at fault if a woman fails to pursue her scientific interests. And I believe that gender discrimination is a matter of still greater importance in graduate school when relationships with older scientists, with future patrons, are first established—relationships that are critical to a scientist's en-

tire career. (p. 221)

Sex discrimination problems at the college and university level often involve the same issues as in elementary and secondary school (Sadker & Sadker, 1994). Both male and female faculty treat their students differently based on sex. Dr. Bernice Sandler, director of the Association of American Colleges Project on the Status and Education of Women (PSEW), indicated that this treatment subtly undermines women's confidence and academic ability, lowers their academic and educational expectations, inhibits learning, and generally lowers self-esteem. In the report *Classroom Climate: A Chilly One for Women* (Hall & Sandler, 1982), research conducted on differences in the educational system and the work force for males and females discussed the chilly climate and silent sexism in many university classrooms. To explain why some women become discouraged in the college classroom, researchers cited that professors' overt behaviors such as disparaging, belittling, and crude remarks; obscene jokes; and remarks about physical appearance or clothing were undermining the women's education. This PSEW study found approximately 30 different types of subtle behaviors which all tended to reinforce men's confidence while undermining women's.

At many universities, there is widespread acknowledgment about what causes many females to drop out of both math and science majors, but little has been implemented to bring about change. At the University of Connecticut, The Chancellor's Commission on the Status of Women recently asked that a section of a dorm be reserved for women who major in math, science, or applied mathematical fields such as engineering or computer sciences. The Commission hoped that peer support will help to alleviate some of the discrimination issues facing young women in their academic classes. In interviews with young women at the University, the Commission has found that female students perceive that some faculty consistently ignore women and instead call on men. Female students believe that both male and female faculty call on men more often, use their names more frequently, give men more time to answer, and show more respect in their consideration of these responses. By their actions, the professors provide more positive reinforcement for men's responses than women's.

On a committee charged with examining why so many female math and science majors later switch their majors, I had the opportunity to listen to male professors discuss the University's inability to keep talented undergraduate women involved in math, science, and engineering majors. Some male professors in these areas told members of our committee that the reason so many young women changed their majors was that these science and math courses were just too difficult and that the women preferred easier alternatives such as English. "These girls just don't want to work hard," one male science professor complained. "They are the problem, not us!" another male professor agreed. "They want to take the easier classes in English or history," another male professor explained.

According to recent research, even in college or university classes in which women outnumber men, women are outtalked in class. Catherine Krupnick (1984, 1992) studied talented women at Harvard and found that they speak less and are interrupted more. She also studied the classroom dynamics of coed seminars that resulted from the decision to change Wheaton College to a coeducational environment. She had expected to find greater classroom equity than she had seen elsewhere because the student body and faculty were still predominately female. Her results showed the opposite however, as even when men made up just one to two ninths of the seminar classes she studied, they did one third to one half of the talking.

Work in the Home

Another external barrier many women experience as they attempt to realize their potential is the burden of responsibilities they often shoulder at home. A greater of amount work at home occurs when women enter relationships: "Marriage creates work, far beyond the apparent practical need, in order that work may create marriage" (Bateson, 1989, p. 123). Bateson's explanations of the customs of work created in marriage have been echoed by many talented women I have studied. Coming home from a day of work, they encounter a "second shift" of work assigned to them because of their sex. As Betty Friedan so eloquently stated, "Equality in jobs, without domestic equality, leaves women doubly burdened." Unfortunately, the cycle of inequality continues as mothers do most of the household work and their children watch.

Of course, exceptions exist. Some partners, husbands and fathers work diligently at home and support their spouses, but many do not. Bateson believes that part of the work existing in a marriage emanates from the common creation of patterns when adults live together—men do some tasks while women do other tasks which frequently involve more work. Other sociologists concur. Hartmann (1981) compared statistics on different types of households and found that the presence of an adult male creates more work for a woman than the presence of a child under ten, even when the man believes himself to be sharing the housework equally.

A study reported in *Newsweek* (Beck, Kantrowski, & Beachy, 1990) indicates that women also face the issue of caring for aging parents, estimating that the average American woman will spend 17 years raising children and 18 years helping aged parents. These added responsibilities will occur because of increasing longevity in our elderly population. These issues interact with many of the personal decisions women have to make on a daily basis.

THE INTERACTION BETWEEN EXTERNAL BARRIERS AND INTERNAL BARRIERS

Kate Noble (1987, 1989), a clinical psychologist who focused on the problems of gifted females, summarized data obtained from interviews with her clients, as well as the results of a survey of 109 women who attended a conference on gifted women. These data and a review of the literature on gifted females indicated that many gifted females are unaware of, ambivalent about, or frightened by their potential. She traced these findings to three sets of problems: interpersonal obstacles (rejection from family, teachers and peers; underestimation of abilities by families), sociocultural barriers (inadequate academic preparation, double messages), and interpersonal factors (self-doubt, disclaiming the label of giftedness). These problems, defined in different ways, have also been cited in the literature by other researchers (Arnold & Denny, 1985; Callahan, 1979; Eccles, 1985; Fox, 1977; Hoffman, 1972; Hollinger & Fleming, 1988; Horner, 1972; Kerr, 1985; Reis, 1987; Rodenstein, Pfleger, & Colangelo, 1977).

A conflict may exist for gifted females because of the differences in value systems between men and women, such as the ethical sensitivities of women investigated by Gilligan (1982). Women seem to understand and recognize the importance of interpersonal relationships and connectedness in a way that causes them to believe that the relationships in their life are of primary importance. For gifted women, pursuing their own talents in a way that will enable them to nurture and realize their capabilities at the risk of taking time from their children or family may be a difficult, if not impossible, task (Reis, 1987).

Gifted and talented females face conflicts and barriers that exist between their own abilities and the social structure of their world. These conflicts include (a) their inherent knowledge that society considers many challenging jobs to be masculine, (b) their multipotentiality in many academic areas which may prohibit appropriate career counseling and cause them to delay or avoid crucial decisions, and (c) the encouragement that they need is often hidden in a variety of mixed messages from their families, friends, and society in general. For younger girls, these mixed messages result in difficulty in learning what is special and good about being female.

Dr. Cynthia Mee (1995) interviewed 2000 middle school students in grades 5 through 8 in 15 schools in New York City, Illinois, Wisconsin, Florida, California, and Ohio. She found that many girls had difficulty answering the question, "What's the best thing about being a girl?" The most common responses were:

- "I don't know,"
- "can't think of any,"
- "nothing,"
- "a better selection of clothes,"
- "being pretty"
- "we don't have to go to war,"
- "boys,"
- "going shopping,"
- "having babies,"
- "don't have to pay for dates,"
- "fooling around with hair and makeup."

The most common responses for boys when asked "What's the best thing about being a boy?" were "not being a girl" and "we can do more things." Mee (1995) summarized her research by indicating that both boys and girls thought that boys could do more, are viewed as better, have different expectations, and have different restrictions. The boys thought of themselves as having a great deal to enjoy just by being a boy (p. 5). Mee further explained:

> The girls in my study struggled to find good things about being a girl, and easily identified a variety of negative aspects; they were very aware of society's different expectations of and the responsibilities imposed on each sex. The average middle school girl thinks that boys can do more now and that they will continue to be able to do more as they grow up, they will have higher status career expectations, they will get paid more, and will have more fun and less do-

mestic responsibilities. (p. 5)

The effects of such feelings on all girls are negative, but the further effects on gifted girls who have the potential to realize the highest career expectations can be devastating. It is important to examine research that discusses all girls and then look more closely at research that focuses on gifted girls to see what in particular may affect this group differently.

Jeanne H. Block (1982), a pioneer in gender research, believed that a fundamental task of the developing individual is the mediation between internal biological impulses and external cultural forces as they coexist in a person's life space and life span (p. 2). She further believed that the socialization process, defined as internalization of values, appears to have differential effects on the personality development of males and females. Socialization, Block asserted, narrows women's options while broadening men's options (p. 220). Unfortunately, as girls get older, many of them learn that their perception of reality differs from the life experiences they encounter.

The most difficult conflict faced by the majority of gifted women I have studied revolves around their relationships, the knowledge of their relationships, and especially their understanding that they may become mothers. Career plans and decisions are always made with the knowledge that today's women still bear the major responsibility for organizing a home and raising their children. These external barriers often interact with internal barriers causing many gifted women to lower their expectations.

CHAPTER THREE

~:~

PERSONALITY FACTORS, PERSONAL ISSUES & DECISIONS FACED BY TALENTED FEMALES

*It is obvious that the values of women differ very often
from the values which have been made by the other sex.
Yet, it is the masculine values that prevail.*
—Virginia Woolf

My research with talented females has revealed a number of
personality factors, personal priorities, and decisions which have
consistently emerged as the reasons that many either cannot or
do not realize their potential. These factors, priorities, and personal decisions were identified in hundreds of interviews that I
conducted with girls and women at various ages, stages, and occupations. Of course, not all women experience the same priorities and decisions, but commonalities do exist in many of the
talented women I studied, including dilemmas about abilities
and talents, personal decisions about family, decisions about duty
and caring (putting the needs of others first) as opposed to nurturing personal, religious, and social issues. It is difficult, if not
impossible, to discuss gifted girls without discussing gifted
women because many young gifted girls believe that they can
"do it all" or "have it all," while many older gifted females have
learned that they cannot.

Perhaps the most compelling way to introduce these issues
is through an excerpt from an interview with a researcher named
Miriam, a professor who was widely acknowledged to be very

successful. She published widely, was well-respected by her colleagues and graduate students, and seemed to have overcome many of the obstacles described by other women I studied. During one conversation, however, Miriam indicated her frustration at not being able to finish many of the projects she had begun in the last several years: "I have the primary responsibility for the care of my aging parents, in addition to our youngest daughter who is in eighth grade. My sister is involved in her own life and my brother will provide any financial help I need for my parents' care, but he can't provide what they need most, time and attention."

I replied, "Well, at least you know that you have been able to accomplish what many other women only dream of—you completed your doctorate, you have a respected profession, and have conducted important research resulting in books and articles."

Miriam smiled and responded, "Oh, it's not what I've done that is the issue, Sally. It's the work left undone at this point in my life, and what I could do with more time. But it can't and won't be done in time that I take from my parents and my daughter. I will not look back and wish that I had given them more of myself." This brief statement exemplifies the personal compromises described by many of the talented women in my research.

These personal issues occur across the lifespan. Some affect the youngest girls I have interviewed in the primary grades and some are only apparent to women who have become involved in serious relationships in their college or graduate school years. What is essential to note, however, is that I have found that most of the personal issues discussed in this chapter are resolved by the older talented women I have studied. The age of fifty seems to be a key age for understanding and resolving most of the dilemmas that face many gifted women, although some did find solutions earlier. It is also important to understand that some of these dilemmas cannot be resolved to the satisfaction of everyone involved. Rather, some dilemmas end with changes in a woman's life, such as the maturation of her children and, in some cases, the dissolution of a relationship, the reemergence of other relationships, and a change in environments at work or home.

CAN'T I DO IT ALL?

Consistent trends found in interviews with many young gifted women indicate that they grow up believing that they do not face the barriers that their mothers and grandmothers encountered. When and how do women learn about the barriers which can affect achievement? Hollinger and Fleming (1984) found no sign of recognition of internal barriers affecting accomplishment in women in 29% of the 284 gifted adolescents they studied. Perhaps, as these results indicate, women's internal barriers have been somewhat reduced since the advent of the women's movement. I have found, however, that the conflicts and barriers become more apparent as gifted girls mature and face decisions relating to marriage, career, and children at critical junctures in their lives. In fact, the intersection of these factors—ability, age, career choice, and personal decisions relating to marriage and children—may result in additional internal barriers.

In one interview conducted almost 15 years ago, a gifted teenage girl named Maria became angry with me as I asked her questions about perceived barriers she might confront in her future. Maria told me she faced no barriers, that the women's movement had paved the road and that she could certainly have it all. I remember her youthful enthusiasm as she explained to me that her dreams were not dreams at all, but rather a road map for her future. Her map included an education at a first-rate women's college, a graduate degree, a university position teaching to support her while she wrote the great American novel, and a husband and children. Last year, almost 20 years later, I interviewed Maria again. She had finished her undergraduate degree and fallen in love during college. She had not gone to graduate school, but had financially and emotionally supported her husband, whom she loved deeply, in his pursuit of his career. She spoke about his talents in glowing terms and showed me photographs of their young child who was the joy of her life. When I asked her about her plans for graduate school and for her writing, she paused and said, "Oh today, I am much more realistic about my goals. I try to get through the week and take care of my family. I also am devoted to my husband's dreams." As I paused to think of a way to tactfully ask another question, she spoke quietly, "You know, I bought the whole superwoman thing, but it's just not right to put my own needs ahead of the needs of my child and my husband. He has such dreams about his work." Instead, she deferred her own dreams, and only time, perhaps decades, will tell if they will reappear again or simply change.

Young girls often believe they can do anything and everything. For them, a direct battle would be easier to fight than the subtle messages laden with guilt that they encounter later. Some young women today are in a more difficult position because they aren't able to take the hard-line stance against discrimination that their mothers' generation did twenty years ago. In previous decades, women could find some satisfaction in being strong, in being a rebel of sorts, and they could appreciate gains when that behavior was recognized. These days the obvious foes to women's rights may be gone because of the success of the Women's Movement, but the reality of confronting more subtle obstacles and barriers still remains. Women today are supposed to have won the battle for equality, and to have no more glass ceilings to break through. Unfortunately, women keep encountering them anyway. It's as if there aren't any real windmills to conquer because in many cases the windmills are far too hazy, and we really can't see them until we run into them, as did Maria. Ambivalence about feminine ambition is also an issue. Many women encounter negative stereotyping and feedback from parents, peers, and other women, in addition to the population at large, about being ambitious and pursuing their goals and begin to feel that being ambitious is synonymous with being selfish.

Even those women who have made it to the pinnacle of their field suffer from decisions about priorities. In an article about elite female Olympic athletes, Martha Ludwig (1996) paints a poignant portrait:

> Many female Olympic athletes attempt to juggle the pressures of competition along with a career, a romantic relationship and parenthood. In spite of the assumed sociological strides made toward equality between women and men in the 1980s and 1990s, high-performance female athletes continue to encounter the obstacles of traditional gender roles. (p. 31)

Ludwig (1996) found that female Olympic athletes report that their spouses often do not provide enough support at home. These women carry the primary responsibility as wife, mother, homemaker, career person, and elite athlete. Even if the athletes balance these responsibilities well, Ludwig has found that they believe that their spouses may not understand the sacrifices required of them: "Many female athletes face the consequences of identity overload and must struggle to determine the priorities and balance of daily life within a non-supportive environment. Gender continues to make a difference" (p. 32). Ludwig also found that many of the elite female athletes delay relationships and childbirth rather than shoulder these responsibilities alone.

Some of these personal issues described in this chapter affect both young girls and older women and have been identified in my research as well as in studies by other educators and psychologists. It is difficult to pinpoint exactly when many of these issues surface in younger girls and women, but my research indicates that many of the difficult personal choices and dilemmas facing younger females are resolved as women age. With reflection, discussion, supportive friends and partners, and the right environment, younger girls and women can also address and perhaps resolve many of the difficult choices they face. These discussions can be guided by an examination of the critical personal issues they face and personality factors they possess.

Gilligan's Concept of a Different Ethic of Caring

The work of Carol Gilligan (1982), a professor at the Harvard Graduate School of Education, had a profound impact on my thoughts regarding gender and achievement. Prior to reading her work, I had found that many talented and gifted girls and women faced a difficult, almost unsolvable dilemma: how to put their own talents first when their entire life had been based upon the importance of relationships and the tacit belief that women always put *others* first. According to Gilligan, women not only define themselves in a context of human relationships, but judge themselves in terms of their ability to care for others. Historically, women have nurtured, taken care of, and helped their children and spouses. They have developed networks of relationships which are vital to them. K. F. Gauss, a legendary 19th century mathematician, lived his life in a haze of productivity. His biographies reveal a flood of ideas that kept him in a constant cycle of activity. When told his wife was dying, he is said to have been so involved in his work that he exclaimed, "Tell her to wait until I am through." Few, if any, women could imagine behaving as Gauss might have. As care and relationships are linked with a woman's integrity, this scene would be unthinkable for most women.

Women have been found to be much more concerned than men about relationships and to understand their own need for interdependent relationships. The talented women I studied understood that if they developed their own talents, there would be an impact upon those they loved. They often were frustrated with their own inability to resolve the need to do two things: support, care for, and maintain relationships with those they loved while simultaneously pursuing a talent or a gift to its fullest level. Many only resolved their frustrations about their inability to pursue their own talents at a later age.

In her book, *In a Different Voice*, Carol Gilligan (1982) pointed out that a woman's sense of integrity is entwined with an ethic of care, and for some this ethic of care is confused with either seeking or needing approval from loved ones. She explained that making the distinction between helping and pleasing frees the activity of taking care from the wish for approval by others. At that point, responsibility can become a self-chosen anchor of personal integrity and strength. Gilligan warned that mid-life changes in family and work can alter a woman's sense of self and her feelings of connectedness to family and others, possibly leading to deprecation and despair. I have found that some talented women were only able to pursue their dreams to a limited extent during the early years of building a relationship, caretaking and nurturing, and seeking financial security. These women welcomed mid-life as a time that often brings opportunities to pursue their chosen work in a more focused way. Mid-life may also help erase the boundaries between self and the need to care and nurture others. Unfortunately, as Gilligan explained, if this time is not perceived to be an opportunity for more freedom, and the caring needed to raise a family is no longer required, mid-life can become a time of loss and, potentially, of bitterness and angst for some women.

The ethic of caring described by Gilligan accompanied by women's belief in the importance of relationships is often the single greatest issue to address for gifted females who also have their own unique dreams and aspirations for important work. The majority of the gifted women in their 20s, 30s, and 40s who told me their stories were torn by guilt over what they want to do for themselves and what they believed they should be doing for their families and for those they love. Most struggled with finding time to do their own work and often compromised by putting their work off until they met all family obligations. As a result, they often had little time left for their own creative work. As one of the artists in my study explained, she can work only:

> . . . *when my life is in order, the kids are happy,*

> *dinner is cooking, the house is clean, the laundry is caught up, and there's a semblance of calm in the household, it just seems like ideas flow. I can sit down and write poetry just like that. I can sit at the computer and turn out two or three pages of a screenplay.*

CREATION OF A SENSE OF SELF AND A FEMININE IDENTITY

One of the older gifted women I interviewed was most eloquent as she explained her search to find herself.

> *I was never called by my own name until my husband died. As a young girl, I was always Arthur's daughter. When I married, I was Charlie's wife. When I had children, I was Sarah and David's mother. It was only after my children grew up and my husband died, that I was recognized as Berice and called by my own name. I realized I had lost my sense of self as a young girl, and only regained it as an older woman.*

Most young girls in elementary and middle school do not have an understanding of self. They begin to learn who they are in high school and college, only to have their sense of self waver as they become involved in a relationship.

A sense of self is critical to the development of talent in women. Profound changes in a woman's personal life can completely alter her sense of self; an early marriage and a resulting name change, for example, may erode her sense of self. A famous geologist explained to me that she had changed her name after marrying her first husband in college and did not want to change it when she divorced because of her numerous publications and growing name recognition in her field. When she was to be honored with the distinction of having a mountain named after her, her mother asked her if she really intended to name the mountain after her husband's family instead of her own. She made the difficult decision to name the mountain using her own family name, but now, she explained to me, "Nobody realizes it is named for me."

If women marry at young ages and have children early in the marriage, they often have little or no time to regain their sense of self. Gifted women must create a sense of self and an understanding of their identity if they are to realize their potential. Gaining a sense of self and a belief in self was consistently mentioned by the gifted women I interviewed who had been able to develop their talents in adulthood. Women who marry at a later time, in their late 20s or early 30s, are able to establish a stronger sense of self and are more often able to maintain their understanding of and belief in self after they become involved in a relationship and have children.

THE DEVELOPMENT OF SELF-EFFICACY

Albert Bandura developed the concept of self-efficacy in 1977. According to Bandura, self-efficacy is a person's judgment about his/her ability to perform a particular activity, and Bandura has found a significant, positive relationship between self-efficacy beliefs and academic performance (1986). Sources for increasing self-efficacy include past performances, the vicarious experiences of observing models who are like yourself, verbal persuasion, and physiological clues (Bandura, 1986). Some stop trying to achieve because they seriously doubt they can do what is required. Despite assurance of their capabilities, others give up working to achieve because they expect that their efforts will not produce any results in an unresponsive, negatively biased, or punitive social environment. While those with perceived low self-efficacy will readily let go of their dreams should their efforts fail to produce results, self-efficacious individuals will intensify their efforts and, if necessary, try to change inequitable social practices. Bandura also reported that people with positive views of their self-efficacy approach new tasks willingly, persist in the face of difficulty, and believe that they can succeed. Those with low self-efficacy tend to avoid new learning experiences, give up quickly, and focus on feelings of incompetence.

Because of the external and internal barriers they confront in life, many gifted females do not have the opportunities to develop self-efficacy. They receive less verbal persuasion from their parents and friends, observe fewer role models, and produce less creative work. Many more women must visibly achieve in diverse ways before the self-efficacy of other girls and women can be developed and increased.

MULTIPOTENTIALITY

Women who demonstrate multipotentiality usually have an eagerness to learn or an endless thirst for knowledge (Ehrlich, 1982); uniformly high scores across ability and achievement tests (Sanborn, 1979); multiple educational, vocational, and leisure interests at comparable intensities; and complex personality factors. Women with high potential and multiple interests often have multiple academic, career, and leisure possibilities, and these choices constitute multipotentiality. For some, having many choices is beneficial because they result in a variety of options. Others, however, often can not find their niche, make it on their own, or choose a vocational path (Fredrickson, 1979,1986; Jepsen, 1979; Kerr, 1981; Marshall, 1981; Sanborn, 1979b; Schroer & Dorn, 1986). Many women with multipotentiality find decision making difficult since it is not possible to do all that they would like to do and are capable of doing.

Personalogical factors may also affect girls and women who demonstrate multipotentiality. Perrone & Van Den Heuvel (1981) found that multipotentiality may lead students to commit to a career too quickly in order to reduce tensions caused by a vast array of competing options. Other multipotential women may have career choices externally imposed on them by their parents or teachers who believe they know the appropriate field (Silverman, 1993). Still others may simply become engrossed in a single subject area at a very early age and waver little from this choice, deliberately closing doors to many unexplored possibilities in order to eliminate the likelihood of any unwanted confusion (Marshall, 1981; Silverman, 1993). A connection between personality attributes and the "overchoice syndrome" seems to exist (Clark, 1992; Schmitz & Galbraith, 1985). The areas of self-exploration, self-criticism, intellectual maturity, and the presence of complex value systems all interact with multipotentiality. Women with a wide range of personality characteristics and perspectives often have a difficult time understanding themselves and making appropriate choices for career and advanced training.

The Development of Resilience and its Relationship to Work

Theories about resilience attempt to explain achievement among those who are subjected to negative psychological and environmental situations. Rutter (1987) defined resilience as "the positive pole of individual differences in people's response to stress and adversity" (p. 316). Resilience is not a fixed attribute in individuals and the successful negotiation of psychological risks at one point in a person's life does not guarantee that the individual will react positively to other stresses when situations change. Rutter discussed four processes that protect individuals against risk and enhance the development of resilience: (a) reduction of risk impact by altering either the risk or exposure to the risk, (b) reduction of negative chain reactions that follow risk exposure, (c) establishment and maintenance of self-esteem and self-efficacy, and (d) opening up of opportunities. Werner (1984) described the characteristics of individuals with resilience as an active, evocative approach toward solving life's problems; a tendency to perceive experiences constructively, even if they have caused pain or suffering; the ability, from infancy onward, to gain other people's positive attention; and a strong ability to use faith in order to maintain a positive vision of a meaningful life.

The gifted women I studied used successful resilience strategies and achieved while others of similar ability who faced similar problems did not. These gifted artists, scientists, authors, politicians, activists, and scholars took control of their own learning. Their lives were characterized by determination, insight, independence, initiative, humor, and creativity. One of the older women had endured a series of disappointments and endings in her life. When asked how she had gained the courage to continue her work, she answered, "My dear, what was the alternative? I just got up the next day and kept at it." Another participant in my study (a famous author) indicated that she worked much harder to "get even" with those who wanted her to fail and explained that she had been consistently denied opportunities: "So many people tried to keep me from accomplishing my goal. The best revenge was my own success." Still others continued to work because of a sense of seeking fairness for all women. A famous female composer interviewed for the older women's study explained that music appreciation and music history books were filled with male composers and it was time for more females to enter those pages. Others believed they simply had to compete: "Only one other person has written a book on this and I didn't believe it was a very good book. I set out to write a better book." Still others excelled out of a sense of being a rebel. One scientist explained, "I was the only woman in my science classes. My parents insisted I major in education or business. I majored in science as a pure act of rebellion."

Many women I studied had great talent, but failed to achieve at levels that they believed were commensurate with their potential. They were discouraged by their perceived previous failures, or explained that they were overwhelmed by family and life factors and their poor use of time management and planning skills. Fear of failing again or being negatively viewed or receiving poor feedback or evaluations all seemed to have an effect on their inability to develop resilience. Several explained that their fear of criticism or negative feedback separated them from their male peers. "My male colleagues enjoy a good fight and are proud when their work is singled out for criticism. They believe this kind of criticism draws scholarly attention to their work and helps them to become better known," explained one female academic scholar. "I, on the other hand, hate criticism because it hurts me. I back away from fights, avoid publicity, and seek quiet acceptance to continue to do my work."

What factors contributed to the development of resilience? Strong family and relationship ties, friendships with other women and men, love of work, and a passion to continue doing what they love were all attributes of the resilient, gifted females I studied. Likewise, the realization that defeat sometimes provided an opportunity for learning to occur also contributed to developing resilience. One older participant in my study, a prominent college president, explained that she is constantly criticized by faculty, students, and the press. She indicated that she understood that this criticism was a "part of the territory" when she accepted the position. She expected criticism and regarded it as the predecessor to positive action.

The process of doing work they considered important also helped develop resilience in the gifted women I studied. One artist described her daily struggle with the creative process of her art and her attempt to form her vision as a vital area of both comfort and security in her life. The work was essential to her well-being. "There's still so much more to accomplish," she explained. The talented women I studied who experienced pain and unhappiness acknowledged these difficulties and then moved on to continue their work as quickly as possible. A chronically ill poet who participated in my study of older women explained that she got over her pain and physical discomforts and forgot them as quickly as possible. "I just get on with my life and am happy for another day. I figure with another day, I may have another poem. There are still so many other poems in me, just waiting to get out." Meaningful work that mattered and made a difference was essential to the development of resilience in these women.

Fear of Success and What Might Accompany Success, or Fear of Never Finding a Partner who Celebrates Your Success

Some researchers believe that the "fear of success" syndrome first introduced by Matina Horner in 1970 is a key factor in understanding the problems facing gifted women. Fear of success may cause some females to believe that they will be rejected by their peers or appear undesirable to the opposite sex if they are too competent or successful. Horner explained that many capable young women change their plans to accommodate a less ambitious, more traditionally feminine role, away from role innovation. The women she studied may have experienced fear of success and withdrawn from the actual achievement of it because they believed that success in an innovative role may rule out success in a traditional and expected role—affiliation with the opposite sex (pp. 66-69). Her research, conducted originally as her doctoral dissertation, stated that fear of success, also known as success anxiety, "exists because for most women the anticipation of success in competitive achievement activity, especially against men, produces anticipation of certain negative consequences, e.g., threat of social rejection and loss of femininity" (p. 125).

My research provides evidence that negative consequences to success do occur for some gifted women. One negative consequence involves partners who may feel threatened by the success of a competent, intelligent, successful women. Many of the women I studied have been divorced, separated, or involved in unhappy relationships. Some could not fulfill their potential and achieve success until they were divorced or their partners had died. The reasons for these relationship problems varied, but the one most frequently cited in my research revolved around men who were threatened by a very successful wife. In one candidly honest article, Joe Kane (1985) wrote, "For all the supposed enlightenment of the last decade, there is still no accepted place in our culture for the man whose mate is a more powerful figure than he is." He also elaborated on the secret fear which was expressed in many of my interviews with both younger and older women.

> Come on, admit it: when you meet an ambi-
> tious, successful woman, and the man in her
> life is not an achiever of equal note, you figure
> him for a wimp, don't you? And your judg-
> ment of him is far more severe than your judg-
> ment of her would be if the situation were re-
> versed. (Kane, p. 52)

Kane's article, written about his own relationship with a talented woman who was about to graduate from an Ivy League law school addresses this issue head on and with considerable honesty. "Do I feel threatened? You bet. Ugly questions are rearing up, demanding to be answered" (p. 52)

What is the role for men in a society in which women are rising to new heights? Is it an accident that some powerful women, such as Secretary of State Madeline Albright, are divorced? Were their positions of power reached because they were able to develop resilience from their experiences, enabling them to forge ahead and create new lives for themselves? Many women who want to live lives with vital relationships have to make difficult choices about their own talent development. Our society still does not have a common model about the spouse or partner in a relationship with a very successful woman, unless the partner is equally or even more successful.

Georgia Sassen (1980) reexamined success anxiety in women, finding that the climate of competition may result in anxiety instead of success. She suggested that this anxiety might be a reflection of an essentially female way of constructing reality and called for a way to restructure society and institutions so that competition is not the only avenue to success. However, my research with women in their late 20s, 30s, and older indicates that these women do not fear success, but often regard it with some ambivalence. This ambivalence occurs not because they fear rejection from either peers or individuals in whom they may have a romantic interest, but rather because they don't desire the trappings which may accompany success. In the women I studied, these trappings include overexposure in a too public life, an inability to balance success with time for family and other loved ones, an overt dislike of the perceived competition that may be necessary to achieve success, and a strong dislike of the types of behavior that may become necessary to maintain success. Women consider some of these behaviors—a need for power, a "good ole boy attitude," egocentric behavior, and a tendency to monopolize meetings and conversations—to be negative male characteristics, and they do not want to emulate them.

Although some women overcome fear of success, many others never do, and it would be inaccurate to simply dismiss fear of success as something which declines with age. I have found that some types of fear of success or ambivalence about success affects women at all levels of accomplishment, from the most eminent to those who are in the beginning of their rise to success. Even female Olympic contenders experience fear of success. In an article on women in the Olympics, Martha M. Ludwig (1996) discussed fear of both success and failure, indicating fear of failure is manifested in a similar manner by both men and women, but that fear of success is primarily a female issue. "Fear of success for women seems to initiate from a cognitive belief system that sometimes becomes an insurmountable obstacle to success" (p. 31).

Learning how some women gain the confidence necessary to actively seek success will help parents and educators work to inspire confidence in young girls. Many of these fears or concerns, which accompany what has traditionally been defined as success in work, diminish in some women with age and experience, according to my research with older women. I have found that for many talented women, reaching the age of 50 provides a renaissance period, enabling the further understanding of self, ambition, and success which can be obtained without detriment to loved ones. Other women learn that for them, success in life should not be measured only by how well they do in their careers or work, but rather, how well they do in the areas they determine to be important, which may include their relationships with their families, their parenting, or work.

Fear of success at an early age, however, may lead to a change in confidence in one's ability and can have devastating effects if it occurs during college or graduate school. Although my current research suggests that fear of success can be eliminated in many women with age and experience, results in a study of high school valedictorians by Karen Arnold (1995) found that female students who had done well in high school lose confidence in their ability after a few years of college. In their second year of college, the female valedictorians lowered their assessments of their intelligence. The effects of this loss of self-confidence can influence the rest of a young woman's life if it causes changes in college plans, goals for graduate study, or choice of partner or career. Arnold's conclusions parallel my own about the gender differences in intellectual self-esteem of talented females who realize that their career decisions will interact, perhaps negatively, with both their relationships and motherhood.

ABSENCE OF PLANNING OR POOR PLANNING

Another issue affecting young talented females is their inability to plan for the future in a realistic way. Many young women ignore or are unaware of the economic reality that most will have to work their entire lives to support themselves and/or their families. (Older women comprise the single, largest, adult poverty group in the United States.) Many never consider long-term planning for a career or the financial implications of their choices as they erroneously believe that someday Prince Charming will come along, take care of them, and support them. Males, on the other hand, grow up realizing that they will have to work for a lifetime and select more appropriate long range career goals.

Because some women do not learn to plan, they often have

not thought about how to juggle a marriage, career, family, graduate school, and/or advanced study. Some talented girls I interviewed have unrealistic beliefs that they can go through college and graduate school, begin a career, and then interrupt that career to marry and have children without consequence to their career choices and advancement. Could a talented young male executive or scientist interrupt his newly developing career for seven or eight years without serious ramifications? Females need to be aware of these consequences and encouraged at an early age to begin considering and planning their education and thinking about their choices. These choices may include careers that will allow them to flourish both professionally and personally. It is important that this planning begin early enough so that young girls can internalize their career options and realistically plan future directions. Parents and teachers must consider planning as a way of working with young gifted females to help them establish clear goals which will guide them if they should become involved in a relationship and consider deferring their own dreams. A few lines worth practicing with younger gifted girls might be "I would love to have a relationship after I finish graduate school" and "Me first, for as long as I am in school."

Talented young women have to learn that to plan for themselves is essential and not a selfish act. Personal planning interacts with other personal concerns which affect success in women. In 1891, Charlotte Perkins Gilman wrote in *Women and Economics*, "Where young boys plan for what they will achieve and attain, young women plan for *WHOM* [caps added] they will achieve and attain." We must ask if the current situation of talented women is so different today. In a recent seminar with 60 honors students at the University of Connecticut, of whom approximately 40 were women, I asked what some considered their major block to success. Several of the young women instantly called out "relationships" or "my boyfriend." Many talented females put their own dreams and hopes on hold once they are involved in a relationship and especially after they have children.

It is difficult to pursue one's talents when others must inevitably come first. Lack of careful planning often causes these difficult choices to occur much earlier than they should. Planning for one's education and personal dreams should provide the tools necessary to enable talented girls and women to have choices, as well as to understand the ramifications of decisions to discontinue an education or change a career plan because of a relationship, especially a relationship that occurs between the ages of 17 and 23.

HIDING ABILITIES, DOUBTING ABILITIES, AND FEELING DIFFERENT

Thomas Buescher and his associates (1987) studied gifted adolescent boys and girls a decade ago and found that while 15% of boys hide their ability in school, 65% of girls consistently hide their talents. They also found that boys sought ways that they could be recognized for their abilities in areas such as athletics, student council, and in honors classes while girls did not. My interviews have consistently found that young girls do not want to be considered different from their friends and same-age peers. Indeed, a tendency exists for many females, regardless of age, to try to minimize their differences. Both young girls and older women have a greater need to be accepted and a need to have people who are like them. *Defying the Crowd*, the title of a recent book on creativity by Sternberg and Lubart (1995), illustrates a fundamental difference in creative endeavors for women. Defying the crowd is the last thing that many women would seek to accomplish. If women either feel different or are different, most want to minimize differences through quiet work and failing to call attention to themselves. Most talented women I studied have wanted to create and produce quietly, preferably in an environment in which their differences do not appear so obvious and they are not singled out. Parental influences such as teaching daughters to be modest or polite seem to confound this issue. In many of my interviews with young and adolescent gifted girls, they explained that they did not like to share the news of a high grade or a special accomplishment because it would seem as if they were bragging.

In one especially poignant interview with a first grade gifted girl named Jennifer who was reading at a fourth grade level, I learned why she had tried to hide her reading ability from her first grade teacher. Her mother had called me and explained that Jenny had been reading Nancy Drew books at home. But in school, she pretended that she could not read, spent her time looking at picture books, and began bringing home picture books with little or no print. When I spoke to Jenny, I asked her pointedly if she was trying to hide the fact that she was an excellent reader from her teacher or her friends. She paused momentarily before answering, "Both," and then explained that she did not want to hurt her friends' feelings who were not yet reading and did not want to appear different to either her teacher or her friends. She also explained that it seemed like she was showing off if she read "bigger, harder books than anybody else in the class." The solution to this problem was simple as we found a first grader from another class who read at a similar level and could be paired with this precocious reader for reading instruction and free reading time.

For many girls, however, the problem is more difficult as they become women and their talents and gifts set them apart from their peers and friends. If the school environment is one in which academics take a back seat to athletics or other activities, the issue may be exacerbated. Learning why females mask or hide their ability is often critical to addressing the problem, and finding environments in which success is celebrated and individual differences are respected is crucial.

In addition to hiding abilities, some gifted and talented women begin to doubt that they really have abilities. In a study about female graduates who attended a school for gifted students in New York City from 1920 through the 1970s (Walker, Reis, & Leonard, 1992), three out of four women did not believe in their superior intelligence. Consequently, if women do not recognize their potential, they usually will not fulfill it. In this study, we also found that these gifted women selected mediocre and gender stereotypic jobs, often due to pressure from parents and teachers.

It is difficult to live within a community when you either feel or are different. Wanting to create or do one's work instead of going out for lunch, spending time with friends, and being involved in community often sets older talented women apart. Many told me the same story. They are constantly asked why they can't be happy with their life. "You have a lovely home, a nice husband, and a good life. Why do you need to do more?" is a phrase that many repeated to me in one variation or another. "Why can't you be happy with your life as it is?" is another question often asked of these women by their families and their friends. A congresswoman in my study of older eminent women told me that her female friends asked her in amazement each time she ran for reelection, "Why do you do this to yourself?"

An unfortunate by-product of a creative productive life is the reality of few friendships. Over and over, many of the talented women told me that they did not have time for friends. At age 50 and over, as other relationships ended and children grew up and moved out, some patterns of friendship were renewed and the feelings of separation, for some women, diminished. But the feelings of being different seldom left these women. Again, finding environments in which success is celebrated and individual differences are respected is essential both when girls are in school so that they can learn and later in life so they can produce creative work and find personal happiness.

SEARCHING FOR PERFECTION

Too many females spend their lives trying to be perfect. In addition to investing considerable energy in trying to be the best athlete, the best dancer, the best scholar, the best friend, and the best daughter, young girls and women often feel that they must also be slender, beautiful, and popular. This perfectionism is often a result of parental pressures, as well as pressures from the media, and a conscious or unconscious desire to try to make everyone happy. A perfectionism complex can cause talented women to set unreasonable goals for themselves and strive to achieve at increasingly higher levels. It also can cause women to strive to achieve impossible goals and spend their lives trying to achieve perfection in work, home, body, children, wardrobe, and other areas.

Perfectionism can also be regarded as a positive influence in one's life. Hamachek (1978) viewed perfectionism as a manner of thinking about behavior and described two different types of perfectionism, normal and neurotic, that form a continuum of perfectionist behaviors. Normal perfectionists derive pleasure from the labors of effort and feel free to be less precise as the situation permits. Neurotic perfectionists are unable to feel satisfaction because they never seem to do things well enough. Hamachek identified six specific overlapping behaviors describing both normal and neurotic perfectionists: depression, a nagging feeling of "I should," shame and guilt feelings, face-saving behavior, shyness and procrastination, and self deprecation.

In a recent study on perfectionism in gifted adolescents in a middle school, Schuler (1997) found that perfectionism can be viewed as a continuum with behaviors ranging from healthy/normal to unhealthy/dysfunctional. Order and organization, support systems, and personal effort were the factors that impacted the healthy perfectionists. All of the healthy female perfectionists had been aware of their perfectionist tendencies since they were young, with their first memories related to school activities. Barbara, one of the participants in Schuler's study, expressed this need to have work organized and in correct order, "I know I was really worried when I was a little kid ... [that] everything had to be perfect."

While this need for order was pervasive among these gifted girls, there was also a feeling that they felt supported by their families, friends, and peers. They received encouragement to do their "personal best" academically, told that mistakes were acceptable parts of learning. The comments they heard from their parents were typical of Barbara's experience:

> They want me to succeed. They expect me to succeed . . . my parents think, believe, if you expect failure, you'll get failure . . . but they also don't want to set [goals] so high that it's like without control over your own life. So they expect me to succeed and to try my personal best, and to do well and to finish what I started, and that kind of thing. But they don't expect that it's going to be perfect and excellent . . . (Shuler, p. 159)

Personal effort was perceived as an important aspect of the healthy gifted females' perfectionist behaviors. Doing one's "personal best" and working hard were synonymous, and while participants acknowledged their high abilities, they believed their drive for perfection and their hard work made them successful. They continued to work harder to relieve their frustrations if they made mistakes or had difficulties. The healthy female perfectionists were considered responsible, cooperative, organized, considerate, and conscientious workers by their teachers. Since elementary school, they all had been a "pleasure to have in class."

On the other hand, concern over mistakes, perceived parental expectations, and perceived parental criticisms were the salient factors for the gifted unhealthy/dysfunctional female perfectionists. They possessed a fixation about making mistakes which resulted in a high state of anxiety. Their definitions of perfectionism focused on not making any errors. The meaning one participant in Schuler's (1997) study named Mary gave to perfectionism and the accompanying feelings were representative of the unhealthy female perfectionists when she said, "I believe perfectionism is when someone must be on top, right, accurate at all times. When they are wrong they feel they haven't succeeded. Maybe after that, they feel less confident."

Unlike the healthy female perfectionists, the unhealthy females' earliest memories of being perfectionistic centered on making mistakes. Phoebe, for example, still felt angry about being teased by a teacher in front of her elementary class for handing in less than her usual perfect work. These unhealthy female perfectionists were concerned about making errors both because of their own high standards and those of their parents. To make a mistake would be an admission that perhaps they weren't so bright after all. They would become angry with themselves when work or test scores didn't meet their personal standards, especially if others would notice. They feared embarrassment, either in school or at home. Mistakes were not opportunities to learn, but humiliations to be avoided.

The majority of the unhealthy female perfectionists worked to please others—teachers, peers, or parents. Unlike the healthy female perfectionists, they viewed their parents' perfectionism negatively, and perceived parental expectations as demands to be perfect in everything they did. Comments such as "don't fail," "do the best," "where are the A's?" and "you should do better" were not interpreted as motivators, but as criticisms of their efforts, leading them to be highly critical of themselves and possess an intense concern over making mistakes.

The unhealthy female perfectionists believed that their teachers, friends, and peers also expected perfection from them. The pressure to work hard was a result of their intense sensitivity to others' reactions to everything the perfectionists did. They perceived their efforts to be under the microscopic review of family, teachers, friends, and themselves. If they could not be perfect and meet their own and others' expectations, they believed they would be criticized. Most of these gifted females lived in a high state of anxiety and doubted their actions because they never knew if what they were doing was going to be good enough. They were afraid of failure in school performance, as they did not want to disappoint others who they perceived would be upset if their performance was less than the best. As Annie remarked:

> Because I have the image of being a straight A student, that's who I am. And if I don't do well, or if I fail or something, then I don't know who I am. And no one else does either. Everyone else is just kind of like, whoa, you know. Like she's not who she used to be . . .

Even sadder, these girls sometimes equated maintaining grades with maintaining friendships. Earning high grades were important because they ensured the existence of friendships. Lower grades might threaten them. Mary, an exceptionally talented student, stated "I don't think I would feel as good, and that . . . I didn't belong with some of my friends who got straight A's . . ."

Not only were they critical of themselves, they were also critical of those whom they wanted to impress, especially a parent or other perfectionist peer. Their own inappropriate expectations, added to the pressure these girls faced not to fail. The consequences for the pressure were self-doubts, procrastination, repeating work over and over, taking an exceedingly long time to complete tasks, and constant anxiety and worry.

The findings of this study illustrate the complexities of perfectionism in the lives of gifted female adolescents. While all of the participants were straight A or A⁺ students and envisioned themselves in professional careers, their degrees of perfectionism varied, as did their coping strategies. The healthy female perfectionists used more positive techniques, including problem-solving, self-talk, talking with peers, helping others, pacing their work or setting time limits. The unhealthy female perfectionists, on the other hand, displayed a number of depressive symptoms. Anxiety, sleep problems, withdrawal, temper tantrums at home, and guilt feelings were common, yet none had a major decrease in school performance. None sought social support when they were stressed out. They worked harder to become more perfectionist or neater, sometimes blamed others, or took extraordinary amounts of time to do things. All wanted to be in control of situations and had difficulty when they weren't. They were in distress, but because they hid their "imperfections" so well, no one was aware of their pain. They had perfected the art of camouflaging their feelings. Like the healthy female perfectionists, the unhealthy females were a "pleasure to have in class."

Schuler (1997) found that perfectionism is a trait that exists on a continuum with definite behaviors and attitudes. It is not a problem to be cured, but a trait that can be either beneficial or harmful. To help gifted female adolescents move away from the unhealthy end of the perfectionist continuum, parents, educators, and counselors need to examine various interventions and strategies to address the consequences faced by these young women.

What I have called "The Honor Roll Syndrome" connects in various ways with perfectionism. Many talented girls become victims of the honor roll mentality imposed by schools and bought into by parents, especially if the honor roll is published in the local newspaper. Many young people come to believe that it is necessary to strive for A's in all subjects in order to make the honor roll. As a result, they have to do well in every area instead of putting particular emphasis on what they like most or in what they have the greatest interest. This mentality sometimes translates into life experiences later when women strive to do well in all areas of life. Many successful female scientists who have written about their careers discuss how they considered switching majors because they got their first B or C in a difficult class. Talented girls and women need to realize that success and professional goals can be attained with average grades in some content areas, that they must choose the areas in which they want to excel, and that excellence cannot and should not be expected in all areas. These lessons are critical for girls in high school because when they go to college or beyond, they must begin to understand that their success will be due to effort rather than ability, as many of their peers will have similar ability. In my interviews I have found that many do not have the time to contribute the required effort for top grades in every content area, and they must make decisions about where they will focus their energy.

THE IMPOSTOR SYNDROME

A fascinating anomaly of perfectionism occurs when females achieve high levels of success—labeled by psychologists Pauline Rose Clance and Suzanne Imes (1978; Clance, 1985) as the "Great Impostor Syndrome." This syndrome describes a low sense of self-esteem which occurs when females attribute their successes to factors other than their own efforts and see their outward image of a bright successful achiever as being undeserved or accidental. "I was lucky," "I was in the right place at the right time," "I really didn't do as well as it seems," and "I had a lot of help" are all statements made by talented females complemented on their successes. This reaction to compliments and success does not seem to affect males to the same degree. More talented males of all ages have been found to attribute their achievements to their own efforts, saying "thank you" when they are complimented, while more girls attribute their accomplishments to external forces and not to themselves.

In my research, some female college students who believe they are impostors were afraid when they entered college that they didn't belong academically (despite the fact that their grades were actually better than those of the non-impostors) and also afraid that they would fail socially. Clance (1985) has estimated that about 70% of all college-educated people experience the impostor phenomenon sometime in their lives, often when they get a promotion or start a new job. However, 40% of this group are not able to lose the sense that somehow they don't belong and think that the next time, they "will be found out" or "will blow it." Females tend to attribute their successes to effort or external factors such as luck while failures are explained as internal faults or as due to lacking certain abilities. On the other hand, males attribute their success to their own capabilities and failure to external factors. Attribution theory indicates that the masculine attribution pattern is more likely to provide a greater motivation for performance than the feminine pattern. Weiner (1986) has found that attributions can influence emotions, self concepts and subsequent behaviors.

This gender difference has recently been noted in a research study Karen Arnold (1995) conducted with high school valedictorians. Arnold found that by the second year of college, over a quarter of the high school valedictorians she studied had lowered their self-rankings of their intelligence, indicating that they were merely average in intelligence. This phenomenon did not occur with the male valedictorians whose self-rankings remained consistent or actually improved. The women Arnold studied continued this pattern at graduation from college. None of the women placed herself in the highest category of intelligence while men, in sharp contrast, steadily increased their self-ratings (p. 106).

Clance and Imes (1978; Clance, 1985) identified four elements of the origins of the Great Impostor Syndrome in childhood and family background: (a) the family image of the child was not the image held by the world and the inconsistencies produced confusion in the child; (b) the impostor's family valued smartness above all; (c) the child was a "square peg" and was different from others in the family; and (d) the family did not praise the child enough and did not celebrate and reward the child for his or her accomplishments and abilities. In my interviews with talented females, some believed that their parents contributed to the absence of their belief in their own abilities by telling them that they were the beauty of the family while their brothers were more intelligent. When these girls became more successful than their brothers in school, they later looked for explanations for why they contradicted their parents' beliefs or the myths within their family structure.

Some women actually begin to believe that they have accomplished success because they have fooled other people, or have been successful due to having the right mentor, a happy disposition, or an act of chance. In some cases, this feeling of accomplishing success due to luck or chance has occurred because talented girls and women can often accomplish a great deal without the effort which is often required from their less capable peers. If ability is high and less effort is warranted, many women begin to feel that they are lucky rather than academically gifted. The women I have studied often attributed their successes to external factors—the right schools, the best teachers, and fortunate circumstances or chance. In my research I have found that many impostors come to believe they are not really talented. Therefore, they believe they had better not put themselves in situations in which talents are required for success as they will fail.

Self-reflection, discussion, and time are often necessary to overcome the Imposter Syndrome. Supportive environments, counseling, and peer support are also important for understanding that success is attained in different ways.

Confusion about Effort and Ability

Linked to the Great Impostor Syndrome is the difficulty experienced by many talented women in understanding the complex relationship between effort and ability. Most people believe that effort and ability are the reasons that they achieve or underachieve in school or life. Effort and ability are both internally perceived causes, according to attribution theory (Weiner, 1986a), and understanding the relationship between them is important. Many high achieving students tend to attribute their successes to a combination of ability and effort and their failures to lack of effort. On the other hand, individuals who accept their own failure often attribute their successes to external factors such as luck and their failures to lack of ability.

Before the age of 10, children are usually unable to distinguish effort from ability. However, as they approach adolescence, they begin making a distinction and gender differences emerge. Boys more often attribute their successes to ability and their failures to lack of effort, while girls often attribute their successes to luck or effort and their failures to lack of ability. The academic self-efficacy of young males is enhanced based on their belief in their ability and is maintained during failures because of their attribution of failure to lack of effort. The same does not appear to be true for young females. Girls may accept responsibility for failure, but not for success. Researchers believe that although girls may perceive themselves to be bright, they interpret any failure quite negatively, believing that it is caused by lack of ability (Dweck, 1986).

Developing a strong belief in one's ability in the elementary and middle school years is important because "by the end of elementary school, children's [perceptions] . . . of ability begin to exert an influence on achievement processes independent of any objective measures of ability" (Meece, Blumenfeld, & Hoyle, 1988, p. 521). Many gifted adolescent girls believe that their high ability means that they will achieve excellent grades without effort. Students often believe that if they must work hard, they lack ability (Dweck, 1986). My research has indicated that during adolescence, talented girls move from self-confidence to self-consciousness and often have doubts about their ability.

Teachers contribute to confusion about effort and ability. As early as first grade, teachers tend to "attribute causation of boys' successes and failures to ability and girls' successes and failures to effort" (Fennema, Peterson, Carpenter, & Lubinski, 1990). Teachers also contribute to confusion by stressing the time assigned for tasks or tests. Girls all too often learn that being fast equals being smart. This time pressure may be discouraging to girls who are often more reflective and take longer to think.

Researchers have found that teachers' feedback about work is a better predictor for children's self perceptions about their ability and effort than are other types of interactions with teachers or with peers (Pintrich & Blumenfeld, 1985, p. 654). My colleague, Del Seigle, and I (1998) recently conducted a study in which we found that teachers still rate adolescent gifted females higher than gifted males on effort. Schunk (1984) found that children who initially receive feedback complimenting their ability, rather than feedback complimenting their effort, developed higher ability attribution, self-efficacy, and skills. This finding clearly indicates that parents and teachers should praise girls for their ability, thereby helping them come to understand that they have ability. Parents and teachers must provide students with activities in school and life which require real and sustained effort. If these activities are not provided, students may come to believe that when work becomes challenging and they do not excel in it, it is because they are not smart. It is essential that young girls learn early about effort and understand that the most talented people expend a great deal of effort to be successful at challenging pursuits.

PRINCE CHARMING MYTH AND SELECTING PARTNERS

Many bright young girls believe that their major goal and dream in life should be to find their prince. The Disney movies that children watch and the fairy tales that they read somehow convince many girls that they really deserve a handsome prince who will rescue them from a humdrum life, support them, and take care of them, leaving them free to do . . . what? Even if women are fortunate enough to find a loving partner who will support them emotionally, they should still have dreams and hopes to pursue. Many young women have yet to realize that attaining the relationship is not the dream, rather, it is the work that they can pursue within a committed relationship that is the dream. Many young women defer their hopes and dreams when they fall in love and support their partner's dreams and hopes instead. When Prince Charming isn't so charming, many end up as single parents and the sole support for their children.

Parents and teachers spend too little time discussing with

young women the types of partners they should seek in their future. At conferences for young girls, I often tell them that women spend more time considering the characteristics they want in a pet than they do in identifying the characteristics they want in a partner for life. In an attempt to make these young women laugh and reflect further on the topic, I mention some of the questions we ask as we contemplate whether we want to take on the responsibility of a puppy for the next 14 or 15 years: Does it shed? Is it good with children? Does it like to play? Is it easily trainable? These are all questions we ask about a pet, but we seldom help young women think about the important questions to ask a partner that they consider having for life.

Young girls must learn that these kinds of questions are absolutely critical for the important decisions they face which affect the rest of their lives. Many of the older talented women I studied realized their goals despite negative input and feedback from their families and partners. Most of them, however, struggled for years and often divorced or separated mentally, if not physically, from their partner before they were able to pursue their dreams or their work. Those who had supportive partners had a much more pleasurable road. While still facing obstacles in the form of time, children and other responsibilities, they often reported that their partner's support and encouragement enabled them to continue their work and keep their dreams alive.

Scarlett O'Hara Syndrome

The Scarlett O'Hara Syndrome, named after Scarlett in *Gone with the Wind*, refers to the ways in which some women and some young girls have learned to achieve a goal by using their appearance or by manipulating others to get ahead. Instead of relying on their own skills and strengths to reach a goal, individuals who experience this syndrome rely upon manipulation to achieve. Advice such as "butter him up," "flirtation works best," "be cute," or "use your looks" all underscore the issues faced by talented women who may not know how to achieve goals through effort and, instead, begin using strategies which they may have seen other women use.

These strategies are counterproductive to the development of talents in young girls and to the development of character and moral beliefs about what is important in life. Teenage girls who wear suggestive clothing such as skintight jeans and midriff blouses may have an entirely inappropriate idea about what is important in the life and character development of young girls. Parents and teachers must work to help young women become more concerned with what is in their hearts and minds than what is on their backs. Parents and school personnel should enforce dress codes and provide information sessions for both parents and teachers so that they can have an opportunity to discuss the problems facing young girls related to appearances and the inappropriate use of flirtation or one's looks to achieve goals.

DIFFERENT MESSAGES FROM HOME AND SCHOOL

Many young girls have problems reconciling messages that have emerged from different environments. For example, if a teacher tells a girl to speak out in class, raise questions, and be assertive in pursuing her talents, this teacher's message may directly conflict with what this girl has been told at home. Parents often have strict guidelines about manners for their daughters at home such as not being too aggressive and acting like a "young lady." However, looking like a little doll, "minding their manners," and being polite and "ladylike" may conflict with characteristics which are necessary for girls with high potential to evolve into successful women who make a difference. My research has indicated that in order to evolve into successful women, girls need to challenge convention, to question authority, and speak out about things that need change. The very characteristics I have found to be associated with older talented women (determination, commitment, assertiveness, and the ability to control their own lives) directly conflict with what some parents encourage as good and appropriate manners in their daughters. The manners taught to some daughters and sons are, of course, influenced by the cultures in which we live. While not wanting to eliminate what is unique to each diverse culture, a discussion of some of the issues related to strict implementation of a code of manners and behavior for girls (as well as boys) is warranted.

Some young girls are willful and determined, and many parents with whom I have worked strive to correct the very behaviors that will be sorely needed as their daughters grow older. From the time she was barely old enough to talk, I have enjoyed watching the growth and development of a young girl in our church. We have a children's message each week and all of the children who are in fourth grade or younger go to the front of the church where they listen to a special message. This young girl delighted me and the rest of our congregation on a weekly basis, often calling out funny responses to our minister's questions. Her verbal creativity and outgoing personality never failed to make all of us smile. One day after she had answered two or three questions, I overheard her mother reprimand her, explaining that she had, once again, monopolized the conversation and brought attention to herself. Too many parents squelch their daughters' enthusiasm and spirit under the guise of manners. Some of the passion and the excitement that gifted children feel simply bubbles to the surface.

Dabrowski (1967) is one of the few theorists whose personality theories have been applied to gifted individuals. Dabrowski believed that some people display supersensitivities or overexcitabilities in several areas: psychomotor (increased levels of physical activities), intellectual (increased levels of intellectual activities), sensual (expanded awareness), imaginational (high levels of imagination), and emotional (intensified emotions). Research conducted by Silverman (1993) has indicated that very young children often have passionate beliefs about social injustices in the world and feel deeply about issues affecting certain segments of the population.

Talented young girls may experience some of these overexcitabilities and often, in my experience, have expanded awareness in the sensual, imaginational, and emotional areas. Too strict a behavior code may directly conflict with their emotional nature and could be difficult for parents to enforce and for children to obey. Parents who demand a certain behavior code at all times sometimes squelch the passion and the love of questioning and talking from their outgoing, spirited daughters. I often encourage parents to try to channel the overexcitability, determination, willfulness, or stubbornness they find in their daughters to something positive such as social action or improving some aspect of life. Girls can apply energy to sports, hobbies, music lessons, or any personal interest area.

As girls watch and learn from their own home and family dynamics, confusing messages result. Many of the teenage gifted girls I have interviewed express their ambivalence about being like their mothers when they get older. Some whose mothers are busy professionals say they never want to work as hard as their mothers or have as little time for their families. One gifted woman told me that she had selected teaching as a career because her mother, who was a physician, had also been a martyr:

> I never want to work as hard as my mother did and enjoy martyrdom the way she did. Everything was done perfectly, but with no joy at all. Rather, a long drawn out sigh accompanied every task. "Of course, I will be at your school play. I will have to rearrange all of my patients and redo my entire schedule, but I will be there, despite all of the work it will take."

Other adult talented females have told me that their mothers encouraged them to "have it all." These talented women, however, also understood that their ideas about gender roles had been influenced by watching their fathers go to work while their mothers' careers dwindled because they assumed the major responsibility for home and child care issues. Others reported that their mothers were perfectionists about their weight, homes, and children, causing them to develop conflicting feelings about their own dreams as they watched their mothers grapple to do everything perfectly. Clearly, the answer lies in balance. It is better for girls to have both paternal and maternal role models who have challenging work and spend enough time with their children. Parents should show their daughters that their work is enjoyable while also showing they still have enough time to spend with their families.

My research indicates that the primary mixed messages gifted and talented girls receive emanate from the interaction of family variables, their parents' relationship, and their parents' expectations that their daughters have certain types of manners and behaviors. Many of the girls from urban areas, including those from culturally and linguistically diverse family backgrounds, loved their mothers but did not want to have lives like theirs. They knew that an education and a challenging career would separate them in some ways from their families, but hoped that they could realize a different type of life—one in which there was a balance and their parents and their siblings *could* still be actively involved.

Locus of Control

A woman's or girl's belief that she has the ability to control her own life is critical to success. Locus of control is usually defined as an individual's sense of how the environment either hinders or facilitates her goals. Callahan (1979) first discussed the ways in which locus of control might affect gifted women, indicating that studies of gifted women who achieved in college showed that when compared to less successful gifted peers, the higher achieving women had greater self-confidence, ego strength, greater rebellious independence, and greater rejection of outside influence. Locus of control in elementary and secondary male and female students is similar as both girls and boys believe they can determine their own destinies, but after high school, according to earlier research by Maccoby and Jacklin (1974) a shift occurs. During college, men begin to exhibit greater internal locus of control as well as confidence in their ability to succeed while women's belief in their ability to control their own destiny begins to diminish. This diminished locus of control may occur because of both relationship issues and other issues cited earlier, such as lowered confidence in one's academic ability and susceptibility to criticism.

UNREAL EXPECTATIONS OF FUTURE CAREERS OR PART-TIME WORK FOR A FULL-TIME FUTURE

Some young girls want to be doctors, lawyers, or scientists when they grow up, but don't know how to plan to achieve these goals and have no idea about the time commitment involved or the requirements of these careers. Many have not considered how to integrate personal relationships with this process, and when they fall in love, few are prepared to make decisions to enable them to have these challenging careers. Instead, they often put the interests of the person they love ahead of their own interests. The increasing number of women in graduate schools offers more opportunities for role modeling and support groups. But the fact remains that many younger talented girls have no clue about how to plan a career, how to investigate options beyond college, or the realities of combining graduate school with a relationship. Many talented young women lower their aspirations, choosing less demanding careers that they believe will enable them to marry or be involved in a committed relationship. Many leave work to raise their children and plan to reenter the workforce at a later time. To this end, they may choose not to pursue careers in math or science or they may decide to postpone their completion of advanced degrees in a professional career. Instead, they may select a more traditional female service career such as teaching, medical technicians, secretarial, or childcare which they believe will enable them to leave and return to work when their children are older.

In the study of high school valedictorians cited earlier, Arnold (1995) found that the highest-aspiring women differed from their peers in their expectation that they would have continuous careers. Aspirations for top careers, professionally related experience, and mother's education characterized the females who planned to pursue the most challenging careers. These women with higher career aspirations also planned more continuous labor force participation as well as later marriage and childbearing than their female peers. At the age of thirty-one, three-quarters of the women who had held the highest aspirations were found to be working at the highest levels. This group included physicians, attorneys, professors, scientists, and business executives. Another group included women in middle-ranked occupations such as nursing, physical therapy and pre-college teaching. The third group of women were working in nonprofessional jobs that did not require a college degree or raising their children full-time (p. 116-7).

Many women take time off from their careers during their mid-twenties to mid-thirties to raise children, and unfortunately, this time is precisely when most careers escalate. It is possible, in some careers, to take time away to raise a family. It is impossible in other careers, however, and this reality results in one of the most difficult decisions facing women. The ten years between age 25 and 35 has also been found to be the strongest predictor of lifetime earnings. Lester Thurow, an economist, made the point poignantly in a *New York Times* article written almost 20 years ago, indicating that between the ages of 25 and 35 women are most apt to leave the labor force or become part-time workers to have children. When they do, the current system of promotion and skill acquisition extracts an enormous lifetime price. Despite the need to have an uninterrupted career in certain fields such as science and math, not everyone should have to make a full-time work choice during critical personal periods of one's life. Our society needs new models of the ways in which women can work, have families, and still be successful.

Job sharing, reduced hours, work at home, flexible scheduling, and a variety of creative solutions all address the dilemmas facing women who struggle with these issues. As more women pursue these various future directions, businesses and institutions should continue to develop new suggestions and strategies for promoting female success.

SELF-DOUBT, SELF-CRITICISM, AND COMPARISONS

From the earliest ages, as young as primary grades, girls have been found to lack confidence when compared to boys of the same age. Judith Bardwick (1972) found that girls who were as young as 1st through 3rd grade lacked confidence and expected to fail when compared to boys of the same age who expected to achieve. "Shortchanging Girls, Shortchanging America," a study commissioned by the American Association of University Women (AAUW), included a poll of 3,000 students in grades 4-10, which found that as girls get older, their self esteem drops dramatically. Enthusiastic and assertive at ages 8 and 9, they begin to lose confidence in their abilities at ages 13 and 14 and emerge from high school with measurably lowered goals. The same study indicated that the decrease in girls' self-esteem is three times greater than boys.

Karen Arnold's study (1995) showed that as female valedictorians got older, they lowered their self-rankings and seemed to have more doubts about their own abilities, despite receiving higher grades throughout college. She cites Meredith, a Phi Beta Kappa graduate in mathematics and music, as being deeply insecure about applying to graduate school: "I thought no one wanted me" (p. 107). Arnold's findings about the insecurities of talented females parallel my own research in which at almost every age level beginning with adolescence, females, as compared with males at similar ages, express more doubt about their abilities, compare themselves more, and criticize themselves and others more. Unfortunately, this critical nature often extends to withholding support from other women. I have found that many gifted women perceive other women to be their worst enemies, both in college, work, and in their personal lives.

Even the most talented women worry about criticism and sometimes doubt their work. Maria Goeppert Mayer had to be pushed to publish her work. She was reluctant to present a detailed account of her ideas to the scientific community at large, fearing that her ideas were not original (Gabor, 1995, p. 144). She published a brief explanatory letter about her findings in *Physical Review,* and only later submitted lengthy articles about her discovery of the shell model for which she later won the Nobel prize.

Several different researchers have found that a lack of confidence in girls seems to increase with females who are more intelligent, and this pattern may continue into mid-life. The roots of the problem are deep and complex. Charmaine Gilbreath, a rocket scientist at the Naval Research Laboratory in Washington, D. C., heads the electro-optics technology section. Her work involves shooting laser beams at rocket plumes to study reflected light and learn how particles in rocket fuel react with the atmosphere. After completing her first college degree in communications and humanities and deciding to become a lawyer, she changed her plans, deciding she liked physics and geometry. She recalled:

> . . . it took me two years to get up the nerve to take a pre-calculus class. I was surprised that it wasn't that hard. I aced it. Then I took physics and calculus courses, and they weren't all that hard either. That's when I first realized I'd been buffaloed. (Cole, 1994, pp. 58-9)

When she returned to school to get her degree in physics and engineering, she found her biggest obstacle was her own lack of self-confidence: "Girls think they have to always get As. If a girl gets a B or C, she thinks she can't do it. But boys get Bs and Cs and go on to be scientists and engineers"(Cole, 1994, pp. 58-9). Explaining the success of some of the current crop of female scientists, Dr. Gilbreath, who completed her Ph.D. at Johns Hopkins, explained:

> I had to put psychological blinders on, and not listen to the external stuff, because before, the external stuff had been wrong for me. Those of us who made it are those who learned to ignore society's traditional expectations of women. (Cole, 1994, p. 59)

Numerous studies have documented the difference in self confidence between men and women relative to achievement (Erkut, 1983; Gold, Brush, & Sprotzer, 1980; Vollmer, 1986). In addition to having less confidence in their own abilities, the talented girls I studied were overly critical of themselves and listened more to advice given by others, took it more to heart, and often followed it. Psychologist TomiAnn Roberts (1991) has found that women look to others for evidence of their competence more than men do and are more sensitive to the evaluations they receive from others (Roberts & Nolen-Hoeksema, 1989, 1994). Research has also found that women take criticism much more seriously. Roberts and Nolen-Hoeksema believe that women are more influenced by the evaluations they receive than men, perhaps because of differing perceptions of the informative value of those evaluations. If a guidance counselor tells a young girl that an advanced math class will be too hard, she may not take the math class. If parents tell their daughter that medical school is beyond her capabilities, she may believe them. If she ignores what her parents have said and eventually applies and goes to medical school or pursues other advanced opportunities, she may either suffer from the impostor syndrome discussed earlier or subconsciously begin to believe that her parents were right and that she may not be able to succeed at anything difficult.

My research has indicated that girls and women also compare themselves to others more and often assess how they stand in various areas as compared to others. The influence of relationships and comparisons on women is complex because some women who experience self-doubt and compare themselves to others may actually cause themselves to be less successful. And those who are successful often ask the most questions about how their success influences others. This view is shared by Jean Baker Miller who wrote *Toward a New Psychology of Women* in 1976. Miller, a psychiatrist, found that the women she saw in her practice were preoccupied with how their actions affected others, questions about connecting and giving, and whether they were perceived as being selfish or measuring up. Her female patients' problems ranged from anger that they did not have the time to pursue their dreams to those who reached their goals but were lacking in personal connections and relationships and believed that they were missing something essential in their lives (Miller, 1976).

Many of the gifted females I interviewed also wondered aloud if their success had been gained through compromising what they have done for others. Why do so many women feel guilty and/or selfish about pursuing their own talents? Why, even when they have been successful, are they plagued with guilt and concerns about the impact of their success on those they love? Perhaps the answer lies in what they have been taught as children or perhaps it lies in what seems to be fundamentally important to women—that is, the relationships in their lives. The importance of relationships may explain the happiness of the many women who have had to give up some of their career dreams or professional aspirations and instead created (or "composed," in the words of Mary Catherine Bateson, 1989) a happy and fulfilling personal life, rich in relations with their partners, children, and their families. Again, however, the paradox emerges as I have also interviewed gifted females who look back with deep regret on dreams left unfulfilled. I have found that happiness for gifted females depends upon their belief that they have achieved a combination of a happy personal life and meaningful work. These women often have a sense of destiny and a need to find appropriate work in order to feel that their lives have somehow made a difference. At the same time, they also seem to realize that work without relationships leaves a woman unhappy in her personal life. The contrast provided by the passage below is indicative of understanding what is needed for the "entire trip":

It is very sad to see how little is left for a man who has devoted his life to making money when that motive is removed . . . No wonder women outlive men. We have had to be responsible for the shape of our lives from the beginning. Even women with jobs face a full work load every day at home. Every woman knows that making a living is just the first step. But for too many men it is the entire trip. (Hailey, 1978, p. 255)

RELIGIOUS TRAINING

Let a woman learn in silence with all submissiveness. I permit no women to teach or to have authority over men; she is to keep silent . . . Yet women will be saved through bearing children. . . —I Timothy 2: 11-15.

Men are superior to Women. —The Koran

Blessed are thou, O lord our God and King of the Universe, that didst not create me a woman. —Daily prayer of the Orthodox Male Jew

To the women he said, I will greatly multiply your pain in childbearing; in pain you shall bring forth children, yet your desire shall be for your husband and he shall rule over you. —Genesis 3:16

If the woman grows weary and, at last, dies from childbearing, it matters not. Let her die from bearing, she is there to do it. —Martin Luther

> A wife is to submit graciously to the servant leader-
> ship of her husband, even as the church willingly sub-
> mits to the headship of Christ." —the 18th Article
> of the Baptist Faith and Message (June 10, 1998)

Many of the talented women I have studied who have firm religious backgrounds and beliefs have grappled with the religious training they received as young children. This religious training may conflict with what is required if they are to develop their own talents. Selflessness, modesty, turning the other cheek, and the subjugation of individual pursuits for the good of others are lessons some women learn from their earliest interaction with religious training, and these lessons may conflict with experiences that occur later in life. An example from the life of Rose Kennedy may help to illuminate some of the conflicts.

Archbishop William O'Connell helped to convince Rose Kennedy's father that Rose should not attend Wellesley College and should, instead, attend a small Catholic school with the nuns of the Sacred Heart. The Archbishop held a profoundly conservative view of a woman's purpose in life, insisting that a woman was to bear and raise sons of deep faith who would go out into the world as women could not. Her father's decision that she could not attend Wellesley, Rose later told historian Doris Kearns Goodwin, was monumental: "My greatest regret is not having gone to Wellesley College. It is something I have felt a little sad about all my life (Leamer, 1994, p. 61).

Upon the occasion of Archbishop O'Connell being named a Cardinal in the Roman Catholic Church, Rose heard him deliver a speech in which he said:

> Every Christian woman ought to have two
> things always at heart. First, the welfare of her
> husband, her children, her home, or, if unmar-
> ried, of the immediate family; their happiness
> must be her most sacred duty-a duty which she

can not shirk, even under the pretext of care
for others, and secondly-she must every day,
after the duty is done and before she permits
herself any merely selfish consideration, do
something, no matter how slight, which in some
even small degree will help on the happiness of
someone else not of her immediate encourage.
(Leamer, 1994, p. 116)

Concerns about pursuing one's talents being misconstrued as "selfish consideration" have been mentioned repeatedly by many of the gifted women I studied who had religious training throughout their childhood and adolescence. Many still struggle with their learned beliefs that to pursue their own talents is self-ish. Guilt seems intertwined with many women's struggle to understand the relationship between their own talent development and what they learned in their religious training about their responsibilities to those they love. The guilt they feel, perhaps, explains why selecting work that results in social change or the improvement of the human condition is so important to some talented women with strong religious backgrounds.

ABSENCE OF SUPPORT FOR ONE ANOTHER AND LONELINESS EXPERIENCED BY TALENTED WOMEN

In many of the interviews I conducted with both older and younger gifted females, they described their feelings of loneliness and betrayal by other women. When asked about friendships, a successful college president replied simply, "I have none." Some of the reasons that many talented women have few friends and are often lonely revolve around the extremely limited amount of time they have for friendships and the ambivalence of other women to talented women who achieve at high levels. In interview after interview, successful women recounted situations in which their success was viewed negatively by both other women and men. Women who had successful careers often reported that they were pitted against women who stayed at home and worked to raise their families.

The talented women I studied who achieved eminence recounted situations in which other women actually seemed to look for specific examples of deficiencies in their talented counterparts. "She actually said to me, 'Well, of course you earned a law degree, but your marriage fell apart,'" confided one woman, describing her best friend's comment after her painful divorce from her husband who had been having an extramarital relationship. Many talented women consciously hide their accomplishments from friends and families and often seem to feel guilty about being able to accomplish a great deal. Several described to me the ways in which their friends consistently drew comparisons. "I don't know how you do it, I certainly can't," "How do you get so much done?" and "Look at what you have accomplished as compared to what I have accomplished" are frequent comments made to talented women by their peers and friends. These types of remarks seem to imply that there is one secret to being successful instead of what has contributed to achievement in most of the women I studied—hours of sacrifice, time spent on work instead of other areas, and choices, often painfully made, about what to give up so that one's work can be completed. Many women need and look for support from females and male peers and instead find comparisons, hostility, and a continued absence of friendship. Some women do not extend support to other women and, in turn, rarely find the support they need for their own individual choices. Talented females need to establish a network of support and encouragement from their parents, siblings, and friends. They need someone to be proud of their efforts and the results of their work. Without this support, they will continue to be lonely and isolated.

PHYSICAL ATTRACTIVENESS
In a recent interview, former Congresswoman Pat Schroeder remembered her frustrations with how difficult it was to find a position as an attorney after graduating from Harvard Law

School in 1964. She could not secure a single interview with a Denver law firm. The Denver firms were interested in her husband who also had a law degree, but not in her. She also reported that the Harvard placement office which, at that time, took for granted the masculine marketplace, did not help her either. Schroeder remembered the placement officer telling women to look ugly, to roll their nylons down around their ankles, and to look dowdy, as an attractive woman would be a detriment in law offices, but an unattractive woman could be stuck in a back room taking care of research files.

Clearly, times have changed, but for some of the most physically attractive females I interviewed, their most challenging conflicts have been about personal issues and choices. Teenage girls who are considered attractive are sought after by young males, increasing the likelihood that they will have more decisions to make about relationships and, perhaps, more options to marry younger. They are also more sought after for friendships by other females. Girls who are considered less attractive by their male and female peers may have more time to pursue their own choices and can devote more attention to their academic work without facing some of the difficult issues about relationships. In my research with high school and middle school girls, those who were considered attractive by their peers were pressured by other students for dates, attention and relationships with both male and female peers. They had little time for introspection about what is important in life.

In research with gifted teenage girls (Reis & Diaz, in press), some very attractive young women invented boyfriends to give them an excuse not to date, allowing them more time to pursue their work in school and their own interests. Gifted young women from Puerto Rican or other Latina groups reported that inventing boyfriends enabled them to achieve while being able to exist within their culture, a culture in which relationships are crucial. Rosa, one of the young women in my study of high school gifted girls, did not date at all until her junior year of high school and then she invented a boyfriend who was away at college, explaining that for a talented Puerto Rican female to date would mean she would have to put her hopes and dreams on hold and pay attention to her boyfriend: "It's not that I'm not interested. It's just that I see myself doing my thing first. Males always have to be first in a relationship. And, sometimes, they don't like that you're smart" (Reis, Hébert, Diaz, Maxfield, & Ratley, 1995).

While beauty has long been considered a positive attribute in the psychological literature, Heilman and Stopeck (1985a) have found that it can be detrimental for women in the corporate world. In one study using 113 randomly selected men and women, participants were asked to review career descriptions and photographs of fictitious important corporate executives. While attractive male business executives were perceived as having more integrity than unattractive men, attractive females were considered to have less integrity than unattractive ones. Attractive male executives were believed to have ability and effort directly related to their success, while the success of attractive females was attributed directly to luck, not ability. Heilman and Stopeck also found that all unattractive female executives were believed to have more integrity and to be more capable than attractive female executives. In another study, the same research team found that attractiveness was advantageous for women in nonmanagerial positions and disadvantageous for women in managerial positions. Physical attractiveness had no effect whatsoever on males in the same types of positions (Heilman & Stopeck, 1985b).

In my studies, I found that the talented females who were considered by their peers to be the most attractive had the most options to choose from about the future and were the most ambivalent about their own talent development. If they began to date, they deflected attention from their studies and their belief in self. Those who were less attractive had more freedom to be studious and to continue with their academic plans. None of the gifted girls I studied wanted or would have chosen to be unattractive, but if they were, they usually had more freedom to pursue academic work and to have a challenging subsequent career.

Holland and Eisenhart (1990), authors of *Educated in Romance: Women, Achievement and College Culture*, found similar results in their study of women in a southern university. Many of the women they studied viewed boyfriends as a source of prestige and romantic relationships as positive, normal, and desirable. However, women in this study also admitted to having difficulty with achieving a balance between their romantic relationship, work, academic classes, and their peer involvement. Holland and Eisenhart found that contrary to popular belief, women who fell in love did not lower their ambitions because they fell in love. Rather, they lowered their ambitions and *then* they fell in love. Holland and Eisenhart found that the peer culture of the women they studied was critical and that the enemy of ambition in some of these high achieving young women was their own peer group of other women. Almost all of the women studied by Holland and Eisenhart gradually experienced a decline in their ambitions and their aspirations, pointing again to the importance of planning for gifted girls across their lifespans.

CINDERELLA COMPLEX

When Collette Dowling ("The Cinderella Syndrome," 1981) wrote *The Cinderella Complex*, she was interested in learning why many young women had begun to realize that they did not want to live alone and why they felt dependent on a relationship. As Dowling defined it, the Cinderella Complex is about psychological dependence, both the conscious and unconscious belief that girls are brought up to depend upon a man, to feel that they cannot stand alone, and even to be frightened without a man in their lives. Dowling's premise seems to have stemmed from a variety of psychological studies indicating that girls receive less encouragement to be independent than boys, as well as more parental protectiveness and fewer opportunities for independent exploration of their environment.

Dowling also believed that these dependent tendencies are deeply buried and denied. The Cinderella Complex may lead to inappropriate or ineffective behavior on the job, anxiety about success, or the belief that independence will lead to the loss of femininity. Until two or three decades ago, femininity was defined by one's dependency, and Dowling believes that many women continue to hold vestiges of this complex without even realizing or acknowledging it. Some parents raise their daughters to be dependent on family and parental input for every decision. This belief conflicts with the skills necessary for independent planning, decision making, and problem solving for gifted girls and women.

CHANGING THE TIMELINE FOR PRODUCTIVITY IN WOMEN

Albert Einstein said, "A person who has not made his great contribution to science before the age of 30 will never do so." It is almost routinely pointed out that Einstein developed the first theory of relativity at age 30, Isaac Newton figured out universal gravitation at 24, and Charles Darwin developed his theory of evolution in his late 20s and early 30s. Some studies have indicated that people in a wide variety of fields are most productive in their early adulthood, the time during which most women have children. Lehman (1953), in his study of men in almost all areas of intellectual achievement, found that the most creative period for the quality of achievement is between 30 and 45 years of age. He also acknowledged, however, that a person's quantity of productivity is often greater after the age of 40. His research also acknowledged that a steady decline occurs in productivity after that time. This study, and most others dealing with productivity, have almost universally been based upon the accomplishments of men and have addressed male cycles of productivity.

I have found different patterns of peak productivity in

women, many of whom have worked slowly and carefully throughout their lives in a manner which enabled them to do what was also essential to them, that is, maintain relationships and care for those they love. More than a century ago, psychologist G. M. Beard (1874) wrote that productivity was the combination of enthusiasm with experience. Enthusiasm is abundant in the beginning of professional life, then gradually declines, while experience grows throughout life. Beard believed that enthusiasm without experience renders original, but unfocused effort, while experience without enthusiasm results in uninspired work. During those years when the two curves intersect, according to Beard, creativity can peak. What Beard did not address was the critical issue of time. Maria Goeppert Mayer did not begin to realize her full scientific potential until relatively late in her career, although her intensity and single-minded dedication to physics was evident throughout her life (Gabor, 1995). I believe that women's experience, enthusiasm, and limited availability of time at certain points in their lives may indicate that their timeline for highly productive work may be quite later than the timeline for men. And, because most women live longer, they may have the time to enable thoughtful, experienced work to emerge much later in life.

Diverse Expressions of Creative Productivity in Females

Yet . . . any objective chronicler of the history of Western culture will have to report sadly that women's contributions to its aggregate have been dismally few. This is true in the arts and the sciences. (Singer, 1984, p. 159)

The lower adult creative productivity of women has been consistently cited in many fields of study. I have argued for a different view of talented women and an understanding of the different ways in which creative productivity can be demonstrated in addition to work, as related to family, relationships,

home, and interests. As women still assume the primary responsibility as family nurturer and caretaker, their many creative energies are directly channeled into their family and home
while their spouse's creative energy may be free to be directly
applied to his work. Completing creative work requires long
periods of concentration which are not available to many women
in their peak work and childbearing years.

Arlie Hochschild (1989), a sociology professor at the University of California at Berkeley, studied 52 couples over a 10-
year period. Hochschild installed herself in the homes of these
couples for hours at a time and interviewed them over the decade. Her results, summarized in *The Second Shift*, indicated that
most working women return home each evening to inescapable
domestic responsibilities amounting to an extra month of work
every year. Women, she found, worked an extra 15 hours more
each week than men.

Hochschild (1989) found that four out of five men did not
share the work at home, and if they did help, they did not do
daily chores such as fixing meals. Women were more likely to
do two things at once, such as cooking and talking to their children. Even when husbands happily shared housework and other
responsibilities, the women *felt* more responsible for home and
children. More women than men kept track of doctor's appoint-
ments, arranged day care, camp activities, and their children's
schedules. Family members often indicated that their mother
rushed them, urged them to get their homework done, get ready
for school and served, Hochschild found, as the "lightning rod"
for family tensions, the enforcer of the rules, the nagger about
homework, and the person responsible for the "toxic details"
which run households. She also found that the women she studied were often exhausted and talked about sleep the way a hungry person would talk about food.

Hochschild (1989) found the happiest two-job marriages
were ones in which both men and women shared the housework and parenting, which included taking care of the family,

going to the school play, helping a child read, cooking dinner, grocery shopping, and a host of other daily jobs that maintained both the home and the family. If gifted girls are to mature into women who can transform their gifts into meaningful work, it will be in part because their spouse or partner shares equally in responsibilities at home.

When asked about the diverse manner of creative production in women's lives, a participant in my study of older women, one of the first female producers on Broadway, indicated that she believed women's creativity evolves in a different pattern than men's: "Women spend their lives moving from one creative act to another, and they can find satisfaction from their creative expression [in] many different outlets." She then spread her hands and wove them in and out several times to illustrate the various creative acts some women undertake. "Men, on the other hand," she continued, "see an end goal and move toward the pursuit of that creative goal." To illustrate that point, she moved her hands in a straight upward path to a high point above her face and stopped. "that is why men are able to achieve goals and fame more quickly than women, but I think that women have a richer creative journey, find joy in the diversity of their creative acts, and in the end, enjoy the creative process so much more."

I have found that female creative productivity in work may also be directed at less high-profile products and often more to service for the common good. While their male counterparts produce plays, write articles or books, undertake deals, and continue to be high professional achievers, many women make either conscious or unconscious choices to work in a more facilitating background role. They also often make creative contributions that seem to be on a much smaller scale, but which, in reality, have a different type of impact on society. They take on leadership roles in church groups or PTA, develop curriculum units they want to use in a classroom, volunteer in community organizations, become involved in charity events, help friends or family in need, or take care of sick friends, relatives or elderly parents. Women's service work runs this country and improves the quality of life. The contributions of women who use their creativity and gifts in these ways cannot be understated or underestimated, yet we may never know their names or see obituaries which chronicle their accomplishments.

Another reason that certain kinds of female creative productivity may be less visible relates to a value decision that some women make about their choices. Important personal issues that need and deserve their time may take precedence over professional creative productivity. A child who demands attention, elderly parents who need care, a friend who is ill, and a host of similar personal choices often cause talented women to make a decision about what they have to do for themselves and what seems to be most important to them.

Confusion about Passivity and Assertiveness and Ambivalence about Ambition and Accommodation

What should be the personality attributes of women who are ambitious and who want to succeed? Confusion about how to balance success seems to trouble many talented women with a "feminine" personality. Maria Goeppert Mayer once had a conversation with her son in which she was critical of at least one woman whom she considered a "pushy" female scientist at the University of Chicago. One of her biographers reported that she told her son Peter, "I was like that once . . . so I pulled back and then everything came to me" (Gabor, 1995, p. 142). Being perceived as pushy, aggressive, or even ambitious is troubling to many talented females who often consciously or unconsciously refrain from speaking too much for many reasons. Fear of sounding too aggressive or too smart, stereotypical views about who should speak more often, manners which have been instilled by parents, and other issues related to negative perceptions from the opposite sex cause smart women to become confused about their roles. This confusion confronts young girls almost from the moment they consciously begin to understand that there is an opposite sex. What kind of person am I? Who do I act like? If I talk too much and am reprimanded at home, why should I speak out in school?

In the thought-provoking book, *Mother Daughter Revolution*, Elizabeth Debold, Marie Wilson, and Idelisse Malave (1993) state the problem succinctly: "Mothers grapple with the harrowing task of reconciling their overriding desire to keep their daughters safe with their desire to keep them strong and free in a world that insists on women's inferiority and subordination." I have found in my interviews both with young girls and older women that too much attention paid to manners in childhood can cripple a talented girl's attitudes and her ability to question and speak out. "Don't interrupt," "don't ask so many questions," "don't raise your hand so much," "don't be so aggressive," "don't be so bold," and "show respect for your elders"—females in my generation have heard all these statements, and I have found that smart girls today hear them, too. Unfortunately these types of admonishments from parent to child plant the first seeds of passivity which may eventually create a young woman who doesn't ask questions, doesn't raise her hand, and gives up speaking out in class.

In an undergraduate honors seminar I taught a few years ago in the School of Education at the University of Connecticut, I had sixteen students who were in their final year of preparation for becoming teachers. Fourteen were women and two were men. After three weeks of the seminar which met twice each week for one and a half hours, I observed aloud that the two men in the class of sixteen had spoken for approximately 80-90% of each class. I discussed some of the issues raised in this chapter and asked all of my students to react in writing about why they thought the women in the class were so much more silent than the young men. The reactions of the women were troubling and similar to each other. They all agreed that many did not speak and almost all indicated that this had been a learned behavior. One student explained, "I was very outspoken when I was young and then learned that this was negatively perceived by my peers." Another young woman wrote, "As I became older, I learned to speak less and listen more, and now I find it hard to speak at all in a public forum." This response was fairly representative of most of the other women in the class. Several wrote that the men like to talk more and particularly enjoyed hearing themselves talk, so why not let them have their fun? Others expressed their anxiety, or, at least, their concerns about competing with men for attention from a professor, "He seems to need to have you listen to him more. Far be it for me to deny him what he needs. I know you listen to me and would rather speak to you in a different way."

Still others wrote, "It's just silly to fight for time to talk." However, time for talk in classrooms across the country is too often devoted to boys. As students get older, some girls lose opportunities for learning if they do not learn to express themselves in academic situations, ask questions when concerns arise, and clarify issues they may not understand. In some situations, the early silence of girls breeds the later passivity of women. Accompanying the silence are questions about other personality attributes which interact with women's pursuit of their talents: modesty, pushiness, ambition, and assertiveness are those characteristics mentioned most frequently. How to act, when to speak, and the ramifications of speaking out are all areas gifted females grapple with as they pursue the development of their talents.

So What Comes First? My Work or Those I Love? (Mommy-Track, Daughter-Track, and Wife-Track)

In my research, the greatest conflicts for talented women in their 20s, 30s, and 40s concerns the interaction between their career and personal lives. This intensely personal struggle to try to develop their personal talents while they also try to meet the needs of those they love causes gifted women the most conflict, guilt and pain. Maric Mileva Einstein, Albert Einstein's first wife, was a gifted mathematician with extremely high potential and a fellow classmate at the prestigious Swiss Federal Polytechnic. In a biographical study of her life, Andrea Gabor (1995) found that "the more insecure Maric became in her relationship with Einstein, the more she came to identify her interests with his, ultimately putting Einstein's welfare ahead of her own" (p. 12). After she married Albert and had their children, her life changed drastically. Friends recalled that she often spent all day cleaning, cooking, and caring for the children and then would busy herself in the evening proofreading her husband's work and doing mathematical calculations to help him in his writings.

Lee Krasner, a very talented artist, married Jackson Pollock and followed a similar path, defined by biographer Andrea Gabor (1995) as the Invisible Wife Syndrome: "In her marriage to Jackson Pollock, she succumbed to a potent brew of upbringing, social expectations and precedent by deliberately choosing to exercise much of her artistic devotion through the work of her husband" (p. 58). It was only after his death that Krasner created art that seemed to be a reaffirmation of life. Unfortunately, this creative energy in art stemmed from her loss of this complicated man she so deeply loved. Constructing a personal and professional life for gifted women is an intensely difficult challenge, and putting the needs of their husbands or partners ahead of their own needs is an ongoing personal decision that has not often been effectively reconciled in many women's lives. Consider the reflections of Mary Catherine Bateson (1990): "As a young woman, I never questioned the assumption that when I married what I could do would take second place to what my husband could do" (p. 40).

Relationships with children and family are firmly rooted in the lives of gifted females and interwoven with their accomplishments. When Margaret Sanger was in England, prior to her trial for circulating information about birth control, her five year old daughter Peggy died of pneumonia in the United States. Instead of abandoning her work and feeling guilty for the rest of her life, Sanger turned more deeply toward her cause. In responding to the thousands who wrote sympathy letters, her biographer Joan Dash (1988) quotes her as saying, "This contact with the source . . . which had taken me out of my maternal corner two or three years before, renewed my desire and gave me the strength to carry on" (p. 47). Maria Goeppert-Mayer often remembered her father's advice: "Never become a woman!" Her husband, who was also a scientist, provided support and encouragement, but little role modeling as a primary caretaker of their children. Although she loved her children, she also loved her work. "I know if I ever had to stay home because a child was sick, I did it and hated it," (p. 279). This statement, stark in its honesty, may be offensive to some but it captures the dilemma for women who love their work and also have children. Mary Catherine Bateson (1989) addressed the same dilemma:

> The assumptions made about women and girls when we were children, which still linger today, are bound to leave wounds. Prosperity is not sufficient to remove these problems. The daughters of successful fathers may indeed incorporate that achievement into their image of themselves, but they may equally well receive the message that achievement is not for girls. Devoted care is not sufficient. Most women today have grown up with mothers who, for all their care and labor, were regarded as having achieved little. Women with a deep desire to be like their mothers are often faced with the choice between accepting a beloved image that carried connotations of inferiority or rejecting it and thereby losing an important sense of closeness. (p. 28)

This choice may result in the cultural dilemma described by Susan Faludi, the author of *Backlash*, who believes she is leading the life her mother was denied. When Faludi was growing up, she was torn:

> I would look at the women in my neighbor-
> hood, and they were all mothers, Cub Scout
> leaders and cooking chocolate chip cookies, and
> part of me wanted to grow up and have a sta-
> tion wagon. But the other part of me wanted
> to be mayor of New York City. (Pogash, 1992,
> p. 67)

Doris Kearns Goodwin (1997), a noted historian, had similar feelings which developed after spending a day at work with
her father, a bank executive:

> Before this day, I had felt that my father and
> the other men had moved in a world of inter-
> ests inaccessible to me; now I had glimpsed the
> other side, and I resolved someday to enter that
> larger world. I would go to work like my fa-
> ther, and yet I would somehow keep house the
> way my mother did, preparing lunch when the
> kids came home from school. How I would
> accomplish this I did not know, but the desire
> stayed with me. (p. 105)

Most women take on the responsibilities for childcare, after-school care, summer activities, camps, homework, and other
related child issues. In an interview with one of the most successful and most highly-rated pediatricians in New England, I
asked about childcare for her two children whose father was also
a doctor. "I do all of it," the pediatrician responded. Her husband, a physician who had far fewer working hours each week,
she said, became pressured when the schedule could not be easily arranged, "He sees this as my responsibility, although he does
spend many hours with the children."

Sandra Day O'Connor became the first woman to serve as
the majority leader of a state senate. What is described as an
extremely hectic work life by biographer Andrea Gabor (1995),
though, never interfered with her family life. "Come 4:30 or 4:45,

she would collect her handbag and say in that matter-of-fact way of hers: 'I have to go home now and get dinner ready." (p. 261). Day O'Connor made accommodations, however, including having full-time household help, hiring teenagers to drive her children to their sports lessons, and finding other types of support. However, Sandra Day O'Connor seemed to always have made time to keep a schedule that even her sons found exhausting. She went to PTA meetings, checked homework, and typed all of her children's papers until they took typing classes at school. Surviving on limited sleep, she worried about her sons and seems to have paid attention to every detail of their childhood while simultaneously trying to let them develop their own independence (pp. 261-3).

In addition to the responsibilities of children, more recent years have seen an added wrinkle to the complex decisions facing women. Just when many enter the time in which their responsibilities to their children decrease, they struggle to cope with the responsibilities of taking care of aging parents. A different pattern has emerged for women and men regarding care of elderly parents. While sons typically offer financial assistance, daughters and daughters-in-law offer the hands-on care. Elaine Brody, a leading researcher affiliated with the Philadelphia Geriatric Center, believes it will continue to be women's responsibilities:

> And it's going to be primarily women for a long time. Women can go to work as much as they want, but they still see nurturing as their job. There is a powerful, almost primordial feeling that they have to provide all the care, no matter at what cost to themselves. With many more very old people, and fewer children per family, almost every woman is going to have to take care of an aging parent or parent-in-law. (Lewin, 1989)

As a result, having children grow and leave home does not

always guarantee time to pursue one's passions—as older parents will continue to need and receive care from their daughters.

SUMMARY

The accomplishments of some gifted females and the underachievement of others is a complex issue dependent upon many factors, including personal choices and decisions. Our current societal structure virtually eliminates the possibility that the majority of gifted females who are married and have children can achieve at a similar level as their male counterparts, at least for the 18 year commitment they make to raising a child, and now possibly, another commitment they make to caring for aging parents. While the importance of maternal or family giftedness to our society cannot be underestimated, it is often not enough for women who want more, or women who have a sense of destiny about making a difference in the world. While our society has a critical need for those who excel in traditionally female careers such as teaching and nursing, decisions to pursue these careers should be considered by those who have been exposed to the full range of options available to them.

Gifted young females should explore careers, further education, and plan and pursue professional opportunities that will challenge their intellect as well as fit into their personal plans for the future. Families, schools, businesses need to offer talented women across the lifespan opportunities that will enable them to continue to examine and pursue their personal choices. Talented women should learn to assess and determine whether they are finding the time needed for their own talent development. If they are not able to develop their talents, they should learn to examine why and be proactive about what is required to help them to realize their potential. How adults do daily work, the types of decisions they make about labor and the division of responsibilities, and the ways in which new patterns of family life can evolve in the future are all aspects of life which we must reexamine and for which we must carefully consider new models.

The exploration and discussion of the personality issues and personal choices facing talented girls and women should be encouraged. Personality development is intricate and complex. What one young girl regards as an impossible obstacle may be regarded as an intriguing challenge by another. Many of the women I interviewed were negatively influenced by their parents' lack of support for their career preferences so they changed their career plans; a much smaller percentage of women were so angry that their parents tried to steer them away from their dreams that they rebelled and became eminent in their selected areas of endeavor. How the same obstacles differentially affect girls and women provides the fascination of researching their accomplishments. Resilience, rebellion, multipotentiality, different cycles of creativity, and extremely high achievement in the face of obstacles such as poverty and a complete absence of support characterize many of the gifted women I have studied. Yet, they persist. Can this type of persistence, determination, and inner will be learned or is it the result of innate personality traits? Many of the women I studied developed these characteristics throughout their lives, and it is precisely this act of development which creates their success—an active, evolutionary success learned throughout their lifespan. Exploring how and when they develop these characteristics will help teachers and parents guide gifted females in their journeys.

Part Two

~:~

Case Studies of Gifted & Talented Females throughout the Lifespan

CHAPTER FOUR

~:~

MY BOYFRIEND, MY GIRLFRIEND, OR ME?
GIFTED GIRLS IN ELEMENTARY &
SECONDARY SCHOOL

No trumpets sound when the important decisions of our life are made.
Destiny is made known silently.
—*Agnes De Mille*

Like a broken record, many of the gifted women I interviewed repeated a similar story: they were extremely bright in
school, but as they got older, ambivalence about their future
caused their hopes and career dreams to waver. They began to
doubt what they previously believed they could accomplish.
Why? Some have suggested that belief in ability and self-confidence of talented females is undermined or diminished during
childhood or adolescence. In a recent qualitative study of five
talented adolescents, not one participant attributed her success
in school to extraordinary ability (Callahan, Cunningham, &
Plucker, 1994). Other recent research has indicated that despite a degree of "feminine modesty," some gifted students acknowledged their abilities despite admitting to having fears about
the future (Reis, Hébert, Diaz, Maxfield, & Ratley, 1995). What
factors help some smart young girls become self-fulfilled, talented adults who can achieve at high levels and enjoy personal
happiness? Studies of gifted women provide essential information about what may happen to smart girls during childhood
and adolescence to cause confusion about their future career and

personal goals. During the last two decades, educators have speculated about the differences between males and females and about how to help all females achieve at higher levels.

CURRENT RESEARCH ABOUT THE DIFFERENCES BETWEEN MALES AND FEMALES

In their study, Linn and Peterson (1986) examined possible underlying differences to explain the undisputed sex differences in occupational choice—the lower representation of women in mathematical, scientific, and technical occupations. First, they pointed out that spatial ability has been the "cognitive ability of choice" among those trying to explain these sex differences despite the lack of evidence that spatial ability, independent of general ability, is related to science or math achievement. Then they note that spatial ability is not, in fact, a unitary concept and point out that the definition and type of instrument used has great influence on whether or not sex differences are identified. Finally, they concluded that on traditional tests normally thought to measure spatial ability, few gender differences are found and that larger differences are found on tasks calling for mental rotation of block forms. However, they argued that even those findings do not warrant conclusions that spatial abilities account for differences in adult achievement in mathematics and science.

The popular press often publishes reports about brain differences and differences in intellectual capacity. During the last ten years I have collected and reviewed over 100 articles on this topic from major popular magazines and journals including *Time, Newsweek, U. S. News and World Report, Redbook, Reader's Digest,* as well as a selection of different parenting magazines. An article published in 1988 in *U. S. News and World Report* entitled "Men vs. Women" (McLaughlin, Shryer, Goode, & McAuliffe) made the following claims: women respond better to stress, women are more attracted to people and males to objects; boys have a shorter attention span; boys and girls differ in their approach to moral problems, men are more aggressive and competitive than women; men dominate discussions and spend more time talking and less time listening; females have a better sense of smell; boys get 90% of all perfect scores on the Scholastic Aptitude Test in Math; boys are far more likely to be left-handed, nearsighted, and identified as dyslexic; men tend to be more autocratic and make decisions on their own; and in politics, men are more prone to support a strong defense and capital punishment while women support spending to solve domestic problems such as housing and poverty.

"The Female Brain," a 1998 article in *Ladies Home Journal* on female brain differences (Hales, 1998), claims to discuss some of the most recent research findings and quotes psychiatrists, neurologists, neuroanatomists, psychologists, and science popular press writers. This article suggests that women use more of their brains; the female brain responds more intensely to emotion; the female brain is wired for expression, not aggression; the female brain has more facility with words; sexual pleasure may register in a different location in the female brain; women notice more than men and navigate differently; and that a woman's vision is more acute and her hearing, more sensitive.

The discussion of biologically based gender differences is controversial and the cause of much academic attention. Chipman (1988), in her review of previous studies of sex and gender differences, suggested that the important issue is no longer whether or not there are sex differences. Pointing to the infrequency with which these differences are identified and the relative lack of predictability from those that are identified (as estimates of the variability in adult achievement accounted for by these statistically significant abilities range from a low of 1% to a high of 5%), she suggested that research needs to be reoriented toward potentially more productive questions, such as how we capitalize upon the strengths that women and men currently display.

The focus of research in these areas should address factors that mediate gender differences in achievement and environmental variables which can be changed to ensure that neither male nor female development is inhibited or choices limited. We must examine the individual differences within both sexes and, for girls in particular, determine those characteristics likely to be influenced by the environment, as well as those experiences and conditions which enable full development of potential in all areas. Conducting research is critical in areas such as career choice, parental encouragement, the effects of family on career or personal choice, and the issues of personal/professional achievement and life satisfaction in gifted females.

Because studies in these areas can be contradictory or based on outdated assumptions, we need to conduct more research. Clearly each sex has strengths and it is up to all of us to ensure that everyone has the opportunities to realize their unique potential. Although the topic of gifted females has gained some attention in recent years, issues about their school experiences are rarely discussed or investigated, and many teachers have no idea that they may be inadvertently discouraging young girls from realizing their potential. This chapter provides an overview of some of the important issues and some current research related to gifted and talented girls in school, beginning with two case studies (Reis, Hébert, Diaz, Ratley, & Maxfield, 1995).

~: NICKI :~

Nicki was a small, slight girl with a shy smile and a reserved manner. She had light brown hair and a light complexion, and was the older of two sisters who lived with their mother. Their father was an alcoholic, divorced her mother when Nicki was seven, and lived about an hour away. He saw Nicki and her sister irregularly. Neither parent had attended college, and her father did not graduate from high school until after time in the Navy. Her mother was a clerical worker for an insurance company, and her father was a mail carrier. Nicki indicated that she was not at all close to her mother and, in fact, felt some anger toward her. She perceived that her mother expected perfection from her and that a different set of expectations existed for her sister, who was three years younger and failing one class in the high school she and Nicki attended.

Nicki lived with her mother and sister in an apartment on the third floor of an older house in a neighborhood of two and three-family houses in the city. A family with several children lived in the apartment below her, and her descriptions of these children resulted in one of Nicki's rare smiles.

Nicki participated in an elementary gifted and talented program during 5th and 6th grade and remembered many of the activities in the program, including the writing activities. She was also enrolled in a summer program at a private school in which she took advanced math and science classes. She remembered classroom teachers from her elementary school, and her freshman English teacher had such an impact on her life that Nicki decided to become a teacher. During her junior year, Nicki ranked second in a class of 350 students. She was involved in the National Honor Society, softball, swim team, track, and had taken years of dance. She also was involved in community services, was a lifeguard, and participated in food drives and the beautification of her high school. Nicki took all honors classes during her last two years of high school and her senior classes were Honors Spanish, Honors English, Honors History, Honors Pre-Calculus, Accounting, and Graphic Arts.

Nicki won first prize in a statewide essay contest sponsored by a large insurance company for an essay she wrote about her father's battle with alcoholism. Below is an excerpt from the essay, for which she received a $10,000 scholarship.

> We entered the house like one might enter an unknown country, with silence and apprehension. The stranger isn't there. Upstairs, my mother set foot in my room and stood gaping at my bed. A look of ire and vexation was plastered on her face. That's when I noticed it too. Carved on the wooden head post of my bed were the words "I love you." The dark sur-

face of the wood was scratched so it looked as if the
words were a different color. I kept staring at this
message from the stranger. While my mother was
distressed, I was glad. Some light spewed into my
dark head. One empty question was answered.

Nicki applied to several prestigious New England colleges
and was accepted by all of them. She received scholarships from
most and decided to attend a small private highly selective college. Nicki explained that her mother and father wanted her to
go to the state university because it was slightly less expensive,
but she also indicated that her parents did not understand that
with the scholarship package she had received, it would actually
be cheaper for her to attend the private college. She wanted to
be a teacher and was committed to working in an urban setting
in the future. Nicki was determined to succeed, although she
worried about whether or not she could do the hard work required of her in college. She also knew that she had to address
some issues in her life, such as her difficult relationship with her
father and her distant relationship with her mother. She looked
forward to going away to college and starting a new life.

~: MARY :~

Mary was a senior in a large urban high school, and both
faculty and students admired and respected her. She was outgoing, honest and direct. She spoke quickly, with great confidence, and was able to communicate her ideas well. A tall, attractive young woman with reddish hair and a light complexion,
Mary was an academic superstar. She ranked first in her class,
was taking all of the most advanced classes, had won numerous
awards, and was President of the National Honor Society. Her
mother was a teacher and her father, a social worker with a
master's degree. Mary had one younger brother, a freshman at
the same high school. Her report card indicated that her teachers had consistently considered her to be a delightful student,

and she had always excelled in school.

Mary was involved in many activities involving sports and extracurricular clubs, including swim team, softball, a peer writing program, peer counseling, and numerous activities as a part of the service component of the National Honor Society. She did not date, but had many close friends and sought help for one close female friend who had been a high achiever, but was not progressing in her search for an appropriate college to attend. Mary was afraid that her friend was beginning to enter a period of underachievement and that her grades might fall, hurting her chances for a scholarship.

Mary was committed to her urban education but had concerns about the level of academic rigor in her high school. During her junior year, the high school administrators changed policies about honors classes, opening them to all students who might have an interest in taking them. Because of that policy, Mary indicated that the degree of challenge in her honors classes had changed dramatically from one semester to another. She found that the classes required less work, and she did not find the same level of discussion and challenge. Mary decided to attend a small private religious college with an outstanding reputation after she received an acceptance letter for early decision in the late fall of her senior year. She planned to major in social work and indicated that she was committed to a helping profession.

These two young women from diverse life situations were both high achievers in school and anticipated lives with many successes and challenges. Not all gifted girls leave high school as committed to success and achievement. My interviews with over 200 gifted and talented girls in elementary, middle, and high school during the last fifteen years have indicated that many have excellent insights about the changes they experience as they mature in school. In one recent interview, a seventh grader who had been identified and placed in a gifted program in first grade explained:

> *I don't know what has happened to some of my*
> *friends. Consider Lisa. She acts so different around*
> *boys. She gets all giggly and silly and seems to act like*
> *such a jerk. She's cooing and trying to be all sweet*
> *and everything. She's started to act like she isn't smart*
> *at all. Her grades are horrible and she just isn't her-*
> *self anymore.*

The seventh grader who was discussing her friend lived in a very supportive home, had an excellent relationship with her parents, and had been able to remain true to her own personality during her three years of middle school. Many of her friends had not.

I have also interviewed students who had been involved in gifted and talented programs for a long time and had worked with teachers who were devoted to helping them continue to develop their gifts and talents. Many of these girls withstood the pressure to change and were able to successfully integrate their abilities with their school experiences and personal life. Others had a more difficult time integrating their talents into the cultures of their schools. Two gifted high school students commented:

> *I think the whole society is still designed for males. I*
> *see so many girls in the high school typing papers for*
> *the guys, letting them borrow notes, letting them bor-*
> *row homework. It seems like girls do the homework,*
> *and they copy. We do the schleppy work and they get*
> *the credit.*

Young girls' confusion about their abilities, the importance of their appearance, and the way they are regarded by boys emerged in many interviews. It seems that what these talented young women believe about their ability is influenced by what happens with their peers, especially male peers. A female student who was identified as gifted and who had published several poems said:

> *I developed my self-esteem. I didn't have it when I*
> *was younger. It may sound petty, but it really started*

to change when boys started getting interested in me. You see your friends in junior high school who have boyfriends, and you don't, and then you get to high school, and there are older boys there and they think you are cute. I think I really developed my self-esteem when people began thinking I was cute and when they started telling me how thin I was. Oh yeah, I also was excelling in writing and doing well in my classes, too.

Society's general increase in negative attitudes toward academic achievement can especially affect higher achieving students in school (Renzulli & Reis, 1991). These attitudes may cause some students to try to be like everyone else and under no circumstances appear to be different. Other students work to get good but not outstanding grades. My interviews with middle school gifted girls indicated that they rarely share their grades or discuss their accomplishments with peers unless they believe their peers to be of a similar achievement level. The peer pressure often negatively affects smart girls, as is clear from the following comment offered by a high school senior who was writing to her local newspaper in support of the gifted program which was targeted for budget cuts:

> In my twelve years in Torrington Schools, I have been placed in many average classes, especially up until the junior high school level, in which I have been spit on, ostracized, and verbally abused for doing my homework on a regular basis, for raising my hand in class and particularly for receiving outstanding grades. (Peters, 1990)

Do Young Girls Lose Their Beliefs in Their Abilities?

As a teacher of gifted and talented students for many years, I watched as girls I had known since kindergarten lost, to varying degrees, their enthusiasm for learning and their courage to speak out and display their abilities. Some research and reviews of research (Arnold, 1995; Bell, 1989; Cramer, 1989; Hany, 1994; Kramer, 1991; Leroux, 1988; Perleth & Heller, 1994; Reis, 1987; Reis & Callahan, 1989; Subotnik, 1988) have indicated that some gifted females begin to lose self-confidence in elementary school and continue this loss through college and graduate school. These girls may grow to increasingly doubt their intellectual competence, perceive themselves as less capable than they actually are, and believe that boys can rely on innate ability while they must work harder to succeed. Some of this research also indicates that girls try to avoid competition in order to preserve relationships, even if that means that they don't take the opportunity to use their skills. Some research suggests that talented girls choose more often to work in groups, are more concerned about teacher reactions, more likely to change their behavior to fit adult expectations, and are less likely than boys to describe themselves or to be described as autonomous and independent. These behaviors aren't necessarily negative. Bright girls can use affiliations and relationships to assess their level of ability or to achieve at higher levels, and it is natural for children to desire peer approval and to believe that their grades will be higher if their teachers like them. In many girls, however, these behaviors can also indicate low self-confidence and self-esteem.

Bell (1989) identified several dilemmas facing gifted girls which may contribute to personality development issues later in adolescence. She found that gifted girls often perceive achievement and affiliation as opposite issues because to girls, competition means that someone wins and someone loses. The gifted girls that Bell studied encountered great difficulty with comparisons and downplayed their own accomplishments. The girls also feared social isolation as a consequence of their success.

Kline and Short (1991) found, in a review of the literature, that the self-confidence and self-perceived abilities of gifted girls steadily decreased from elementary grades through high school.

Buescher, Olszewski, and Higham (1987) found gifted boys and girls were more alike than peers not identified as gifted except in one critical area—the recognition and acceptance of their own level of ability. Interviews with middle school gifted females revealed that girls avoid displays of outstanding intellectual ability and search for ways to better conform to the norm of the peer group (Callahan, Cunningham, & Plucker, 1994).

While some gifted girls are competitive and want to succeed, many seem to value their own personal achievements less as they grow older. This change in values may indicate that for gifted girls, growing older and approaching adolescence and early adulthood has a negative impact on both achievement and self-confidence. Since girls' self-perception of ability is a key factor in keeping gifted girls involved in advanced level mathematics and science courses, this trend is troubling.

Being identified as being bright or talented may create social problems for females (Bell, 1989; Buescher, Olszewski, & Higham, 1981; Eccles, Midgley, & Adler, 1984; Kerr, Colangelo, & Gaeth, 1988; Kramer, 1991; Reis, 1987, 1995; Reis, Callahan, & Goldsmith, 1996). Some research indicates that gifted girls believe it is a social disadvantage to be smart because of the negative reactions of peers. Fearing their peers' disapproval, bright young women may deliberately understate their abilities in order to avoid being seen as physically unattractive or lacking in social competence. In other words, they may "play dumb." Parents may also send negative messages about how girls should act, how polite they should be, how they should dress, and how often they should speak out and in what situations.

Recently I received one of the many phone calls I get from the parents of smart daughters. This call was similar to hundreds of others. "Her teacher told me that she keeps raising her hand and wanting to answer," the mother explained apologetically to me. "She always wants to talk in class and is rarely content to sit and listen. What can I do to make her understand that she has to give others a chance?" My usual response to this type of query is to tell parents that the last thing their smart daughter needs is more negative feedback from her mother and/or father. Parents should encourage their daughters as much as possible to both raise and answer questions in class.

The current research on girls in school indicates that while some progress has been made, we are still far from creating an equitable environment in which all children can learn. Research on teacher-to-students and student-to-student classroom interaction patterns, reviews of curricular materials, and data on participation in extracurricular activities suggest that the school climate is less encouraging for girls and young women than for their male classmates. Even testing and assessment procedures may give an inaccurate picture of girls' abilities and thereby limit their options.

Do Smart Girls Score Lower on Tests Than Boys?

Differences in scores on standardized tests between talented males and females still exist. In a recent meta-analysis (Hyde & Fennema, 1990), the magnitude of gender differences on tests of mathematics achievement and aptitude was studied as a function of the selectivity of the sample. Results indicated that more highly selective samples had larger gender differences favoring males. Hyde and Fennema also concluded that gender difference is a function of ethnicity, with the largest difference favoring males found among American Caucasians and Australians. The importance of environmental influences on these differences is clear as Hyde and Fennema also found that the gender difference for Asian-Americans favors females, indicating that talented Asian-American females outperform males.

Further evidence that sex differences exist among high ability students on standardized tests is presented by Becker and Forsyth (1990). In examining gender differences in a longitudinal study of score distribution on the Iowa Tests of Basic Skills and the Iowa Tests of Educational Development across 10 years (grades 3-12), they found that males performed significantly better at the upper percentiles (90th and 75th) in vocabulary and mathematics problem solving across all grade levels. Female advantages were noted at all levels and across all grades in language usage; at the 90th percentile, however, the advantage was less and "males consistently scored higher than females in vocabulary at the upper percentiles of the score distribution across all grades" (p. 7). The advantage of females over males in the upper percentiles in grades 3-8 was reversed to a male advantage in grades 9–12. Finally, the differences between males and females across grades 9–12 in social studies and science consistently favored males, although there was a slight decline in the differences across those years.

This score differential has serious ramifications for females. Lower scores on the traditional college admissions exams can deny opportunity for admission to selective colleges, and they may also deny access to certain programs for the gifted and talented—particularly at the secondary level. In New Jersey, PSAT scores have been used as part of the selection process for attendance in the Governor's Schools program and the New Jersey Scholars Program. In Washington, DC, students who earn high scores on the SAT-Q are provided the opportunity to attend college courses in mathematics during the summer. Many summer programs offered by colleges and preparatory schools base admission on SAT or PSAT scores. Invitations to attend the 1987 Johns Hopkins summer program were extended to 2,594 boys, but only to 1,082 girls—even though equal numbers of boys and girls took the exam (Rosser, 1989). Lower scores may also have had an impact on girls' selection of careers, as the majority of girls who took the SAT in 1990 turned away from math and science, indicating that they planned to have careers in the social sciences (Sadker & Sadker, 1994). Achievement tests that many young people take with the general SAT exam, which are, according to Sadker and Sadker, "a male landslide" (p. 141), may also effect career selection. For example, in 1990, boys scored higher on 11 of the 14 achievement tests. In 1991, the largest point gap was in physics (62 points), but in 1990, males scored 60 points higher in European history, representing the largest gap for that year.

Test scores may have even more detrimental effects on gifted females than previously believed. Rosser (1989) found that both boys and girls estimate their math and English abilities closer to their SAT scores than to their grades, suggesting that girls underestimate their own abilities. Rosser also found that "girls planned to go to slightly less prestigious colleges than boys with equivalent GPAs" (p. iv). This result, in conjunction with the findings of Boyer (1987) that 62% of students questioned said they lowered their expectations after receiving their standardized aptitude scores used for college admission, suggests a chain reaction that is detrimental to females, especially those in high school. If girls' SAT scores are lower, they may lower their expectations, apply to less prestigious colleges, and consider less challenging careers.

GRADES IN SCHOOL

Researchers have consistently found that girls get higher grades in both elementary and secondary school (Achenbach, 1970; American College Testing Program, 1989; Coleman, 1961; Davis, 1964; Kimball, 1989). How does this affect gifted and talented females in particular? This phenomenon, if it still exists, is not necessarily positive. Girls' attainment of higher grades, when contrasted with their lower scores on some standardized tests, may contribute to talented girls' beliefs that they are not as "bright" as boys and can only succeed by working harder. Also, since the majority of school teachers are female, there may be sex-based biases or preferences involved in the grading process. The grade disparity may also simply indicate that girls are, in general, more proficient than boys at some school-related tasks (completing homework assignments, for example) than others (standardized tests) and that educators should perhaps take differences in male and female learning and performance styles into account when designing curricula.

However, this female grade point advantage may be changing. My colleague, Del Siegle, and I (1998) recently conducted a research study of 543 gifted male and female students and did not find the higher grades reported for gifted females in previous research. This study investigated whether teachers perceived male and female gifted students differently with respect to the quality of their work, as measured by grades, effort, and ability in all content areas. Results indicated that teachers consistently rated female students higher than males on effort and quality of work. However, teachers did not believe males or females had different abilities, nor did they assign different grades to males than they did to females. Perhaps the grade disparity never existed, or the attitudes and practices of teachers and students that previously led to females' getting higher grades are changing.

PARENTAL INFLUENCES ON TALENTED FEMALES

We sometimes forget that young children's most important lessons take place not in school but in their homes. Recent research has established the importance of parents' attitudes and beliefs about the academic self-perceptions and achievement of their children (Hess, Holloway, Dickson, & Price, 1984; McGillicuddy-De Lisi, 1985; Parsons, Adler, & Kaczala, 1982; Stevenson & Newman, 1986). In some studies, parents' beliefs about children's abilities had an even greater effect on children's self-perceptions than previous performance (Parsons, Adler, & Kaczala, 1982). Phillips (1987) confirmed this finding in her study of high ability students, and a recent study of parental influence on math self-concept with gifted female adolescents as subjects found consistently significant correlations between parent expectations and student math self-concept (Dickens, 1990). In these cases the research findings are common sense: parents who expect success from their children and who teach them to expect and work for that success are more likely to raise motivated and confident children.

Problems can arise when parents transmit harmful or limiting gender stereotypes to their young children, especially girls, as noted earlier. In the community where I grew up and later taught for many years, it was not unusual for my gifted female students to tell me that their parents were saving for college for their brothers, and since the money was limited, it would be spent on the boys' education first. My most talented female students often repeated jokes their parents made about the MRS degree that would be of little use to a female after marriage (implying that the girls would never use their education and that college was just a way to find a husband). College was a dream for many in this working class community, but a far more approachable dream for males than for females. In later chapters, the memories of how parental comments haunted talented women decades after they left home provide compelling evidence of the difficulty of addressing this problem. Parental opinions matter greatly to young girls, and the messages sent by subtle and not-so-subtle verbal and nonverbal interactions may encourage or discourage girls for life. Even the most well-meaning parents unconsciously reinforce these stereotypes through different expectations for their daughters than they have for their sons.

CAREER CHOICE

Gifted females continue to reject math and science as courses of study—a decision which influences their career choices. For example, in 1989 only 1% of females taking the ACT exam before college indicated that they planned to pursue a major in one of the physical sciences, 0% indicated an interest in a career in mathematics, and only 2% indicated interest in either the study of engineering or the biological sciences (ACT, 1989). These remarkably low percentages of career interest in mathematics and science occur despite data cited earlier suggesting that females receive consistently higher grades in elementary school, secondary school, and in college in related subjects.

This pattern is also true for high ability female students who score at the highest levels on the SAT quantitative exam. Only about 15% of the Caucasian females who scored above the 90th percentile planned to major in a "highly quantitative field, namely mathematics, physics, or engineering" (Grady, 1987, p. 1). Schmurak (1996) found that the pattern of decreasing interest in nontraditional careers across grades 9-12 characterized females in both single sex and coeducational private schools. Further, the women had little sense of career awareness or educational requirements of careers in math and science. Dolny (1985) studied 228 gifted students in grades 10–12, finding no significant differences between females' and males' aspirations for professional careers or their plans for marriage and children. Female students foresaw no future work and family conflict for themselves, and half of the males expected such conflict only for their spouses, which, of course, points to issues to be resolved in the future.

Leroux (1988) interviewed 12th grade students and their teachers and guidance counselors. She reported that although girls were more academically oriented than boys, they selected service careers more often, perceived males to be more successful in mathematics and science, and thought themselves more likely to remain single in the interest of pursuing careers. Interestingly, these same young women described themselves as "aggressive" and as leaders more often than did their male peers, and scored higher in self-perception of ego strength and ability to cope and adapt. Further, the women had little awareness of educational requirements of careers in math and science.

A 1994 United Nations (UN) report issued from the UN Economic Commission for Europe indicated that women were emerging as a "special underclass" in poorly paid, part-time, and temporary employment positions. It also stated that pay for women had dropped since the 1980s and that women continue to be segregated into traditionally female occupations, particularly in service fields. The report also noted that although women's participation in the labor force has increased, a higher percentage of women have *not* entered positions in managerial or decision-making posts. To investigate whether young girls currently want to enter managerial or decision-making positions, my colleagues and I (Reis, Callahan, & Goldsmith, 1996) studied 284 talented adolescent girls and boys in grades 6-8 about three aspects of their lives: expectations about future education, career, and family. We found distinct differences between the boys and the girls in all three areas.

FUTURE EDUCATION, CAREER, AND FAMILY

Almost all the boys (99.3%) and the girls (100%) said they planned to go to college. When asked why, 58% of the girls and 48% of the boys said they wanted a career or a job which required a college degree. More than twice the percentage of boys mentioned a specific career goal as did girls. When asked what they would be doing after they graduated from college, a third of the boys (33.6%) and a quarter of the girls (25%) said they would work, but boys were more likely to name a specific job or career—46.4% of the boys and only 27.1% of the girls mentioned a specific job or career.

Sixty-five percent of the boys and 25% of the girls thought women should not work after they had children. Some girls still thought they would need to support the family (19%), but fewer boys thought that support was important (11%). Fourteen percent of the boys (and none of the girls) explicitly stated that taking care of the children was a woman's responsibility. Only a very small number of the boys (5%) said they expected both partners to work and for them both to share the childcare.

Figure 6 shows a representative sample of responses from participants on the question of whether or not they believe a woman should continue to work if a couple has children. The responses of boys in grades six through eight offer a glimpse of some of the challenges which young girls will face if they eventually marry young men like the male participants in this study. Responses from girls of the same ages displayed a completely

Should a woman continue to work after she has had children?

Many of the boys responded with "no" and offered the following comments:

- "She will need to take care of them until old enough to stay home alone";
- "She will want to take care of them";
- "If she wants to stay home with both the children she may";
- "She will stay home to help the children";
- "Kids come first until older";
- "When they get older yes, when they are little, no";
- "I don't know, that's not my business";
- "I think that she should take care of the kids during the day."

Girls of the same ages generally displayed a completely different perception of work and childcare:

- "[No,] I think your children will be with you for only a fraction of your life time so you should spend as much time with them as you can";
- "[Yes,] Because we need money to raise the children";
- "[Yes,] Depending on how demanding my job is";
- "[Yes,] I know doctors who can work out their schedules";
- "[Yes,] Take a while off and then begin work after my kids have reached an age that I feel comfortable to leave them";
- "[Yes.] It isn't fair to give up your career for children";
- "[Yes,] Because both are important";
- "[Yes,] Because I can stick them in day care centers."

Figure 6. Responses from boys and girls about whether women should stay home after the birth of a child.

different perception of the future and work.

From a selection of 26 professions, the top four career choices of boys and girls were similar. Scientist was the top choice for boys (40%), second for girls (31%). Top choice for girls was doctor (37%) while it was second for boys (34%) Owning your own business was third for boys (27%) and fourth for girls (20%). Lawyer ranked third for girls (27%) and fourth for boys (22%). Astronomer, a scientific career, was fifth for boys (21%), while 12% of the girls chose that career. When asked what their parents wanted them to do, 88% of the girls but only 37.9% of the boys said their career was their own decision. A greater number of the boys (45%) mentioned that their parents had a specific career in mind for them as compared to 24.2% of the girls.

Two general themes emerged in our research from the questions about future education, career and family: one regarding careers and the other regarding expectations of future work and family. When asked directly girls and boys generally chose similar career goals. In questions about their future, however, boys were much more likely to spontaneously mention a specific career goal than girls, and most of the boys also believed that their parents had a specific career goal in mind for them. This goal was often similar to one they expressed. It is not clear whether these responses reflect parents supporting a career goal their sons had expressed to them, or whether the boys had heard their parents' wishes for them and accepted them. Girls, who generally did not mention specific career goals, said their parents would support any choice they made. Again, it isn't clear if parents of girls do not encourage them to consider careers, if they are waiting to support the girls' choices, or if they don't think careers are important for girls.

Both the boys and girls we studied expected to work in their future, but there are differences in how they regarded their family life and work life intersecting. While boys were more definite about their career plans, girls were more likely to mention combining career or work with family. Only a small percentage of boys mentioned their family in their views of their futures. Girls expected, in overwhelming numbers, to work after they were married, and 75% of them thought they would work after their children were born. The majority of boys believed women should stop working when they have children.

While the boys thought they would do household chores when they were married, and 75% said they expected to share the chores equally, both men's and women's choices of chores reflected traditional gender role stereotyping. Stereotypical male chores such as paying the bills, maintaining the car, fixing things, and mowing the lawn are done infrequently, once a week at most. Women's chores such as cooking, doing the laundry, shopping, and driving the children are done much more frequently, often daily. These gender choices certainly did not reflect sharing equally. The perceptions of young gifted males and females differ in relation to career opportunities for females after marriage and children. Adolescent males indicated that their wives would stay home with their children and postpone or delay their careers until their children are grown. It is apparent that these girls, whose perceptions and beliefs are quite different, will have to address the traditional views of the young males with whom they may eventually raise families.

In our study we saw definite causes for concern about gifted and talented girls. More boys were encouraged by their parents to pursue a specific career than girls. Boys had a clear belief about their future and their professional goals, and they also believed that their wives, by staying home with their children, would take time off from their careers. The chores selected by both boys and girls certainly indicate that girls will spend more time on a daily basis taking care of children and home. While a remarkably high percentage of the gifted girls we studied are interested in being scientists or physicians, we must ask ourselves, given the current beliefs and attitudes of these young people, how many will actually realize this dream? It is clear that until young people change their attitudes, and males take on more active roles in parenting and household responsibilities, many of these females will find their ambitions thwarted.

SCHOOL AND TEACHER INFLUENCES

L. R. Kramer (1985) found that teachers were usually able to identify gifted boys, but were often surprised to learn that a girl was considered smart. The gifted girls in her study were very successful at hiding their intelligence and in silencing their voices. In another analysis of research about adult perceptions of girls' intelligence, Myra and David Sadker (1994) stated that "study after study has shown that adults, both teachers and parents, underestimate the intelligence of girls" (p. 95). An American Association of University Women (AAUW) report (1992) documenting this silence in the classroom discussed some of these inequities. In their survey of school aged students, 48% of the boys said they speak up in class as compared to only 39% of girls who said they speak up. Moreover, almost twice as many boys as girls, 28% versus 15%, said they always argued with teachers when they thought they were right.

Other research supports the conclusion that teachers are unable to correctly estimate girls' intelligence. Kissane (1986) found that teachers are less accurate in nominating girls who are likely to do well on the quantitative subtest of the SAT than they were in naming boys who were likely to achieve a high score. Research also indicates that teachers like smart girls less than other students. Jeanne Block (1982), a pioneer in gender difference research, found that girls who achieved at high levels received the lowest level of supportive, ego-enhancing feedback. They also received significantly fewer laudatory statements and significantly more disparaging statements. Block also found that such negative expectancies can be found at all levels from nursery school to college. As early as 1974, Brophy and Good found that when teachers treated boys and girls differently in class, these differences were the most pronounced for talented females.

Similar findings emerged in a study by Cooley, Chauvin, and Karnes (1984). Both male and female teachers regarded smart boys as more competent than gifted girls in critical and logical thinking skills and in creative problem-solving abilities, while they thought smart girls were more competent in creative writing. Male teachers viewed female students in a more traditional manner than did female teachers. They perceived bright girls to be more emotional, more high strung, more gullible, less imaginative, less curious, less inventive, less individualistic, and less impulsive than males. However, male teachers had more favorable attitudes than female teachers toward talented girls in traditionally male courses such as chemistry and physics.

Teachers have been found to believe and reinforce one of the most prevalent sex stereotypes—that males have more innate ability, while females must work harder. Fennema (1990), commenting on the role of teacher beliefs on mathematics performance, reported that in a study she conducted with Peterson, Carpenter, and Lubinski, "teachers selected ability as the cause of their most capable males' success 58% of the time, and the cause of their best females' success only 33% of the time. Most capable females' successes were due to effort 37% of the time, while best males' successes were due to effort only 12% of the time" (p. 178). They also concluded that even though teachers did not tend to engage in sex-role stereotyping in general, they did stereotype their best students in the area of mathematics, attributing characteristics such as volunteering answers, enjoyment of mathematics, and independence to males. One study found that in classrooms where boys had higher expectations of achievement, high achieving boys (as judged by teachers) and low achieving girls received the most teacher attention. High achieving girls received the least attention (Eccles & Blumfield, 1985).

As indicated by some of the research discussed above, teachers seem to expect less from females than they do from males, especially in regard to achievement in mathematics and science. Girls internalize these lowered expectations very early in life. Cramer (1989) interviewed gifted elementary school girls and reported that "most of the reasons found in the literature to explain the male/female disparity—conflicting expectations, lack of confidence, lack of female role models, and especially sex role stereotyping—came to the surface" (p. 128). Stereotyping was also detected in a study by Fowler (1991). Fowler interviewed eight gifted girls in seventh grade and found that girls did not believe that boys are generally better at science, but that boys were innately better at certain science activities. Those girls who believed this stereotype also reported that their parents didn't like science. In addition, these girls consistently reported the existence of stereotypic gender roles in their science classes. Girls who were the better students "acted grossed out" at the teasing and risk-taking activities of the boys. The girls all believed it was more important to attain good grades than to learn a lot about science. They believed they would be least successful when they took science courses in the future and that science would be their most difficult future courses.

Stereotyping has been found in the use of various instructional techniques with gifted females. Webb (1984) and Webb and Kenderski (1985) found that in high achieving classes, males outperformed females and received a greater number of explanations. When females requested help they were likely to be ignored (at a rate double that of males). They reported that females were often ignored by males, especially in groups with only one female. Shucard (1991) also investigated certain classroom conditions for bright girls. Under competitive and non-competitive conditions, 40 gifted girls and 40 gifted boys in grades 6-8 performed line drawing tasks manipulated for success and failure. The competitive condition brought out higher perceptions of their own ability for boys when compared to girls' ratings.

Concern exists about the effect of stereotypes of teachers who refer students to honors' classes or high ability classes. Hallinan and Sorensen (1987) found that "girls with high aptitude in mathematics are less likely to be assigned to the high ability group than boys" (p. 71). As Koehler (1990) has pointed out, if the advantage of ability grouping is instruction at a pace and level commensurate with aptitude, this inappropriate placement of females hurts female achievement.

Single-sex schools or classes have been recommended for gifted and talented girls as one method for reducing stereotyping, but little separate research has addressed why these alternatives may be better for gifted girls than for girls in general. Several benefits have been cited as outcomes of placing females in single-sex schools or classes including the opportunity for positive role models, the promotion of sex-role development, equal access to the curriculum, and order and control (Riordan, 1990). Campbell and Evans (1993) found that girls in single-gender schools enrolled in science and math classes more than their counterparts who attended coeducational schools and had higher self-esteem as well. Ransome (1993) found that single-sex schools provided an atmosphere designed with the female learner in mind. Lee and Bryk (1986) compared male and female students in their sophomore and senior year attending single sex and coeducational high schools and found that the students who attended single-sex high schools had more positive attitudes toward academics and that the girls who attended single-sex schools had the highest attitudes of all groups. They also took more math and science courses and had the highest gains of any group in both science and reading. Conducting a follow-up study, Lee and Marks (1990) found that students who attended single-sex schools were more likely to attend a selective college and the girls were less likely to regard themselves in sex stereotyped roles as adults.

Recently, Mary Rizza (1997) found that gifted girls were able to positively use competition in a single-sex Catholic academy in an urban center. Girls selected carefully the times and situations in which they wanted to invest their energy and talents. One participant in Rizza's study explained how choice influenced competition: "There are times you take a stand and times you let someone else have it. I never try out for anything halfway, if I want something I go after it." Competition was also described as negative when it involved competing with others, especially friends. However, it was appropriate to compare oneself with peers to see how one's accomplishments compared with other's accomplishments, while still maintaining friendships.

Some research indicates that talented females in single-sex settings attain higher scores on tests. Subotnik and Strauss (1995) reported that girls in a calculus class in a single-sex high school outperformed a group of girls in a single-sex classroom within a mixed-sex school (as measured by the BC Advanced Placement Calculus Exam). In spite of significantly lower SAT-M scores, girls in the single-sex school were more active in volunteering answers, were called on more in the classroom than girls in the single-sex class in a mixed-sex school, and were better prepared for a calculus course as measured by the Calculus Readiness Test. Although the authors acknowledged that very different school climates may have been a possible explanation for the difference, they suggest reducing emphasis on SATs as the sole indicator of math ability and encouraging more participation in class by girls.

"Separated by Sex: A Critical Look at Single-Sex Education for Girls," a 1998 study by the AAUW, challenged the notion that single-sex environment helps girls learn better than coeducation, citing no differences in achievement by girls in these settings. The same report, however, indicated that girls in single-sex settings generally like these settings, express a more positive attitude toward math and science, show a greater willingness to take risks, and draw more confidence from their academic ability than their physical appearance. For these reasons alone, some teachers and parents may want to continue to recommend single-sex options, even those which can be organized in after-school settings such as all-girl technology clubs or mathematics support groups.

Research about participation in gifted programs indicates a general trend that girls drop out of gifted programs as they go through school. Females comprise a slight majority of participants in gifted programs from kindergarten through 9th grade, but the trend is reversed starting in 10th grade (Read, 1991). Read identified several factors that discouraged female participation in gifted programs. In most cases, gifted girls mentioned peer pressure as a reason for not continuing in these programs.

In a more recent study showing a potentially positive trend, Crombie, Bouffard-Bouchard, and Schneider (1992) examined girls' and boys' referral to and enrollment in gifted programs. The researchers obtained data on overall enrollment, referral, and referral outcome by gender and grade from five school boards offering gifted programs. While a greater number of boys than girls were enrolled in gifted programs, when researchers examined the referral process for the most recent year, they observed no gender differences in referral or in decision to enroll.

Despite the preponderance of previously conducted studies, Feldhusen and Willard-Holt (1993), recently noted mixed effects of stereotyping on both high ability boys and girls. They assessed students' perceptions and compared boys with girls on school-related attitudes, age, preferences, and aspirations. Results indicated that boys perceived inequities in the classroom to a greater extent than did girls and that boys had greater preference for math- and science-related tasks. They found no gender differences for effort, verbal activity, aspirations, or perceptions of differences in teacher reinforcement.

Hollinger (1991) confirmed the influences of special intervention to counter stereotyping. Gifted high school-aged females who participated in a longitudinal study were asked to identify internal and external, gender-related and non-gender-related barriers they faced. Less than 10% of the high school aged females believed they faced any of these previously discussed barriers (Hollinger, 1991). Hollinger, however, believed that these females may have indicated that they have no barriers because they are idealistic in their youth.

Recently, Callahan, Cunningham, & Plucker (1994) investigated influences of family on the ability of gifted teenage females to face and cope with the barriers, including stereotyping, to their achievement. They found positive influences to be beneficial to addressing and overcoming these barriers. In particular, the modeling of discussion, debate, and decision making, mothers as female role models, and early encouragement of independent problem solving behaviors led to greater effectiveness in compensating for these barriers.

Achievement and Underachievement in Gifted Teenage Girls

Why do some gifted young girls succeed while others of similar ability fail to achieve at levels which might be expected given their potential? In research that my colleagues and I recently conducted (Reis, Hébert, Diaz, Maxfield, & Ratley, 1995), we studied young women who achieved as compared to a group of high ability females who underachieved in school for a period of three years. The talented, young, achieving women who participated in our study were extremely determined to be independent. Several said they wanted a different life from that of their mothers. The female achievers consistently echoed determination to be different and to succeed, and many explained that their parents had helped instill their determination to succeed. Marisa, one of the participants in this study, was strong, outgoing, and became even more independent between her junior and senior years, breaking up with her boyfriend, caring less about her physical appearance than in previous years, and displaying even stronger bonds with her female friends.

Nicki was quite different in the way she displayed her personal characteristics. She was quiet, calm, and explained that she had periods of doubt about her own abilities, doubt which her close friends who would not let her begin to underachieve addressed. Nicki's scholarship to a small, private Northeastern college had enabled her to achieve a dream: no one else in her family had ever attended college, and Nicki was determined to attend and graduate from college:

*I'm not sure exactly what I want to do, but I know
that eventually I'll find out what I want to do. I
know that I want to go to college, and I think that I
want to be a teacher. But if that changes, I won't
have a problem with changing my mind. I don't have
to be set in something to feel confident.*

In addition to displaying confidence, independence, and determination, the young women in this study knew the areas in which they achieved and those in which they were not outstanding, and they accepted these dualities. The high achieving female students we studied rarely dated or became romantically involved, were extremely supportive of other high achieving students, became involved in multiple activities and were independent, resilient, and dedicated to a career. Clear trends emerged regarding parental expectations as mothers, in particular, encouraged their daughters to excel in school.

Although still somewhat limited in scope, current research does seem to indicate that some changes may be occurring with regard to the problems and challenges of young gifted females. These changes, while not drastic, become more apparent when we compare current findings with some of the suggestions and strategies made a decade or more ago. What implications can we infer from this review of more current research on gifted females in elementary and secondary schools? First, it seems clear that research on this topic is still sparse and that, with the exception of mathematics, few researchers are pursuing the area of talent development in adolescent and high school females. The interest generated by the various reports released by the AAUW, the Sadkers' book, *Failing at Fairness*, and Pipher's *Reviving Ophelia* has not extended to a plan of action, and it is not clear which actions may have a lasting impact. Clearly, we need more research (see Chapter 11 for research suggestions).

What does this review of research about gifted females in elementary and secondary school suggest?

1. Some elementary and middle school gifted girls who have been identified and provided with programs may be more confident and secure in their abilities. It may be, however, that they become less confident about their talents at a later time.

2. The loss of confidence in their own abilities may occur less frequently in gifted girls who have been involved in gifted and talented programs and numerous extracurricular activities than in other populations of gifted girls.

3. The achievement scores of some gifted girls are equal to or higher than those of their male counterparts.

4. While the gap in achievement test scores between males and females seems to be decreasing, the remaining gap favoring males seems largely caused by differences in scores among the top 10-20%.

5. The gap between males and females on test scores of high achieving female students may have far-reaching negative consequences, such as fewer females being named National Merit Scholars, being accepted at most selective colleges or universities, and being provided opportunities such as Governor's Schools or other challenging summer programs.

6. Research has consistently indicated that girls receive higher grades than males in elementary and secondary school. However, one recent research study cited in this chapter indicates that this advantage may be diminishing.

7. Parents may provide different encouragement and career advice for their gifted daughters than they do for their sons, encouraging their sons to pursue specific careers while encouraging their daughters simply to go to college. This difference may have negative consequences on the girls' futures.

8. Little doubt exists that talented girls may still face negative stereotyping in school and community.

9. Despite cultural and family stereotyping, many gifted girls emerge from high school with their ambitions intact and are supported in their efforts by their academic peers—creating an atmosphere of achievement which can nurture talents.

10. Extracurricular activities and summer programs help to encourage gifted girls to use time wisely, develop their independence, and expand their choices about college and careers. Studies have found that high achieving girls are involved in multiple activities, including sports, clubs, and in limited hours of after-school employment.

11. Some talented girls believe they can achieve at higher levels if they do not date or become romantically involved in middle and high school. One talented student commented that after a "horribly stressful" high school relationship ended, during which she had "often wanted to . . . fade away." She threw herself into her studies and extracurricular activities. That first quarter after her boyfriend left was her first 4.0 in high school. Many girls can narrow or destroy their potential for future achievement by becoming too involved in romantic relationships at a young age.

12. Some gifted girls enjoy competitive learning opportunities. Using cooperative learning groups should not regularly be suggested for this population. The enjoyment of competition may be a difference between all girls and gifted girls.

13. Regarding future career and family plans, some gifted girls and boys seem to be on a collision course. Gifted girls believe they will work after having families, while their male counterparts believe that their wives will stay at home and do most of the childcare. Boys also indicate that they will do fewer daily chores than girls and unless boys change their expectations, an unequal division of labor in the home will continue.

14. Adverse social consequences in school still exist for smart females, possibly causing them to subjugate or hide their abilities.
15. Teachers perceive that females work harder to achieve success. Some teachers have lowered expectations for gifted females, especially in mathematics and science.
16. Parents of gifted girls who have high expectations and provide love, support, and encouragement for achievement can help their daughters leave high school with their goals and ambitions clearly articulated and their dreams intact.

CHAPTER FIVE

~:~

TALENTED GIRLS FROM CULTURALLY DIVERSE & LOW SOCIOECONOMIC CIRCUMSTANCES

Can't nothing make your life work if you ain't the architect.
— Terry McMillan

Gifted females from culturally diverse and low socioeconomic circumstances face many of the same issues that all females do. They also have some unique challenges. Sadker and Sadker (1994) reported in *Failing at Fairness* that smart girls are least likely to be recognized by their teachers. Their analyses found the students most likely to receive teachers' attention were white males, followed by minority males, followed by white females. Minority females were the students least likely to receive attention. I recently spent three years working on a research project in an urban high school with culturally diverse gifted students (Reis, Hébert, Diaz, Maxfield, & Ratley, 1995) designed to explore why some culturally diverse, low socioeconomic students achieve while others fail to achieve. The stories of some of the girls who achieved are presented in this chapter, as is a discussion of why other talented young women from similar backgrounds failed to achieve at rates commensurate with their ability.

~: ROSA :~
Rosa was an energetic, attractive young female who spoke

quickly and had a difficult time sitting still. She was in constant motion, and it was immediately clear that she had a purpose in life. Rosa lived with her family in subsidized housing less than a mile from the high school. She was the oldest of two girls born to a mother who was a dietary aide and a father who was an unemployed factory worker. Born in Puerto Rico, her mother had completed high school and taken a few college courses. Rosa wanted to be a doctor, having been influenced by the illness of her younger sister who was recovering from cancer.

Her work load in high school was difficult, as she was enrolled in all advanced courses and was extremely active in school. She was ranked sixth in her class and had excelled in both academic and extracurricular activities. Beginning in kindergarten, teachers made comments such as "my best student," "highly motivated," and "best student in the school." During her senior year, Rosa received all A's in Honors French IV, Honors Pre-Calculus, Honors Anthropology, Honors Composition, and Advanced Placement Biology. She served as the editor of the yearbook, the captain of the women's soccer team, and was a member of the National Honor Society, the French Club, and the Russian Club, which enabled her to travel to Moscow and St. Petersburg for three weeks in the spring of her senior year. She also worked approximately fifteen hours a week in the kitchen at the health care facility in which her mother worked. As a senior, she applied to Yale, Boston College, Wesley, and Brown University and eventually decided to attend Brown University on a full scholarship.

Rosa loved art and credited her mother's artistic ability as the reason for her own talent in art. She also reported that her family communicated well and spent a great deal of time together. Rosa indicated that her parents did not pressure her to get good grades or to participate in all of the extracurricular activities: "My parents said they wouldn't care if I get straight B's or C's or whatever. They just want me to do my best. And that's all that counts. They don't pressure me at all." Her parents were very supportive and encouraged her to do her best in all of her endeavors. For instance, because of Rosa's talents, she received many opportunities to enroll in special programs. Some of these programs required staying away from home for several weeks during the summer, a necessity not well received by her family. She explained that although her parents were overprotective, especially her father, they recognized the importance of her participation in these programs and allowed her to attend them. Continuous telephone contact was expected, however. Rosa's parents celebrated her success, expressed how proud they felt of her, and reinforced her aspirations. She remembered, "They were sad because they didn't want to see me go away. They said that they were going to miss me so much ... but they decided, 'well this is going to be very good for your future.'"

Her parents did not socialize a great deal with other Hispanic families or relatives in this urban community because of the perception of pressure to conform to values that they did not adhere to in their home. Rosa explained:

> *I'm happy that I have my mother and father together.*
> *If you look at my family, we are the only ones that are*
> *separated in this little corner. It's almost like we are*
> *hiding out so nobody will know we're there. The other*
> *people are into all kinds of problems. We are staying*
> *to ourselves.*

Rosa believed she had experienced various types of prejudice in the community and occasionally in academic experiences because she is both intelligent and Puerto Rican. The discrimination occurred in school, from teachers as well as students, and outside of the city in the summer programs she participated in for high achieving students which were held at some of the most prestigious private schools in the state:

> *... people sort of see me differently because I'm Hispanic*
> *and I'm smart. I feel sometimes that they want to put*
> *me down. I have had several incidents where people will*
> *look at my skin color and think I'm dumb, and they*

immediately think that "she's not bright, she's not smart.

Rosa also indicated that some other students who were not in honors classes perceived her as conceited and a nerd. She remarked that most of the time she did not pay attention to these comments, but sometimes they disturbed her. In fact, on several occasions, she chose to be more assertive and confront people. In addition, her mother helped her deal with the situation: "It sometimes gets to me, then I go to my mother and she calms me down. She will say, 'just look at your life ten, twenty years from now, look at them and compare."

Rosa's commitment to her studies was obvious. She often spent five hours a night on homework and described herself as a hard worker: "It's a thing with me; if I don't do my homework, I can't go to sleep. I will feel guilty. I do it because it feels good once I have done it."

Rosa felt she had benefited from the gifted and talented programs she had been in over the years and acknowledged the help and encouragement of some of her elementary and high school teachers: "In sixth grade, Mr. Mahan was great. He showed me that I could be as good as anyone else and to try my best."

Rosa was also influenced by encouragement from her high school guidance counselor who was also of Puerto Rican descent. She said that she sometimes "hid from him" because he "was always looking for her" to fill out something for a special program award or scholarship. In addition, she claimed that her guidance counselor would occasionally see her in the hallway with a male friend and "go ballistic" because he was afraid that she was involved with a boy who would distract her from her studies. She referred to him as her "second father" because he expressed so much concern for her. Rosa, however, did not date at all until her junior year, and then she maintained a distant relationship with a boyfriend who was away at college, explaining that for a Puerto Rican female to date would mean she would have to put her hopes and dreams on hold and pay attention to the male:

I don't feel that I'm ready to date a guy. I'm going to

continue with my career until I get there, where I want. My mother asked me, "Don't you want to go out with that boy" It's not that I'm not interested. It's just that I see myself doing my thing first, boys are another thing, and I will try to do my thing until I can get it finished. Boys have ways of coming up and getting your mind away from studying. Sometimes, they don't like that you're smart.

She smiled, after making that comment, and said, "Me First, that could be the name of a club for girls who want to achieve, couldn't it?"

Rosa's friends were from various cultural backgrounds including one Puerto Rican girl who had been her best friend for many years and who had provided constant encouragement and support. Theirs was a reciprocal relationship as they continued to encourage each other to excel. Rosa also believed that the honors and advanced placement classes in which she enrolled during high school were an instrumental part of her success in school, and she credited her friends and peer group that attended classes together. In fact, the peer group of achievers in which Rosa was involved stayed together in their honors classes and many of their extracurricular activities including clubs, summer programs, and sports.

Rosa believed that some people held negative stereotypes about Puerto Rican teenagers and these stereotypes had a negative impact on students. She explained some students conformed saying, "that's how it is today. We have to accept that. We can't do anything about it." Rosa disagreed with this perspective, adding, "It just makes me work harder just because I want to prove them wrong. Why am I going to sit by myself and let it be true?"

❧ CLAIRE ❧

Claire tended to carry her head in a slightly bowed position, but when she raised it slowly, she revealed a broad, effervescent face. Her body language radiated a positive attitude. She was an African American 10th grade student who was motivated to achieve in academics as well as athletics, despite a childhood marked by divorce and disruption.

Claire was born in Raleigh, North Carolina in 1978 and lived there until first grade. She moved to Centerfield, Connecticut, with her brother Colin, her mother, who was in the process of divorcing her father, and her mother's boyfriend. At the time of this sudden and abrupt move, Claire's mother was pregnant with her half-brother, Terrell. Her mother never married Terrell's father, and he left soon after Terrell was born. Claire's father recently told her that if had he known that his children would have been moved so far away, he never would have allowed it. Although they only saw each other several times a year, Claire remained close to her father and had even considered moving back to North Carolina at some point in the future. Her father, a high school graduate, once worked for a computer company but was laid off and was now a truck driver. When he drove through the area, he always tried to see her.

Her mother's perspectives on life had great impact on Claire's 'just do it' attitudes. Her mother attributed her current successes in life to her belief and faith in God. Claire's mother had been promoted several times and was currently a library supervisor at a small college. Also a high school graduate, Claire's mother had attended night school and had enrolled in summer school while Claire and her brothers were visiting their father in North Carolina. Originally the courses were in the area of religion, but she began focusing on a liberal arts degree. A benefit of her current job was that she could enroll as a student and attend classes tuition-free. According to Claire, her mother wanted no special considerations and had chosen to go through the regular application process that all undergraduate students go through. Claire believed that her mother's Christian beliefs helped her to set goals and believe in her hopes for future accomplishment. Her mother hoped to graduate from college in

1996, the same year in which her daughter would graduate from high school.

Like Rosa's guidance counselor, Claire's mother warned her about the impact of romantic relationships. Her mother talked with her candidly, saying "men take time" and "even Christian men can hurt you." Although Claire had many boys who were friends, she had not had the same need that girls her age have to be in a steady relationship. A previous romance ended when she discovered that her boyfriend wanted to date her best friend. When she broke up with him she said that she "got over it by focusing on basketball and . . . studies." She claimed to have no time for serious relationships and felt that she had enough social opportunities through her interests and studies. "People know me! I'm in everything!" she said. "Everything" included soccer in the fall, basketball in the winter, and track and field in the spring. Claire was sustained by the many friendships available through these endeavors.

When she wasn't at an athletic practice, French Club, or a National Honor Society meeting, she was home studying and "watching out" for her brothers, Colin, 13, and Terrell, 9. Home was a triple-decker in a neighborhood which Claire originally hated because "it's all Puerto Rican." When asked if she would move out of the area if the opportunity arose, she responded that she had already started over in various schools and wanted to finish at her present high school, one which she believed had a good reputation and where she was getting a solid education.

In Centerfield's Vine Street School, her most memorable teacher was Mrs. Scott, "an old woman in her forties who wore thick glasses." Described as a supportive second grade teacher, Mrs. Scott would allow Claire to attend special presentations in other classes throughout the school. She remembered interests in anything that had to do with the human body and medicine. It was during elementary school that Claire decided she wanted to be a doctor. "The Cosby Show" was popular at the time and Claire believed that it, too, may have influenced her choice to become a pediatrician. By eighth grade, her goal still had not changed. Her mother, realizing the seriousness of Claire's intent, purchased a set of medical encyclopedias. She inscribed them with these words, "To Dr. Claire, Love, Mother."

From Vine Street School, Claire's mother had suddenly moved her to another town when she was a fifth-grader. "It made me mad!" Claire recalled. She was one of only three African American children in the school. Regardless of how everyone tried to make her feel like she belonged, she "hated it" and felt very much like an outsider. At the end of the school year, her mother moved the family back to Centerfield, where she again attended Vine Street School for sixth grade. In the middle of sixth grade, her mother announced that they were moving again, this time to the north end of Centerfield. Claire never had an opportunity to say good-bye to any of her friends. She felt a real sense of loss and lack of closure on this part of her life. She was pleased when some of these schoolmates walked up to her and reintroduced themselves as freshmen in her high school. It gave her an opportunity to explain her sudden disappearance, and it pleased her that she had made an impression on them, so much so that they remembered her three years later.

In 7th and 8th grades Claire attended a junior high school. She immediately recalled how she was "talked about," the gossip revolving around "an African American person getting all A's!" She was angry but "cooled off and did not fight." Seemingly a non-confrontational person, Claire again applied her emotions to achieving rather than defending her goals. Although initially she could not remember any teachers as being particularly influential, upon further reflection she admitted that there were teachers "who made you learn." One in particular was her 8th grade science teacher. "I learned everything from her. She taught me a lot. She was the first teacher who gave me a C!"

In high school, Claire's guidance counselor encouraged her to gradually enroll in honors courses. This guidance counselor was disappointed if Claire didn't strive. Knowing that she was always academically at the top in her classes, she persuaded Claire to take two honors courses in her freshman year and three as a sophomore. Honors French, Geometry, and English provided her with ample stimulation and homework. She learned that Geometry was hard, "miss a day and you were lost." In a voice filled with amazement, Claire explained that her teacher actually "finishes the book with BOTH honors and academic classes!" She was concerned already about her course selection for the next year, which included the following honors courses: Algebra 2, Psychology, Chemistry, Composition and Literature, and a government course, *You and the Law*. "I'm going to die!" was the comment Claire made after reciting the list. The only course which she thought provided any breathing space was typing, which she was allowed to take with a pass/fail option. She found the typing course very competitive and believed there were many others who were brighter. "Everything comes to them easier!"

She spent every weekend working, up to five hours on the computer alone. On Saturday, "I let my body catch back up with me." Claire listened to music, rode her bike, or went to the movies with friends. Unwilling to schedule her weekends, events tended to happen spontaneously. Sunday meant a day partially filled with track meets and church and choir activities. Upon returning from church, if she realized that "homework had to get done," and if it was a nice day, Claire pulled the shades down, burrowed into the books, and emerged only when the work was done. "It takes me a long time to think," she added. Frequently, this meant that she spent all day preparing for Monday's classes. "You have to work hard to get good grades," admitted Claire, even though at times the work seemed "overwhelming."

The adjustment from academic to honors' courses was not easy. Admitting that the "academic courses were easy" and that "they didn't help me much," the A's were more elusive when she moved up to the honors' level and received B's for most of the academic year, "finally getting an A toward the end of the year." The amount of homework and studying involved in the honors' courses combined with all of the extracurricular activities made Claire believe she was "pulled in a lot of different directions." It was hard sometimes, and she worried about "burnout." She felt guilty when she missed a practice, and she had missed many due to testing for the Upward Bound summer program, special projects, and French club responsibilities. Claire was a sophomore class officer and winner of many awards and athletic letters. She believed that "if you try and fail, that's good. If you don't try and fail, that's stupid!" A male friend recently told her that he was smart, but he was getting D's and F's. She told him that "if you choose NOT to be smart, that's stupid." When asked about the peer pressure at play that makes it cool for kids with ability to underachieve, Claire replied, "girls go dumb when they get to this high school. It must have something to do with boys."

Claire had very strong opinions about male and female relationships. She had been chosen to be part of a health program sponsored by the guidance department called Take Control. She talked with younger girls in her neighborhood about not becoming "accident victims" and sending the message that it's "OK to say no." She believed that many never think of the consequences of disease, pregnancy, and children to raise. She does not feel that mothers and sisters should end up doing all the child-rearing: "I'm too strong! I don't have compassion [for girls who get in trouble]." It was apparent that Claire intended to take the message to the streets.

Claire lived in the same large urban city for ten years, and although she acknowledged that there was violence, she talked in a matter-of-fact voice about the gangs and shoot-outs. She felt that drugs were a problem in the suburbs, that "there was no money to buy them here." After so much moving in her life, she wanted to get her diploma from her high school, but also knew that "anywhere I go, I'll learn." She wanted to do something which will "make an impact" at her school, especially because "there was no school spirit."

College plans included a big school. Her first choice was

Brown, although she planned to apply to other Ivy League schools and to the University of Massachusetts. Somewhat hesitantly, she added that she would probably apply to Spellman and Howard, traditionally African American universities, because, "I'm not cultural. I've got to learn something about my background." She was applying for scholarships and intended to finance college by working during school.

RESEARCH ABOUT CULTURALLY DIVERSE GIFTED GIRLS

Research studies about culturally diverse gifted females are sparse. Those which have been conducted indicate that stereotypes of male and female roles vary from culture to culture. By studying the perceptions of minority or culturally diverse students we can gain a better understanding of how cultural influences affect female accomplishment. For example, Yong (1992) found that female African American middle school students did not have stereotypic gender role expectations regarding mathematics as a male domain. In other words, African American female students perceived that they had good intellectual capacity, did not exhibit fear of success toward mathematics, and were more apt to learn the subject. These findings contradict some earlier studies that indicated that female students tend to downplay their intellectual abilities, and this contradiction might be explained by theorizing that African American students might have different expectations for the sexes than the general population. This theory is true for other groups as well, as Hyde and Fennema (1990) found that Asian American girls scored higher than Asian American boys on mathematics tests.

Little research has examined what contributes to achievement in talented urban female students, and little research has examined achievement of talented female students who are from diverse or low income environments. Current research indicates that females in particular, who may be at even higher risk than males due to pregnancy, suicide, gangs, and poverty, are failing at school and at life (Hine 1991, pp. 19-22). In light of the current economic importance of females in the work force and society in general, it is imperative that we understand why some females succeed in spite of adversity and which factors contribute to that success so that schools can foster an appropriate environment and take appropriate actions. It is also essential to more closely examine the confidence and self-esteem of talented girls from culturally diverse groups. In the AAUW survey of 3000 boys and girls across the country aged 9-15, the self-esteem of Hispanic girls decreased more than any other group, and African American girls received even less attention than other girls (AAUW, 1992). In elementary school, 68% of Hispanic girls indicated that they were happy with themselves, but by high school, this number had decreased by 38%.

One theory that has been widely discussed related to underachievement of diverse students involves work by John Ogbu (1981, 1985, 1987, 1991). He believes that minority students fail in school because of factors that go well beyond cultural differences. Ogbu concluded that an essential difference exists between immigrant minorities who come to our country voluntarily, seeking a new and better life, and nonimmigrant or "castelike" minorities who were brought here because of slavery, conquest, or colonization. Immigrant minorities may experience problems due to social adjustments, but they eventually overcome these social issues and succeed. Castelike minorities, however, such as African Americans or Mexican Americans, experience the same barriers, but find it more difficult to overcome them. Castelike minorities do not seem willing or able to separate attitudes and behaviors that result in academic success from those that may result in acculturation, the loss or replacement of their own cultural identity with that of the White American cultural identity. Fordham (1988) and Fordham and Ogbu (1986) conducted research on high achieving African American high school students in Washington, DC, finding that these students were more likely to identify with the beliefs and values of the dominant culture than the culture of less successful students. Fordham (1988) found that high ability African American high school students may try to hide their academic abilities by becoming class clowns, dropping out, and suppressing effort to avoid being perceived as "acting white or rejecting the Black culture" (Fordham, 1988).

A more recent study conducted by Donna Ford (1992a) examining underachievement in gifted African American students, however, identified psychological factors, not social and cultural factors, as playing the greatest role in underachievement or poor achievement motivation. My work has suggested that a combination of social, cultural, and psychological factors contribute to underachievement in culturally diverse female gifted populations, providing support for Ford's premise that psychological factors play a major role. These factors, however, are developed and influenced by both social and cultural factors.

FAMILY ISSUES

Gender stereotypes within cultures have been noted in other research as well. In a recent investigation of 28 Puerto Rican families, Ambert and Figler (1992) found that Puerto Rican families in the United States are distinguished by a strong sense of cultural identity as Puerto Ricans, a strong sense of family membership, a strong caring element among members of the nuclear family, a desire for more education, a traditional view of gender roles, and feelings of burnout in relationships with others. These findings supported the well-known Hispanic cultural value referred to as *familismo*, which tends to emphasize interdependence over independence, affiliation over confrontation, and cooperation over competition (Comas-Diaz, 1989; Falicov, 1982). Views of self, therefore, can vary within these populations as self is considered intertwined with family. Each of these areas has an effect on gifted females, especially regarding the traditional gender roles and interdependence.

Hispanic families have also been characterized by their focus on the collective. The needs of the family have priority over the needs of the individual. Another deeply rooted cultural value in the traditional Hispanic family is *respeto*, respect (Lauria, 1964). Comes-Diaz (1989) pointed out that *respeto* refers to appropriate deferential behavior in interpersonal relationships, according to age, socioeconomic status, gender, and authority status. For example, elders in a Puerto Rican family deserve *respeto* from younger people and parents expect the same from their children. However, in North American society, the culture nurtures self-reliance and competitive, verbally inquisitive behaviors among young people. These traits appear to contrast with traditional Hispanic values, and for Puerto Rican parents, these behaviors in all children are considered disrespectful (Figler, 1979).

Perrine (1989) indicated that the "dynamic of families in the Hispanic culture is a vital force and must be considered" (p. 15) in planning the academic experiences of high ability Hispanic students. Perrine suggested that this same dynamic needs to include parents themselves, for parental support is a critical factor in determining whether or not young people's capabilities are valued and nurtured. Perrine noted that several factors, characteristic of the dynamic of Hispanic families, have the potential to mitigate against the nurturance of giftedness in school. They include family structure, parental view of the educational process, and the family view of the general value of education and school success. Our research indicates that these factors are particularly influential on gifted girls from Hispanic backgrounds (Reis, Hébert, Diaz, Maxfield, & Ratley, 1995).

Perrine (1989) indicated the structure of the Hispanic family is critical with respect to role modeling. Male dominance in the family setting may not encourage a bright girl's tendency for independent thought and behavior. For example, in a Hispanic family, children are embraced and cared for, but infrequently included in family decisions. Perrine also noted that due to their limited experience with education, many parents of Hispanic students do not perceive participation in "school life" as their domain. Many Hispanic families, whether they have lived in the United States for generations or recently arrived, reflect a different view of parental association with the school and the duties of the teacher than do Anglo-American families. Many Hispanic parents have enormous respect for teachers, and they do not feel they, as non-experts in education, should make educational decisions. Also, if parents believe a teacher's advice that reflects the teacher's inherent stereotypical beliefs about achievement, it may mitigate against female achievement. An additional complicating factor is that a communication problem may develop in the parent-child relationship when the parents conduct their lives primarily in Spanish and their children develop a predominant facility in English.

The view of education held by Hispanic parents may also differ from that of the school with the youngster being torn between the two value systems. Ruiz (1989) explained that Hispanic parents regard the process of education much more broadly. To be *educado* goes far beyond school, or may not involve school at all; it means to be well mannered, respectful, considerate, and knowledgeable about practical things. *Educado* may further negatively influence gifted Hispanic females who believe it is most important to develop these traits (which are also considered essential for females in other cultures).

Hine (1991) examined several family factors that fostered high achievement among gifted Puerto Rican students. Role models outside the family, outstanding teachers, consistently high teacher expectations and an intrinsic drive to succeed proved to be essential factors to the high achieving Puerto Rican high school students in Hine's research and of particular importance to talented females.

PEER AND SCHOOL ISSUES

Ianni (1989) found that peers have a strong impact on children, especially teenagers. For instance, friends' educational plans (aspirations) appear to be more important than teachers' encouragement in affecting students' aspirations and actual attainment. In addition, negative peer attitudes toward school and school-related activities seem to inhibit the realization of potential (Kerry, 1981). In the case of gifted females, if friendship is indeed more important to students, then these students may choose to underachieve to avoid feelings of isolation.

In 1989, Fernández conducted a study of at-risk and dropout Hispanic students who were primarily Puerto Ricans. An interesting finding of this study was that students openly admitted that friends and peers may be an impediment to success in school. This study also revealed that Puerto Rican youngsters depend on support and guidance for academic success not only from parents and relatives but from neighbors and friends in the community as well. Ford (1992b) found that social forces such as discrimination and prejudice also influenced the motivation and academic achievement of gifted African American students.

Steppe-Jones (1986) suggested that the school was the major agency for preparing culturally diverse high ability students for productive citizenship, and the key element was the teacher's ability to recognize and support the student's potential. Crocker (1987) maintained the influence of social factors on underachievement was underestimated and suggested that the problem of underachievement among African American students was due to social forces such as discrimination, prejudice and low socioeconomic status. In a related study examining achievement levels and self-concept, Mboya (1986) investigated the relationships among global self-concept, academic self-concept, and academic achievement of African American high school students and found a significant positive relationship between academic self-concept and achievement. Mboya found that African American adolescents' orientation toward school was different from the way they felt about themselves and that African American adolescents viewed academic achievement as a separate activity which did not greatly influence their feelings of "self."

Lee, Marks, and Byrd (1994) found that high achieving African American students differed from their lower achieving African American peers in several ways. They read more, did more homework, watched less television, and made more positive use of their time. These researchers recommended, based on their research, a more disciplined environment, as well as exposure to science, art, and music. Peers are also critical influences, as studies (Harris, 1998) including three-year investigation I conducted with colleagues (Reis, Hébert, Diaz, Maxfield, & Ratley, 1995) that found that high achieving students had peers who also valued achievement in school.

Pollard (1989) conducted a study of students in middle and secondary schools in a large urban community. Pollard suggested that there are two areas which need to be investigated more fully in other ethnographic studies to understand the success or failure of urban students. So that teachers and administrators can develop appropriate school environments, we first must study factors associated with academic success for these students. Second we need more information on gender issues in minority groups.

Kitano (1997, 1998) studied African American, Asian American, and Latina gifted women in an attempt to identify factors affecting the lifespan achievement of high achieving women from these cultural groups. Most of the culturally diverse women she studied encountered racial and/or gender bias, and many encountered numerous obstacles in their attempts to realize their own potential. Some had supportive families, others achieved despite an absence of family support. The gifted females she studied had both encouraging teachers and some who communicated low expectations. A common characteristic found in Kitano's study was a strong determination to succeed, a trait we found in our research as well (Reis, Hébert, Diaz, Maxfield, & Ratley, 1995).

Cordeiro (1991) conducted an ethnographic study of twenty

successful Hispanic high school students from low socioeconomic backgrounds, ten of whom were female. To be successful in school these students were aware that there needed to be a separation between home and school culture. They accomplished this separation by finding reinforcements from school and role models outside the family. Students associated with other achieving Hispanic students and participated in magnet and honors programs. An important aspect in the conditions for success was what Cordeiro described as the "success-facilitating interpretive scheme," a cultural framework defining success in terms of the dominant culture and not what students believed was "typically Hispanic" (p. 289). Using this framework, the students gained the skills of time management and "playing the achievers game," which included cheating in school (p. 289). Cordeiro also found that the female students she studied experienced "discouragement for academic success from their families (p. 8) and "had role models that usually originated from outside the family structure" (p. 12).

Another study dealt with high achieving female Hispanic young women who, despite formidable odds, graduated with advanced degrees (Ph.D., M.D., or J.D.). Patricia Gandara (1995), author of *Over the Ivy Wall*, a book about the lives of poor, high achieving Mexican American women, found three important aspects in the lives of her participants: emotional support of parents, strong maternal role models, and attendance at highly integrated schools. Gandara found that if fathers were not supportive of their daughter's educational ambitions, their mothers would usually intervene and actively support their daughters. Gandara also described at least one parent as an avid reader. She also found that these young women were comfortable in two worlds, both in their Mexican American and Anglo spheres, possibly due to the fact that they attended a nearly all Anglo school in which they learned to be academically successful.

Gandara (1995) acknowledged the importance of grouping

high achieving females together in advanced or honors classes in high school, a finding also noted in our research with high achieving high school students (Reis, Hébert, Diaz, Maxfield, & Ratley, 1995). She (Gandara, 1995) explained that grouping these talented young people together worked:

> It worked for these subjects; it provided the environment, the encouragement, the peer group, the subject-matter knowledge, and the real-world information that was critical in propelling them forward. It also isolated them to some extent from peers who were headed down a different path. Had these subjects been heterogeneously grouped with their neighborhood peers, it is entirely possible that their life and academic choices would have been quite different. (p. 122)

Both mothers and fathers in Gandara's (1995) study stressed independence in their daughters, encouraging their daughters and having them "doing things on your own, not asking for help, especially outside of the family" (p. 30), a trait identified as essential in my research as well. Love of and proficiency in reading were also key components in the success of the women Gandara studied.

Leppien (1995) studied gifted elementary African American achievers and underachievers to create a profile of high achieving female gifted African American elementary students. These high achieving girls had a strong belief in themselves which was aligned with the academic success profile of the school. They structured their peer relationships and interactions in a way that enabled them to continue their success in school by ignoring negative peer statements and surrounding themselves with peers who shared a similar belief about the importance of school and education. Some of the students who encountered negative peer pressure requested transfers to other classrooms where they would be left alone and be able to work. *All* of the high achieving African American girls Leppien studied believed that boys were disruptive in the classroom and received more attention than did girls. One participant explained:

> Boys are badder than girls. They are just bad.
> I guess they get more attention this way. When
> they are like this, the teacher has to pay more
> attention to them. They are doing something
> that they are not supposed to and the teacher
> has to pay more attention to them than the
> people who are doing what they are supposed
> to. (p. 155)

Some of the girls studied by Leppien (1995) consciously remained invisible in the classroom setting and consistently refrained from discussing their accomplishments in front of their peers. We found similar instances of students hiding their accomplishments in the research we conducted (Reis, Hébert, Diaz, Maxfield, & Ratley, 1995). Leppien (1995) identified several participants in her study who had been teased, threatened, and picked on in school by their peers, yet seemed to be able to achieve despite what happened in their urban school:

> I get picked on at school. The kids say they are
> going to beat me up and they never do and they
> get jealous. . . It's a jealousy thing. I get it for
> doing my homework. I just ignore it because I
> know that they won't touch me because I have
> a big brother that always will protect me. They
> have seen him drop me off at school. If any-
> body approaches me, I tell them you can talk
> now, but if you see my brother you won't be
> talking then. Then they leave me alone. It's
> hard to ignore them sometimes because they
> stay on you. Sometimes it gets so bad that I
> have to hum to get rid of the noise. (p. 177)

Shatoya, a participant in Leppien's (1995) study, was trans-
ferred into another classroom to avoid the anger of her peers

who said they were tired of her doing well on homework and classwork:

> "It started out in second grade. They would make fun of me and mock me and it happened throughout the grades. [Students in this school stayed in the same groups every year.] Finally, my mother got fed up with me coming home crying sometimes, talking about all the things that happened to me. The class I am in now is better. I would say that it [the threats] scared me, but they did not scar me. They hurt me, but not academically." (p. 177)

The school in Leppien's (1996) study provided less than an ideal setting for these talented female students. They were underchallenged and the learning environment was simply too easy for them. Negative interaction and behavior problems with their peers created ongoing struggles for these talented girls, and most wished they could attend more challenging and better controlled schools. Their involvement in extracurricular activities was important to them, as was the encouragement they received from their parents, teachers, and community members.

Nancy Lashaway-Bokina (1996) studied high ability Mexican Americans in an effort to identify high-ability female high school dropouts who exhibited creativity or exceptional talent in academic areas, the arts, leadership, or cultural activities. The major purpose of Lashaway-Bokina's study was to describe the circumstances that influence high ability students to leave school prior to graduation. Her research indicated that some Mexican American gifted females dropped out of school for the following reasons: an absence of goals and role models, an absence of self-confidence and belief in self, and conflicts with school officials.

Each of the young women Lashaway-Bokina (1996) studied knew she was smart. None questioned their high abilities, rather, they did not know what to do with them. Most of the young gifted women identified with their mothers, almost all of whom stayed home and raised their families. Only two of the twelve mothers of these young women were employed; the rest stayed at home and spent a great deal of time watching soap operas. When their daughters dropped out of school, their mothers felt guilty that they weren't better examples, but several also welcomed their daughter's company at home. Television provided temporary relief in their sometimes depressing, unchallenging lives: "Thus, television became their pacifier in life, keeping them dreaming of another life by immersing them in the lives of others" (p. 305). Poverty was also an issue for many of these young women, as was transportation to school.

DETERMINANTS OF ACHIEVEMENT IN CULTURALLY DIVERSE GIFTED FEMALES

My colleagues and I recently completed an in-depth three year longitudinal study of 35 talented students who achieved and underachieved in high school (Reis, Hébert, Diaz, Maxfield, & Ratley, 1995). The talented young people who achieved at high levels in school were proud of their abilities and did not minimize their intelligence. The females in this study also avoided dating and took the time to put themselves first and to pursue their interests and talents while in high school. Rosa, profiled in this chapter, eloquently explained what led to her success. Among the factors were participation in school gifted programs, encouragement from teachers (and particular guidance counselors), and deciding not to date during high school. She commented, "[my teachers] showed me that I can be as good as anyone else and to try my best."

Our study (1995) sought to identify the factors indicated by high achieving female students as being influential in their academic achievement in urban high school. We also wanted to learn about the relationships and support systems which shaped the behaviors, attitudes, and aspirations of high achieving female students in an urban environment. The research was carried out at a large high school in an urban Northeastern city with a culturally diverse student population. The multicultural student body included a transient population with approximately one-third of the students transferring in or out of the high school during the academic year. Located in the south end of the city, South Central High was a 23-year-old metallic brown four-story structure which housed almost 1,700 students and a faculty and staff of 200. With few windows and no name on the front of the building, the high school resembled an industrial plant.

We observed students over a three-year period for a total of 240 days at different times of the day, at school, and in the community. We collected observation and interview data from social, athletic, and academic settings. During school visits, documentation encompassed students' participation in all subject classes as well as in a variety of other settings such as athletic events, after-school clubs, and at home with parents and siblings. We conducted in-depth interviews with the identified students, teachers, administrators, school counselors, coaches, parents, siblings and other relatives, community members, and other parties as they emerged through other data gathering techniques.

The gifted females we studied were extremely resilient, acknowledging their abilities and working to achieve at a level that was commensurate with these abilities. They existed in a community of achievers within a large urban high school which contributed to their efforts to achieve. The factors identified by the participants as influencing their achievement in high school are discussed below. All female participants, regardless of cultural group, identified these factors and support systems as contributing to their academic success.

Resilience to Achieve Despite Urban Problems

All but one of the gifted female achievers came from homes which had been affected by either poverty, family turmoil caused by issues such as alcohol, drugs, and mental illness, or other problems. All participants lived in a city plagued by violence, drugs, poverty and crime. Their school district is often named as one of the worst in the country. The young people profiled in this study survived in the city and excelled in their school. They ignored drug dealers, turned their backs on gangs, avoided the crime in their neighborhoods, and became valedictorians, class presidents, star athletes, and scholars. Some went to Ivy League schools, others attended the most selective colleges in the country, and all wanted to make a contribution to the world. The courage and resilience displayed by these young people seemed remarkable, and yet, they simply accepted their circumstances and pursued the opportunities given to them. Many were committed to returning to their city after earning their degrees, explaining that they wanted to be able to help improve the city in the future.

Belief in Self

The development of a strong belief in self was evident in all participants. The oldest participants in this study exhibited the strongest belief in themselves, possibly indicating that this belief developed over time and intensified because of various circumstances and experiences. The younger students in this study (freshmen and sophomores) were confident about their ability to succeed, but the juniors and seniors exhibited stronger beliefs about who they were, what they wanted to achieve in life, and the direction they needed to take to realize their goals. This sense of self developed despite their often negative urban environment. The young women attributed their strong belief in self to several factors or influences, including supportive adults, extracurricular activities, appropriate educational opportunities, family support, peer support, and the various personal characteristics including sensitivity, multicultural appreciation, realistic aspirations, motivation, and resilience.

Personal Characteristics

A number of other common personal characteristics were

demonstrated by the gifted young women we studied, including motivation and inner will, positive use of problem solving, independence, realistic aspirations, heightened sensitivity to each other and the world around them, and appreciation of cultural diversity. They displayed high levels of sensitivity and a mature understanding of situations, people, places, and the difficulties of urban life. Jana, who was of Puerto Rican descent and had participated in bilingual programs, was extremely determined to be independent. She said she did not want to be like her mother who had given birth to three children with three different fathers, two of whom she had not married. Jana said that although she loved her mother, she did not want to be like her. When asked if she considered herself different, she said, "Yes," and explained, "I just don't want to be like everybody else—just hanging around. I want to make something of myself." She said she would not date for the same reason. Having seen many Hispanic men who want to be "in control of everything," Jana said of her decision not to date, "I'm just not going to let myself be told what to do or anything by anyone, especially a man."

A determination to succeed was consistently echoed by most of the participants in this study, especially the female achievers. Each of the young women who achieved referred to an internal motivation that drove them to succeed in their urban environment. One participant referred to this drive as an "inner will" which contributed to the strong belief in self

Support Systems

Various networks existed within the high school to support the achievement of these gifted female students. These support systems within the school helped the participants in this study to succeed academically. The students who wanted to succeed academically and were willing to work to achieve this goal interacted with each other and with various teachers, coaches, counselors, and administrators. This network was absolutely essential to the academic success of most of the achieving participants in this study and all participants acknowledged its existence in a variety of ways. As students became older, the network became stronger, as their involvement in various extracurricular activities began or intensified. These extracurricular activities included clubs, organizations like the National Honor Society, and experiences such as summer programs at private schools, Upward Bound, and special ceremonies at various universities. The network of high achieving peers supported each others' experiences. For example, the guidance counselors began to realize which students had the ability and desire to succeed academically and provided the opportunities for students who were the most likely to succeed to be together in classes and summer experiences.

Because of the large student load assigned to each guidance counselor, the counselors spent the majority of their time dealing with students problems. It was a common occurrence to see police and drug enforcement officials, social workers, angry parents, and community members in the guidance counselors' offices. So much time was spent on this population with so little success that some guidance counselors indicated that they considered encouraging high achieving students both a responsibility and one of the few successes they experienced in their work. One guidance counselor, upon hearing of Rosa's acceptance and full scholarship to Brown University, hugged one of the researchers involved in the study and said, "This is the joy of my work!" This sentiment was also expressed in interviews with other teachers and administrators who believed that achieving students received "the short end of the stick" because they had to spend so much time and attention on students with academic, social, emotional, and behavioral problems.

All of the participants in this study indicated that the guidance of supportive adults was essential to their academic success. They all cited teachers at the elementary or junior high who had encouraged their success and academic achievement and cared about them as individual students who could be successful in any academic environment.

PARTICIPATION IN SPECIAL PROGRAMS, EXTRACURRICULAR ACTIVITIES, AND SUMMER ENRICHMENT PROGRAMS

These talented young women were also involved in numerous activities held during, and usually, after school hours. All remained in their high school after school to participate in a wide variety of activities on a daily basis. All were involved in more than one sport, and all were also involved in numerous school clubs and activities, including jazz band, foreign language clubs, service groups, and academic competitions. These extracurricular activities and programs had a major impact on these young people as they consistently cited these activities as being extremely influential in the development of their ability to excel academically, to learn to manage time wisely, and to learn leadership skills.

These experiences enriched their lives and, in some cases, helped them in their decisions to attend colleges and universities that were in other geographic areas. Rosa, for example, initially had problems with her parents when she attended a three week summer program an hour from her home. However, after her success in that program, her parents became more supportive of her decision to attend an Ivy League school that was two hours away from her home. Many older talented female Hispanic students in this high school had attended colleges close to their homes as commuters because of parental pressure to remain close to home.

APPROPRIATELY CHALLENGING CLASSES

Another major factor that these students attributed to their successful academic achievement was their involvement in honors classes. When they entered their high school as freshmen, they were assigned to honors classes because of their previous high grades and their level of hard work. The counselors created one or two honors' classes in each academic content area, and students who were high achievers could enroll in these classes. Students who were involved in this study were consistently grateful for the opportunity to take these classes and be grouped with other students who wanted to work and to learn. Students in our study consistently cited the opportunity to participate in advanced classes and to be with academic peers as influential to their later success. They identified the need to be with other high achieving peers in high school who supported each other's academic efforts as critical to their success as it was in Gandara's (1995) research of successful Hispanic individuals cited earlier.

REALISTIC ASPIRATIONS

The aspirations of the females who achieved at South Central High were closely tied to their strong belief in self. They all expressed a desire to graduate from college and pursue a professional career, with a clear sense of what they wanted to do in life. They had dreams and definite goals towards which they were striving and these dreams, goals, and career aspirations were closely connected with their strong belief in self. Their personalities were often reflected in their choices for the future, and all of the young women in the study wanted to enter "helping" professions, such as teaching, social work, or medicine.

FAMILY SUPPORT

Most of the participants in this study appeared to have supportive families that nurtured them in a variety of ways. Some participants had extremely supportive families while other participants' families provided minimal emotional support because of their need to strive for economic survival. It was interesting to find that all of the young women perceived that their parents regarded school and learning as very important as a way to improve their situation in life, but that in almost every case, the parents of these young people had minimal involvement in their high school experience. They rarely, if ever, came to the school and were not active in any way in school activities or projects.

Participants in this study cited numerous examples of how their parents were actively involved in elementary school, but as students entered their secondary school years, parental involvement shifted. Parents would occasionally ask, "Did you finish your homework?" However, parents paid little attention to either the content or process of learning.

DIFFERENCES BETWEEN ACHIEVERS AND UNDERACHIEVERS

This review of research about culturally diverse students who achieved versus those who did not achieve indicated several common findings. Many of those who achieved did not date or become romantically involved, were extremely supportive of other achieving students (especially other female students), were involved in multiple activities, were independent, resilient, and dedicated to a career. Clear trends emerged regarding parental expectations, as mothers, in particular, encouraged their daughters to excel in school without being actively involved in their daughters' education. The majority of the mothers of this group had never been in the high school their daughter attended, but their support was clear. Their daughters did their homework, put their academic studies ahead of their social lives, and often were deeply connected with their families and their churches. They had a positive circle of peers and were supported by these young people to continue to achieve academically. They were independent, believed in themselves and wanted a career that would enable them to use their talents.

Rather than becoming alienated and underachieving in school, some young women created a community of achievement within their school. Some of their teachers, counselors, coaches, and parents were an integral part of this community and helped to create the academic success achieved by the participants we studied. Despite family problems, and all of the difficulties faced in their urban high school, including gangs, violence and drugs, the achievement ideology remained intact for the participants of this study. The community of achievement they created both developed and harbored this ideology, providing them with a haven in which their accomplishments were both valued and protected.

Underachieving females did not have these support systems and many were not challenged in elementary and middle school. Still others simply did not achieve in a manner consistent with their potential and had a number of family and environmental obstacles that they could not overcome in order to be able to achieve at high levels. Without the adult and peer support experienced by the higher achieving girls, those who underachieved simply did not make it.

WHAT DOES THIS REVIEW OF RESEARCH ABOUT GIFTED FEMALES FROM CULTURALLY DIVERSE AND/OR LOW SOCIOECONOMIC ENVIRONMENTS SUGGEST?

1. Some elementary and middle school gifted girls from culturally diverse and low socioeconomic environments receive negative messages about high achievement in school from parents, family members, teachers, and other adults.
2. Females from low income environments may be at greater risk for dropping out than males due to pregnancy, gangs, and negative peer pressure.
3. The self esteem of Hispanic girls may decrease more than in any other cultural group from elementary to high school.
4. The loss of confidence in their own abilities may occur less in African American gifted girls than in other populations of gifted girls.
5. The achievement scores of some Asian American gifted girls are equal to or higher than those of their male counterparts.
6. High achieving girls in diverse, low income high schools may be more likely to identify with the beliefs and cultures of the dominant culture than the culture of less successful stu-

dents.

7. No doubt exists that many culturally diverse talented girls and women still face negative stereotyping in school and the community. Some gifted girls from low socioeconomic environments were teased, harassed, and threatened by peers for their high achievement. Some high ability culturally diverse students may try to hide their ability in a variety of ways to decrease pressure from peer groups which reject them if they appear to be too academically successful.

8. A combination of social, cultural, and psychological factors all contribute to underachievement in high ability girls from diverse cultural backgrounds. This underachievement may stem from several issues. In some cultural groups, the needs of others and of the group are considered more important than the needs of the individual, conflicting with the pursuit of individual excellence. This conflict is especially true for gifted females and it poses a continuing issue which is difficult to resolve for this population.

9. Traditional gender roles and expectations also interact with issues relating to gifted females from diverse cultural backgrounds, causing some to feel conflict with role expectations perceived by their parents, grandparents, and culture at large.

10. Underachieving, culturally diverse gifted females may not have support systems for academic achievement and many are not challenged in elementary and middle school. Still others simply may not achieve in a manner consistent with their potential because of family and environmental obstacles that they could not overcome.

11. Some culturally diverse gifted females drop out of school because of poverty, an absence of goals and role models, poor self-confidence and belief in self, and conflicts with school officials.

12. Academic self-concept is related to achievement in some culturally diverse low socioeconomic groups.

13. Across numerous studies, role models outside the family,

outstanding teachers and counselors, consistently high teacher expectations, as well as an intrinsic drive to succeed proved to be essential factors to the high achieving culturally diverse students and of critical importance to talented females.

14. Parents, and especially mothers, are critical for the encouragement and career advice given to their gifted daughters.

15. The opportunity to participate in advanced classes and to be with academic peers was consistently cited as influential to their later success. The need to be with other high achieving peers in high school who supported each other's academic efforts was identified as critical to student success.

16. Gifted and talented programs and special extracurricular activities can have an extremely beneficial impact on gifted culturally diverse low socioeconomic females. Numerous extracurricular activities seemed to help these young women gain confidence in themselves and in their ability to succeed.

17. Culturally diverse talented girls and women learn how to succeed in school and must rely on support from peer groups and teachers and families in addition to developing a personal plan for success. Many do not date or become romantically involved. They develop a strong belief in self, are extremely supportive of other achieving students (especially other female students), and are independent, resilient and dedicated to a career.

CHAPTER SIX

~:~

TALENTED FEMALES IN
MATH & SCIENCE

*Isaac Asimov's Biographical Encyclopedia of Science and
Technology is subtitled "The Lives and Achievements of 1510 Great
Scientists from Ancient Times to the Present, Chronologically
Arranged." Of the 1510 scientists included in the book, only 14 are
women.*

Math is really hard.
—Barbie, 1992

When Barbara McClintock won the Nobel Prize for Science in 1983, she was only the fifth woman to receive this award in the 80 years since it was established. According to recent statistics compiled by the National Science Foundation, the number of women and minorities pursuing scientific careers has increased in the last fifteen years. Between 1972 and 1982, the number of women scientists and engineers increased 200%. However, in the early 1980s, of the nearly 2 million American engineers, only 3.5% were women and of the 225,000 physical scientists, only 12% were women (Dembart, 1984). Similar trends were apparent in mathematics during that time period and continue today. Research about the decline in both mathematics and scientific ability of females has been well reported and has caused considerable controversy (Fennema, 1974; Fennema & Sherman, 1977; Maccoby & Jacklin, 1974).

Most notable is the attention given to an article (Benbow & Stanley, 1980) which attributes higher math scores of boys to endogenous variables rather than social factors. The controversy that erupted from that article has produced both speculation and further research. Pallas and Alexander (1983) have suggested that females need to be encouraged to pursue advanced course work in math and science in high school in order to overcome their deficiencies. Concerns about the advice young women receive from guidance counselors, parents, and teachers have been noted in previous articles related to talented females (Callahan, 1979; Casserly, 1975; Fitzgerald & Crites, 1980). The Benbow and Stanley research may lead some counselors and teachers to conclude that females are inferior in mathematics and science. The following excerpt from a letter I received from a parent emphasizes an attitude problem that may be more prevalent in our country than any of us realize:

> *My daughter, an honors student who was later admitted to the biology honors program at The University of Connecticut, was experiencing difficulty in a high school Honors Physics class of 10 students. Only two girls were in the class, and when I contacted her teacher (a male), he threw up his hands and told me that girls were never good at physics! I wonder if part of the problem might have been his attitude and lack of understanding?*

There are still no definitive answers to the question of why men outperform women in mathematics, science, and teachers, parents, and administrators must put forth maximum efforts to help both males and females achieve at the highest levels possible. The case studies below illustrate some of the problems associated with talented girls in mathematics and science.

~: Eva :~

Eva loved science and mathematics as a child and her parents were delighted by her excitement and aptitude. When she was four, she asked her mother how long it was until her birthday and her mother replied, "Two months." She immediately asked, "How much is eight times seven?" and her mother answered, "Fifty-six. Why do you want to know?" Eva replied, "I want to know how many days until my birthday." Eva's favorite activities included taking apart radios, clocks, and old appliances and then trying to put them back together. She loved to build with many different kinds of materials—everything from blocks and LEGO's to materials she found in her parents' kitchen such as marshmallows, pasta (uncooked, of course), and cans and boxes of food. She also loved computer work, especially mathematics programs, and routinely requested these types of gifts, while most of her friends were asking for Barbie dolls.

Unfortunately, Eva's interests and talents in science and mathematics and school began to diminish in elementary school. By third grade, she no longer wanted to do related activities at home and repeatedly told her parents that "school" mathematics and science were boring. Because of her attitude and her lack of interest in doing mathematics homework at home, she fell behind in memorizing her multiplication tables and was not even considered mathematically talented by her third grade teacher. It is doubtful that she will be interested in, or even qualify for, a pre-algebra class when she reaches middle school in two years. How could such a promising child lose her motivation to learn and achieve in these subjects? And—just as important—what can educators do to restore that motivation?

~: JENNIFER :~

Jennifer worked with one of my colleagues, Katherine Gavin, was an A student in all subjects, and was in an accelerated seventh grade algebra class—the only accelerated class in her suburban middle school. Mathematics had been easy for Jennifer in elementary school. She paid attention in class, did her homework, and excelled in facts and algorithms. Now, however, she was in a class with the highest achieving students in her grade, and her teacher presented new concepts in challenging ways. She could no longer simply use her memory to complete her assignments. She became confused and frustrated if she did not instantly know the answer or understand the method to solve problems. Meanwhile, other students, especially some of the boys, seemed to call out answers faster and be able to answer the challenging questions posed by the teacher. Jennifer believed that she needed more time to think about these questions and how to get started solving them. She wasn't getting that time in her class, and her anxiety about math grew.

Eva and Jennifer aren't alone. Gifted, young females may not receive the necessary encouragement to achieve in mathematics, science, and in fields such as engineering. A report by the American Association of University Women (AAUW) (1992) concluded that "all differences in math performance between girls and boys at ages eleven and fifteen could be accounted for by differences among those scoring in the top ten to twenty percent" (p. 25). This statement means that many of our brightest female mathematics students are not keeping up with their male counterparts. It is clear from this and other research studies discussed in this chapter that many mathematically talented females perform at levels that are not commensurate with their abilities (Reis, 1987; Reis & Callahan, 1989).

The situation can be improved. Teachers and parents can help talented girls succeed both in mathematics and science. Jennifer, for example, is at a critical point in her mathematical development. While she wants to please her parents and teachers and excel in algebra, she is becoming increasingly anxious about mathematics and is afraid she may no longer make the honor roll because of her mathematics grade. She spends more time on homework, yet she receives fewer A's than before, and she needs for her parents to encourage and assure her that B grades in mathematics are acceptable. She needs support from her teacher to encourage her to use all of the time necessary to think concepts through and to formulate her own foundations of mathematical thinking. She also needs to know that her uncomfortable, challenged feeling occasionally occurs in everyone, even mathematicians, and that mathematical insights, and even discoveries, may emerge from confusion. If Jennifer is to be successful and remain in this class, her teacher must provide a classroom environment in which Jennifer can develop her mathematical abilities and regain her confidence about her ability to do advanced work in mathematics. This environment should nurture creative thinking and encourage risk taking, as well as use alternative assessments such as mathematics portfolios and creative projects. Ideally, Jennifer's teachers should serve as personal sources of support who will encourage her strengths and help her overcome her decreasing self-confidence.

STEREOTYPES ABOUT FEMALES AND MATHEMATICS

Before we can alleviate the problems experienced by girls like Eva and Jennifer, it is important to try to understand the factors behind those problems. The main reason that some girls do not succeed in mathematics is not any lack of ability or effort—it's simply that girls are not expected to succeed in these areas. Stereotypes influence perceptions and performance in school and in life, and are often cited as contributing heavily to some girls' shortcomings in schools. A great deal of stereotyping and prejudice affects girls in mathematics classes. Unfortunately, mathematics and science are often thought of as fields for men, and our society's traditional images of scientists, engineers, and mathematicians are almost always male. In fact, women currently constitute 22% of our nations science and engineering labor force and were 20% of doctoral engineers and scientists in the United States in 1993 (National Science Foundation, 1996). However, single women are more likely than single men to leave science and engineering employment. Married women without children are more likely to leave science and engineering employment than married men without children, and women with children are more likely than men with children to leave science and engineering employment (National

Science Foundation, 1996, p. 66).

More university mathematics professors are male, and evidence exists (presented in previous chapters) that girls are regarded as less capable in mathematics by some of their teachers and parents. Kissane (1986) found that teachers are less accurate in nominating girls who are likely to do well on the quantitative subtest of the SAT than they are in naming boys who are likely to attain a high score. Recent research I conducted with Del Siegle (1995) found that adolescent female gifted students indicated they had higher ability than males in language arts only, while male gifted students indicated they had higher ability than females in mathematics, science, and social studies. How do young people form these opinions?

As early as 1973, Good and Brophy learned that when teachers treated boys and girls differently in class, these differences were the most pronounced for gifted females. Fennema, Peterson, Carpenter, & Lubinski (1990), in their analysis of the role of teacher beliefs on mathematics performance, reported that "teachers believe that ability explains the success of their male students while the cause of their most talented females' success is thought to be effort." They also concluded that even though teachers did not tend to engage in sex-role stereotyping in general, they did stereotype their best students in the area of mathematics—attributing characteristics such as volunteering answers, enjoyment of mathematics, and independence to males.

Current Research about Gender Differences in Mathematics Tests

One source of stereotypes about females' ability in mathematics is probably the fact that they often perform poorly compared to males on standardized math tests. This phenomenon reinforces beliefs that males are superior in mathematics and gives females lower self-esteem and less confidence in their abilities. While this discrepancy in test scores appears to be decreasing over time, it still exists and is especially a problem for more talented girls. Recently, researchers who studied differences between males and females concluded that a decrease in gender differences as measured by standardized measures had occurred in mathematics and science during the last three decades. However, a meta-analysis of studies (Hyde & Fennema, 1990) in which the magnitude of gender differences on tests of mathematics achievement and aptitude was studied indicated that this decrease did not exist for talented girls in mathematics. "The more highly selective the sample, the larger the gender difference favoring males" (p. 4).

Evidence exists that current differences in standardized tests favor males at the highest levels. Halpern (1989) pointed out that "large and consistent differences favoring male students are still found among the upper levels of mathematics aptitude on the PSAT and the SAT" (p. 1156). In 1996, the population of girls taking the Scholastic Aptitude Test (SAT) averaged 46 points lower than boys on the mathematics section of the SAT. The number of top scoring males on the quantitative section of the SAT far exceeded the number of top scoring females. Eight percent of males (39,369) but only 3% of females (19,005) scored 700 or greater (Educational Testing Service, 1996). Sex differences are even more pronounced when one examines the numbers of males and females scoring 750 or higher. Girls also achieve lower scores on the PSAT/NMSQT, which is used by the National Merit Scholarship Corporation for awarding scholarships to promising college students (Rosser, 1989). Only a few researchers have investigated why these differences occur, but time constraints may have some effects. Dreyden and Gallagher (1989) tested the effects of changing time limits and directions on the performance of academically talented males and females on the SAT. Students took either the SAT-Mathematics subtest or the SAT-Verbal subtest under timed or untimed conditions. Female students' scores on the SAT-M dramatically increased when the test was untimed, suggesting that the difference in the scores of males and females on the SAT-M "may be due more to speed of performance than to ability" (p. 196).

In another study, Byrnes and Takahira (1993) used a cognitive process approach to explain gender differences on the mathematics subtest of the SAT. Besides the SAT test, students were also given surveys to measure their prior knowledge of concepts and effective use of problem-solving strategies. Results showed that males performed better than females on the SAT-M, however, students' prior knowledge and use of strategies explained the majority of the differences. Similar results were found by Gallagher and DeLisi (1994) who found that boys' performance in mathematics was consistently higher only on problems which required "unconventional" problem solving. Gallagher (1996) suggested that, based on research findings, the reference to a global "gender gap in mathematics" is much less accurate than "gender differences in solving complex mathematics problems" (p. 463).

Damaging implications directly relate to the different scores obtained by boys and girls on these tests. Lower scores on the traditional college admissions exams have potential for denying opportunity for scholarships and admission to selective colleges.

Kimball (1989), in her review of literature on women's mathematics achievement, found that while standardized test scores favor boys, grade differences favor girls. The pattern of performance on standardized aptitude assessment measures is also very different from the pattern of grades. While males' mean scores on both the verbal and mathematics sections of the 1996 SAT were higher than females', the females who took the test had a higher mean high school grade point average: 3.27 overall versus 3.11 for males (Educational Testing Service, 1996).

How does this gap affect gifted females in particular? Rosser (1989) reported that the higher the grades, the greater the gender gap. "Girls with an A+ grade point average scored 23 points lower on the SAT-Verbal section (9 points lower than the overall verbal M/F gap) and 60 points lower on the SAT-Mathematics section than boys with the same GPA" (p. iv).

Kimball (1989) made a fascinating point about the current measurement methods for mathematics achievement, stating that:

> although there is ample evidence of young women's superior math achievement when grades are used to measure achievement, they have not been considered seriously in the literature on mathematics achievement. I am proposing that it is important to begin to take them seriously. (p. 203)

Kimball suggested that classroom grades reflect what is learned during a particular class and are not influenced by other experiences outside of, or prior to, the classroom experience. Also, the information that girls are not at a disadvantage and, in fact, have a grade advantage in many courses, may be useful in increasing girls' confidence in their mathematics ability.

Role of the Teacher

Other recent research addresses the critical role of the teacher in encouraging girls in mathematics. Leroux and Ho (1994), in a qualitative study of 15 gifted female high school students, concluded that female math teachers who act as role models are significant influences. Teachers who treat both genders equally, provide a warm, uninhibiting environment, and are approachable seem to provide the most 'psychologically safe' environment that is conducive to girls learning (p. 45). Demonstrating the kinds of effects that teachers can have on students, Rogers (1990), in a study of high ability students, found that significant success in attracting females to higher level mathematics courses was achieved by teachers, either male or female, who created a classroom environment open to and supportive of all students, one in which the teacher's style was conducive to the nature of mathematical inquiry.

In a qualitative study of female mathematics majors at a very competitive college, Gavin (1996) found that almost half attributed their decision to major in mathematics to the influence of a high school teacher. In fact, one-third of the students developed and maintained a personal relationship with these high school teachers throughout their college years. Confirming this finding at the graduate level, Rossi-Becker (1994) conducted in-depth interviews with 31 graduate students and found that students frequently described a successful teacher as one who piqued students' interests by providing an enriched curriculum. She concluded that teachers and instruction can make a difference in all students' career choices, demonstrating the importance of the role of the teacher in promoting interest and further study in mathematics. Figure 7 shows a letter that I sent to parents of mathematically and scientifically talented female students who were leaving the elementary gifted program I coordinated and entering a large middle school. Many years after leaving the program, many young women told me that this letter had made a difference in their parents' support and development of their mathematical, technological, and scientific talents.

CAREER CHOICE

It is well documented that more males than females enter and pursue mathematically and scientifically related career fields. Many gifted females continue to reject mathematics and science as courses of study. An examination of the distribution of women in all scientific fields presents a picture of uneven advancement. For example, women are clustered in the life sciences, with far fewer in the physical sciences, mathematics, engineering, and computer science.

Gavin (1996) examined gender issues with specific regard to mathematics as a choice of major and future career fields, In her qualitative study of female mathematics majors at a highly competitive college, she conducted in-depth interviews with students, observed their classes, and talked with their professors to find out what motivated these students to major in mathematics. It was clear from the discussions with students that their

Dear Mr. and Mrs. Jones,

I write to tell you how delighted I have been to work with Heather over the last several years and also to reinforce, once again, what I have told you in the past. Heather is extremely talented in mathematics and science, and I hope that you will continue to help her work in these areas and develop her talents in the future. Heather is now entering a critical period in her life. As an adolescent, she may face some peer pressures not to do as much academic work as she has in the past. I have recommended Heather for the advanced classes in our middle school in both math and science and if for any reason she is not scheduled into these classes, I urge you to contact me as soon as possible. I also urge you to keep in touch with her math and science teachers in an attempt to maintain the involvement you have had in her education while she was in elementary school.

At times during the next seven years until Heather graduates from high school, she may complain about having more homework because she is in more challenging classes. I urge you to support her, but *do not let her drop these classes*. Some talented young girls drop out of these classes if they do not attain the highest grades and Heather may experience these feelings briefly. However, too many girls strive to be perfect in all areas instead of understanding that some slightly lower grades are perfectly acceptable, especially in their more challenging classes. Also, please help Heather to understand that the advanced classes in high school use a weighted grade system so that a B actually translates into an A in these classes. Also, if Heather remains in these classes, she will have the benefit of learning how to work hard, an essential skill that many talented students do not encounter in school.

In addition to having Heather stay involved in these advanced classes, I hope you will discuss careers in math, science, and technology with her. Many fabulous opportunities exist for talented young women in these areas, and fellowships for graduate studies, both at the Master's and Doctoral level are available. Heather could accomplish these goals, if she remains interested in these

continued on page 198

Figure 7. Letter to parents of talented females in mathematics and science.

areas and has your support. Many summer programs and Saturday opportunities also exist as do some excellent biographies and autobiographies of women scientists and mathematicians that you could help her find at the library. All of these opportunities will help her to focus her interests and identify a plan for the future.

It has been a pleasure and a privilege to work with your daughter during the last several years, and I congratulate you on all you have done to raise this wonderful young person. Please do not hesitate to call me in the future as she continues her education. I will continue to be available to meet with you whenever you have questions or concerns. Thank you for your attention to this and for all of your support for our gifted program.

Sincerely,

Sally M. Reis
Coordinator, Torrington Enrichment Program

Figure 7. Letter to parents of talented females in mathematics and science (continued).

excellent grades and placement in honors classes in high school were not by themselves enough to affirm their talent and encourage them to pursue mathematics further in college. They needed someone outside the family to tell them that they had mathematical talent and should continue to pursue it. Even at the college level, two female mathematics professors were frequently mentioned as mentors and role models who had sustained their students' interest in mathematics. Not only did they encourage students, but their style of teaching promoted a nurturing environment where students were free to ask questions and were engaged in learning activities relevant to their present lives. This "personal relevance" was also a necessary ingredient as students looked toward future careers in mathematically-related fields. They wanted to pursue a career in which the content of their daily work had practical relevance and personal satisfaction. Some chose teaching for this reason, while others sought areas in which they had developed a passionate interest, including statistics and industrial physics.

Using a much larger data set from the National Education Longitudinal Study of 1988 (NELS:88), Gavin (1997) conducted another study which examined a cohort of approximately 1,400 high mathematics ability students. As seniors in 1992, these students were surveyed to determine their intended field of study. Although all students had been identified as having high mathematics ability, only 27% expressed interest in a mathematics or science major, with only 1.8 % intending to major in mathematics. The numbers for females were quite revealing: 46 (3.3%) selected engineering, 27 (2%) majored in physical science, 19 (1.4%) mathematics, and only 9 (0.7%) selected computer science. Findings from this study revealed no gender differences with respect to performance or participation in mathematics courses. Males scored significantly higher on the verbal section of the SAT test, while no gender differences were found on the mathematics section. Significant differences were found between parental levels of education and expectation. The more educated the parent, the greater the expectations were for the child's educational goals. Analyses also revealed that high-mathematics-ability females who intended to pursue a quantitative field were more likely to consider mathematics as useful to their future and had more credits in calculus than high-mathematics-ability females who did not intend to pursue a quantitative field.

Data on intended majors for females who took the SAT in 1996 revealed that of those intending to major in engineering, only 19% were female, and in computer or information sciences, only 25% were female (Educational Testing Service, 1996). These remarkably low percentages of career interest in mathematics and science occurred despite data cited earlier suggesting that females received consistently higher grades in elementary school, secondary school, and college.

Although much attention has been given to research studies that have reported equal numbers of males and females who declare mathematics as their major field of study, it is important to examine who actually graduates with a mathematics major and pursues a mathematics career. In an extensive review of interview studies of over 1,500 students from more than 20 colleges and universities, Linn and Kessel (1995) reported that over 50% of the students who selected mathematics as a major eventually switched to other fields. Some of the most talented males and females switched out of mathematics, and more females than males left the major. Although equal numbers of males and females started with a mathematics major, females comprised 43% of those completing the undergraduate mathematics course of study and only 20% of those completing the Ph.D. In terms of related fields, an examination of the distribution of the Ph.D. degrees awarded in 1992 revealed that women were awarded 16% of the degrees in computer science, 11% of the degrees in physics, and only 8% of the engineering degrees (Hill, 1992). And while the number of women in the life sciences fields has grown steadily since the early 1970s, the participation of women in physics and engineering reached a plateau at about 15% and has remained at this level for the past decade (Campbell, 1992).

Three major implications emerge from studies about careers for gifted females in math, science, and technology. In order to encourage females to pursue their talents in mathematics, parents and teachers must foster (a) high expectations in terms of educational and career goals, (b) personal acknowledgment, encouragement, and promotion of individual mathematical talent, including encouraging girls to take advanced classes such as calculus in high school, and (c) a mathematics curriculum designed to promote relevance, enjoyment, and meaning to students' lives, as well as a discussion of future careers and coursework in mathematics.

Parental Influence on the Mathematical Talents of Females

The area of mathematics achievement appears to be particularly susceptible to the influence of parental beliefs and is also characterized by greater gender differences in attitudes about performance (Chipman, Brush, & Wilson, 1985). Compared to parents of boys, parents of girls are more likely to report that mathematics is less important than other subjects and are more likely to attribute good performance to training and effort rather than ability (Parsons, Adler, & Kaczala, 1982).

But what about high ability females? Campbell, Connolly, Lacattiva, and Pizzo (1985) collected data from 751 gifted Caucasian, African American, Asian American, and Hispanic 5th and 6th grade students and their parents, with particular attention to student perceptions of adult attitudes and expectations. Although the researchers found distinct differences among families in each ethnic group, and each group appeared to exert far more pressure to achieve on their sons than on their daughters, Caucasian parents exerted significantly less pressure on their daughters than did any other ethnic group, encouraged them away from more difficult technical fields, and held significantly lower expectations for their daughters' adult productivity than did Asian parents.

Eccles' research (1984) has demonstrated that even when girls and boys were both earning A's in mathematics and English, girls were considered by their parents to be better in English and boys to be better in mathematics. Even when girls had higher grades, higher standardized test scores, and higher teacher ratings in mathematics, parents believed that mathematics was harder for girls than for boys. She also found that parents rated advanced mathematics courses as less important and English and history as more important for their daughters than for their sons. In addition, these young girls had lower confidence in their mathematics abilities than in their English abilities and, as we might expect, lower expectations for future success in mathematics.

The emerging use of computers as an essential tool in nearly all disciplines makes the study of the impact of parental encouragement for females in technology another area of critical concern. Sanders (1986, 1994) reports that males outnumber females 3 to 1 in computer camps and that the sex difference is even greater in the more expensive camps, which suggests that parents are willing to spend more money on their sons' pursuit of careers requiring advanced computer skills than on their daughters'.

FEMALES AND SCIENCE

It was only after Marie Curie won her second Nobel prize that she was admitted to the French Academie des Sciences, an all-male organization that currently has less than five female members. Jonathan Cole (1979), a sociologist at Columbia University and author of *Fair Science: Women in the Scientific Community*, argues that many girls are still advised at a very early age that avocations in science are not appropriate careers for them. According to most sources, the choice of a scientific career must be made fairly early in the educational process and that a student's path is often clearly determined at the end of high school. If girls take fewer science and math courses in high school than males, then the decision is sometimes made for them. Guidance counselors, parents, and teachers often discourage girls who are talented from taking a full four years of math and science at the high school level (Cramer, 1989; Leder, 1990). If a young woman decides to major in biology in college and has not had the science and math sequence, the chance of shifting into the required courses is slim.

In the dozens of books and articles and research studies I reviewed, several factors emerged as the reasons some girls do not pursue science, including whether or not the girl's parents attended college; the "unfriendly" male atmosphere in many college and university classrooms; the mistaken belief that a scientific career requires singular, total dedication and devotion with no time for marriage, children, or a personal life of any choice; and the misconception that scientists are interested in and work only with "things" instead of people, which might lead some to choose a major in the social sciences or liberal arts—fields perceived to involve more human contact.

It is critical that positive feelings about science be encouraged in young girls as Matyas and Dix (1992) have found that the best indicator of science career interest and continuing science education at higher levels is positive feelings about science in general. Science programs which provide enrichment activities that emulate how real scientists work provide excellent opportunities for young girls to learn to enjoy science and these programs should involve creating, analyzing, experimenting, recording, and observing, skills which are normally incorporated into many science fair projects (Brandwein & Passow, 1988). In classroom activities, however, in which boys and girls do science together, researchers have found that boys dominate equipment and hands-on work, while girls are assigned to the role of secretary or helper.

Jane Butler Kahle (1985), who has written on the area of girls and science and has been president of the National Association of Biology Teachers, has studied the behavior of teachers who are successful at getting girls to pursue science and has found that these teachers provide many opportunities for hands-on lab experiments, avoid sexist humor and sex-stereotyped examples, do not allow boys to dominate, provide career information, and describe science as beautiful. Other research (Ost, 1998) has indicated that teachers must interact with parents more to improve student performance and to ensure higher expectations for higher education, careers and self-identify in science and mathematics.

Because the largest drop in persisting in scientific careers occurs when students leave graduate school, we must examine factors that differentially influence males and females at that point. The high value placed on early productivity in careers in math and science may deter more women of childbearing age than males (Linn & Hyde, 1989). Rayman and Brett (1995) studied women's persistence in science after graduation and found parental encouragement and attitudes about work and family to be important determinants. Other factors influencing persistence were encouragement from college teachers, having had a mentor as an undergraduate, an undergraduate research experience, and having a high interest in science. Parental encouragement from either mothers or fathers contributed significantly to whether or not a woman stayed in science after graduation. The odds of science majors staying in science after graduation was 2.6 times greater if one parent gave a lot of encouragement and 6.7 times greater if two parents gave a lot of encouragement. Family characteristics such as parental education and occupation were not related to persistence although they were related to choice of major in science or mathematics. Women who left science or changed to another field were more likely than those who stayed to believe that mothers with infants should not work at all and should enter careers that were more compatible with family life.

Etzkowitz, Kemelgor, Neuschatz, Uzzi, and Alonzo (1994) identified critical transitions in science and engineering doctoral programs in which female graduate students are pushed down to lower levels. After interviews with 155 female doctoral candidates from science and engineering departments, the researchers found that these academically superior women, who had typically been at the top of their undergraduate classes, were shocked upon entering graduate school to find themselves marginalized and isolated. The researchers also found that these talented women tended to internalize difficulties and resort to blaming themselves, in contrast to men's external attribution of the causes of failure. This study also determined that female students often found it hard to establish camaraderie which is very valuable to graduate students with their mostly male advisors. Issues of isolation and disconnection existed in their departments and among themselves. As women ascended the educational ladder in the sciences, they found support in the early stages, but not in the later stages, where they encountered arbitrary, male-dominated authority or simple inattention to women's needs.

The Influence of Science Teachers

Classroom teachers and subject area teachers who encourage girls in science seem to have specific attributes. They avoid the use of stereotypes in their teaching, excessive use of textbooks, and expression of personal beliefs. Specifically, these teachers do not believe that a girl is successful only because she works hard, but rather they believe and demonstrate their belief that a female student who excels in science is *talented* in science. They discuss careers in science regularly and encourage girls to pursue ideas about careers. They discuss professional growth and the opportunities for careers in science by talking about science broadly and discussing environmental science, the human elements of science, changes in scientific research, current controversies in science such as cloning, breeding human organs, and other fascinating topics. These teachers keep abreast of support systems such as new web sites, all girls science programs, and organizations and institutions dedicated to gender equity in science (see Chapter Eleven). They also recruit and/or expose their students to female mentors, scientists, doctors, graduate students, environmentalists either in person, on the Web, or through articles, biographies, and autobiographies.

Successful science teachers who develop talent in their students invite female speakers to their classrooms or get involved in programs that provide role models in science at local universities or women's clubs or organizations. These teachers also use diverse teaching strategies and go beyond lecturing. They use single-sex pairs of students working together, hands-on studies, and open-ended questions. They encourage hands-on learning for girls and encourage using learning centers to enable girls to pursue their interests in greater depth. They encourage the use of how-to books so that girls can get involved in these hands-on learning activities. They communicate with girls' parents about their talents, discuss their strengths and possible careers, and help girls develop a firm plan for their future academic and professional careers. These teachers work collaboratively with gifted education consultants, who are often available for several years to work with talented girls, and they maintain contact with and offer support to these girls long after they leave their classrooms.

Classroom Conditions to Encourage Girls

What type of classroom environment avoids and helps nullify harmful stereotypes and discrepancies in science and mathematics? Eccles (1987) drew several conclusions from the existing literature on mathematics and science teachers who have been successful in reversing stereotypes and keeping females interested in mathematics and science. She notes a pattern of conditions in these classrooms, which includes frequent use of cooperative learning opportunities, frequent individualized learning opportunities, use of practical problems in assignments, frequent use of hands-on opportunities, active career and educational guidance, infrequent use of competitive motivational strategies, frequent activities oriented toward broadening views of mathematics and physical sciences, presenting mathematics as a tool in solving problems, and frequent use of strategies to ensure full class participation.

We have much to learn about which classroom conditions encourage girls. Some evidence indicates that classes emphasizing *competition* result in higher achievement for males and classrooms that encourage *cooperation* result in higher achievement for females (Peterson & Fennema, 1985). However, these results may not apply to some high ability females. In the qualitative study of female mathematics majors at a highly selective women's college mentioned earlier, Gavin (1996) found that talented young women actually enjoyed competition in their high school classrooms, especially when it had involved males. Hernandez Garduño (1997) found similar results in a recent study. After investigating gifted females' and males' achievement and attitudes about an advanced mathematics summer program, she found no differences in achievement between those students in a cooperative learning environment and those in a whole group, competitive structure. In fact, both male and female students in the competitive setting had more positive attitudes towards mathematics than those in the cooperative learning setting.

Research shows that stereotyping may exist in classes for high achieving students as well. Webb (1984) and Webb and Kenderski (1985) found that in advanced classes, males both outperformed females and received more explanations after asking questions. When females requested help they were likely to be ignored—at a rate double that of males. In this study, males often ignored females, especially in groups with only one female, and so it would appear that consistently using cooperative learning and group learning may not be the best strategy for talented girls.

Male "Ability" vs. Female "Effort"

I have discussed issues relating to attribution theory as well as issues regarding effort and ability previously in this book, but there is no greater problem facing girls and young women in math and science than the belief that males have a natural ability in these areas that females do not. Eccles (1987) suggested an examination of stereotyped aspects of our society that seem to influence the differential achievement of males and females, supporting the need to find ways to counteract these effects. Research has been conducted on strong stereotypes existing in our society about the possession of "natural talent." Mathematics achievement, more than achievement in any other discipline, is often linked to innate abilities. Further, our culture subscribes to an assumption that males have more of those innate abilities. In some other cultures, success in mathematics and science is more often attributed to effort. In these cultures, failure is seen to come from not working hard rather than lack of ability. Exploring this possible ethnic difference, Brandon, Newton, and Hammond (1987) examined mathematics achievement across four ethnic groups in four grades in Hawaii. They found that high achieving girls performed better than high achieving boys, with these differences increasing across grades, and they found that the sex differences favoring girls among Caucasian students were smaller than those among Japanese American, Filipino-American, and Hawaiian students. The authors of the study concluded that "the cultural factors accounting for superiority of Caucasian boys over Caucasian girls in mainland United States might be influencing Caucasians in Hawaii" (p. 458). They further support the consideration of the sociocultural factor in any study of sex differences in mathematics achievement.

GIRLS AND TECHNOLOGY

Currently, far fewer girls than boys are learning technology skills. Examples abound in both literature as well as in our collective experiences. For example, only one girl enrolled in "Introduction to Computer" at a local high school during the 1997-1998 academic year, and no girls took part in "Advanced Computer" (Henry & Manning, 1998). Even if there are computers in the classroom, computer use and computer exposure time differs for boys and girls. Some studies have shown that the more experience a student has with computers, the less anxiety and the more positive his/her response to computers, and boys are more likely to have access to a computer and exposure to computer games at home (Mark, 1992). Boys have been found to monopolize computers even in preschool (Nelson & Watson, 1991). When boys and girls are paired together at the computer, research has found that a girl will defer to her partner's wishes (Martin & Murchie, 1992; Schubert et al., 1984; Volman, 1997). Current research indicates that by the 3rd or 4th grade, girls are less technologically-oriented (Nelson & Watson, 1991). Boys are at least three times more likely than girls to be involved with computers during secondary and post-secondary years (Kramer & Lehman, 1990).

Studies have shown that parents influence their sons to use

computers by purchasing computers for them and giving more encouragement to them than to their daughters (Nelson & Watson, 1991; Reinen & Plomp, 1994). Teachers of both sexes unintentionally contribute to gender inequity because of a lack of awareness of their own behavior.

When earlier studies reported gender inequity in computer education, it was first thought that the negative attitudes found in girls were toward computers in general, but researchers did not consider learning style differences (Volman, 1997). Teachers may not be aware of the learning style differences between boys and girls. Some research indicates that boys like to experiment and tinker, while girls are more goal-oriented in school and feel tinkering may be a waste of time (Martin & Murchie, 1992). Boys have been found to have a higher initial comfort level when using computers, while girls need more training to increase their comfort level (Vernon-Gerstenfeld, 1989). Since most math, science, and computer teachers are male, there are fewer female teacher role models with whom girls can identify (Mark, 1992; Schwartz, 1987). Another reason that girls do not take computer courses is that counselors do not recommend computer courses for girls (Mann, 1994). In many cases, irrelevant prerequisites are established for computer science courses. These prerequisites promote the belief by many female students that high level math courses are necessary for computer programming (Schubert et al., 1984).

The ideas that girls formulate, based on their experiences in computer courses, affect their confidence and their self-efficacy regarding technical and scientific abilities with computers. Confidence and self-efficacy, in turn, are likely to be related to whether young women continue to take computer courses. Boys may feel competent in using computers; they attribute their competence to internal factors such as ability and effort. As mentioned earlier, they do not easily attribute problems to their own mistakes; instead, they blame it on external factors. Girls feel less confident in their computer ability. They may hesitate to claim proficiency (Volman, 1997). Girls attribute any problems to their own failures and their successes to external factors such as luck (Mann, 1994; Volman, 1997).

The more advanced the level of computer courses, the larger the gender gap found. Gender differences are not as prevalent when computers are used for word processing, games, or computer-assisted instruction (Mark, 1992). With little to encourage them to explore computers on more than a basic level, girls usually use computers as a tool for word processing (Kramer & Lehman, 1990), while boys may use the computer for higher-level tasks such as computer programming (Mark, 1992; Volman, 1997).

Software continues to be geared toward male interests, with males being the heroes in 63% of the software examined in one study (Nelson & Watson, 1991). Not only is there a need for software in which girls will have an interest, but also girls' interests need to be expanded so that gender-based stereotypes are not reinforced (Sanders, 1994). While the newest software attempts to meet the needs of both male and female students, many schools do not have this software.

Peers may also discourage girls from participating in computer science courses because of negative or ambivalent stereotypes associated with anyone who uses computers frequently (Schubert et al., 1984). In research conducted by honors students in my graduate education courses, high school students described men who work in computer occupations as computer nerds and women who work with computers as secretaries (Henry & Manning, 1998). Boys can overcome this stereotype by being proficient at computer games, but girls have fewer ways to overcome this stereotype (Volman, 1997).

When interviewed by honors graduate students at the University of Connecticut, high school boys and girls do not cite sexism as the reason fewer girls participate in computer classes, but rather an absence of interest (Henry & Manning, 1998). Instead of attributing their lack of participation in computer courses to gender inequality, girls cite their own personal lack of interest in computers as the reason for self-selecting out of computer courses (Kramer & Lehman, 1990; Volman, 1997). School should design gender-inclusive instruction to teach computer education in a way that is both effective and attractive to girls (Volman, 1997).

Conclusion

Our society has begun to address many crucial issues involving gender equity. Far fewer females than males pursue careers in mathematics and related fields, and it is our duty to make high-tech, high-paying professional careers equally available to all students. As pointed out, few talented students of either sex indicate an interest in majoring in mathematics, engineering or science. Chapter 11 provides a number of suggestions and strategies to try to encourage more talented young girls to pursue math, science, and technological studies. The majority of the strategies are recommended by the National Council of Teachers of Mathematics (1989) in their *Curriculum and Evaluation Standards for School Mathematics*. These strategies and activities focus on constructivist, discovery-oriented learning as the key to building mathematical confidence and understanding in all students. In reality, promoting equality in the classroom is also promoting good teaching techniques, developing student problem-solving abilities, and instilling a genuine appreciation for mathematics. Only wider use of these strategies will provide answers to questions about how we can continue to recruit the number of talented persons we need in mathematics in the future. What should be clear to all of us is that few women see a career involving mathematics, science, or technology as an attainable goal, and the importance of encouraging and supporting more females to pursue both careers and interests in mathematics and science in the future.

What does this review of research about

TALENTED GIRLS AND WOMEN IN MATH AND SCIENCE SUGGEST?

1. Many of the differences in math performance between girls and boys are explained by differences among those scoring in the top 10-20%. This difference means that many of our brightest female mathematics students are not keeping up with their male counterparts.

2. Teachers are less accurate in nominating girls who are likely to do well on the quantitative subtest of the SAT than boys who are likely to achieve a high score.

3. Adolescent female gifted students continue to indicate they have higher ability than males in language arts only, while male gifted students indicate they had higher ability than females in mathematics, science, and social studies.

4. Both male and female teachers regarded gifted boys as more competent than gifted girls in critical and logical thinking skills and in creative problem-solving abilities, while they believed gifted girls are more competent in creative writing.

5. Teachers select ability as the cause of their most capable males' success more often than they do as the cause of their best females' success , which is more often attributed to effort.

6. Even though teachers did not tend to engage in sex-role stereotyping in general, they did stereotype their best students in the area of mathematics—attributing characteristics such as volunteering answers, enjoyment of mathematics and independence, to males.

7. Differences favoring male students are still found among the upper levels of mathematics aptitude on the PSAT and the SAT. Eight percent of males (39,369) but only 3% of females (19,005) attained a score of 700 or greater (Educational Testing Service, 1996).

8. Potentially damaging implications directly relate to the different scores obtained by boys and girls on these tests. Not only do lower scores on the traditional college admissions

exams have the potential for denying female students opportunities for scholarships and admission to selective colleges, they may also deny access to certain programs and scholarships.

9. In 1992, boys achieved higher scores than girls on eleven of the fourteen achievement tests. The largest point gap was in physics (62 points), but there were gaps of 30-40 points in Mathematics I, Mathematics II, biology, and chemistry.

10. Parents, teachers, and guidance counselors still advised many girls at a very early age that science is not an appropriate career for them. The choice of a scientific career must be made fairly early in the educational process. If girls take less science and math courses in high school than males, then the decision is sometimes made for them.

11. Teachers who are successful at getting girls to pursue science provide many opportunities for hands-on lab experiments, avoid sexist humor and sex-stereotyped examples, do not allow boys to dominate, provide career information, and describe science as beautiful.

12. Some young talented women enjoyed competition in their high school classrooms, especially when it involved males.

13. Some talented girls with high aptitude in mathematics are less likely to be assigned to the high ability group than boys.

14. Female math teachers who act as role models are significant influences on girls. Teachers who treat both genders equally, provide a warm, uninhibiting environment, and are approachable seem to provide the most 'psychologically safe' environment conducive to girls learning.

15. Many young women who decide to major in mathematics acknowledge the influence of a high school teacher with whom they developed and maintained a personal relationship.

16. Classroom math grades should be important for talented girls in math as they reflect what is learned during a particular class and are not influenced by other experiences outside of or prior to the classroom experience.

17. Some of the most talented males and females switch out of mathematics and more females than males leave the major.
18. The area of mathematics and science achievement appears to be particularly susceptible to the influence of parental beliefs, and is also characterized by greater gender differences in attitudes about performance.
19. Far fewer females than males are using computers in school and at home, taking advanced computer classes, and participating in self-study of advanced technology skills.

CHAPTER SEVEN

~:~

TALENTED FEMALE ARTISTS: ENCOURAGEMENT DENIED

*[I was] eleven or twelve when I started [sketching]. I'd sit down and
try to sketch something like a tree just to see if I could. . . . I came home
one day after school with a picture. . . . My dad wasn't home so I
showed it to my stepmother. I said it would be really cool to be an
artist. [She responded,] 'No, that's really stupid. You can't do that.'*
—*Kristine*

The Anonymous Was a Woman Foundation gives ten un-
restricted grants each year to female visual artists older than 30
who show creative promise and who are at critical junctures in
their careers. The title of the foundation, borrowed from Virginia Woolf's book, *A Room of One's Own,* is a testimony to all of
the female artists in past centuries who may have signed their
work "Anonymous" to protest the discouragement they felt about
how society and other artists denied them professional respect
and recognition. Many art historians and critics believe that
women continue to be left out of the art world's inner circles.
Steven Z. Levine, an art historian at Bryn Mawr College in Pennsylvania, indicated that women "were systematically excluded
from the institutions of art," adding that there are still institutional impediments built into the infrastructure of our society
that make it more difficult for women to succeed (Dobrzynski,
1997).

My colleague Robert Kirschenbaum and I (1997) studied
female artists in their thirties through fifties who had children
while they simultaneously and actively pursued their art. These

artists revealed conflicts over their priorities in life, explaining that both their families and their art were essential for creative self-expression. Their artistic productivity was dependent upon a number of factors including self-discipline, financial support and security, spousal encouragement and support, childrearing responsibilities, job demands, access to artistic materials/equipment, and workspace availability. They indicated that they faced difficult choices about creative expression and development, as their relationships with their husbands, and especially their children, often diverted their attention from their art. Ironically, the obstacles they encountered—such as the absence of support from spouses and parents, financial difficulties, and time necessary to raise their children—were perceived by these women as contributing in some ways to their creative process and the development of their identities as artists.

~: LINDA :~

Linda, 43, was born in Southern California. Her father was a traveling salesman when she was young but eventually became the president of the company, and her mother was a beautician who had stopped working when Linda was born. One of her earliest memories of art was in the second grade:

> [My teacher] told us that we could decorate our papers any way that we liked if we finished early. I always finished early and decorated my paper. One day, she returned my paper and said, 'This is very nice. I like your decorations, but please don't do this kind of art on here anymore. I don't like modern art.' I had doodled and colored in some circles. 'I like this kind,' she said and pointed to a picture of an apple and a ruler.

Although she took no art in high school, Linda majored in art at college after taking a few art classes. She had been doing art at home, copying the works of modern masters like Klée, Kandinsky, and Matisse:

> *I read a lot and was exposed to a lot of artists' names*
> *from literature. I wanted to know what they were*
> *talking about, so I would look them up in the library.*
> *When they asked me what I wanted for my birth-*
> *day, I might say an art book. That was when I was*
> *about fifteen.*

Linda's mother had given her oil paints to use a few years earlier. Her father, Linda's grandfather, was an artist and sign painter who died at the age of 24. When her mother was in her early teens, she had made portraits that she arranged to have sold in a local Woolworth's store. By the time Linda's mother was in high school, she decided she couldn't pursue art and quit school to go to work. Linda said her mother always encouraged her: "I think she probably wished she could have done more in art, but we never talked about it." Still, her mother wanted her to go to business school because she thought it was important that a woman always have a way to support herself.

Linda's academic work was outstanding, and she skipped a grade after having started school early. She attended a private school because the public school refused to allow her to enroll early. Few of her peers knew she had been accelerated because she had reached her adult height by the age of twelve. She attended several colleges and universities, transferring to the last one because her future husband went there:

> *I didn't have any mentors. For the most part, my art*
> *has been self-motivated. I've taught myself by read-*
> *ing, taking workshops here and there, and searching*
> *out people whom I want to learn from. A program*
> *wasn't laid out for me, so I graduated with only one*
> *semester of painting. I tried a lot of things but never*
> *really painted. . . . When I got out of school, I wanted*
> *to pursue art on my own. College sparked my inter-*
> *est and gave me a few skills to start with. The last 22*
> *years, I've been slowly branching out.*

Linda has never held a full-time job, but explained:

I've done a lot of volunteer activities and have given workshops and classes for the Park District and the [local] Arts Commission. I've volunteered to teach English and reading, helped with Head Start before I had children, and did lots of things with the League of Women Voters. I've done a lot to keep busy, along with raising a couple kids.

She works on her art in the fall and spring, and does her most intense work at home:

I do my metalwork in the basement where the power tools are. I don't have a studio room which is entirely my own. I work wherever it is convenient to work. I have taken over one part of the basement because I'm in a clay phase right now. . . . If I paint, I'll use an upstairs room and try to lock it off during the day so my daughter won't get into my paints. . . . [When I get to] the point where I'm tired of [a piece] or have explored the idea as much as I can, then I'll drop it and usually shift media. . . . I let the life cycles direct me. If I have an idea, I'll let it grow in my mind all summer if necessary. . . . I have to think about an idea for months or years in order to be fully prepared. Until they're ready to come out, I can't do anything anyway. . . most of my working time is done in my head.

Her husband, a foreign language teacher, is supportive: "He's positive about [my art]. He writes, so he understands about the creative process." Sometimes her husband takes her children away for the weekend or holiday, and Linda can work at night.

Linda believes that she really "arrived as an artist" when she produced a large enough body of work in order to have what she considered a good show:

Having a large, cohesive body of work definitely con-tributes to an artist's self-confidence. I want people to

> look at my work and see a certain quality that is im-
> pressive. . . . When I looked at my pictures and sculp-
> tures, I saw vitality and experimentation. That was
> the common thread that I projected into my artwork.
> It perked me up to look at them.

Every once in a while she sells a piece after people have seen
them at shows: "Now that I know my art is accepted, it's too
much trouble to do some of these shows. I don't care about
them anymore. What I care about is developing my ideas. When
I feel that I have things to show, I find someplace to do that."

As a child, Linda did not know that she wanted to be an
artist when she grew up. "Everything happened to me very quickly
when I was young. I never formed a coherent, cogent vision of
what I wanted to be." Although she was very shy and introverted when she was young, she is now forthright, confident,
and outspoken. At the center of her life, however, is her family:

> My priority has always been my family. I do many
> things and one of those things is art. I consider myself
> an artist. It's part of my life, whether I'm painting or
> not. If I never do another piece of art, I'll still be an
> artist. . . . If I never produced another thing in my
> life, people would fill my life.

A study of female artists is essential because the majority of
research conducted on creativity and productivity in adult life
has generally concentrated on males. Although very little research exists on talented female artists, Pirto (1991) suggested
one explanation for the absence of many famous women artists:
"Perhaps the reason that few women become famous visual artists might have to do with how intensely they pursue their passions for art . . ."(p. 144). Of course, the major reason that some
talented women who have children cannot pursue creative professional endeavors is the absence of sufficient time and energy,
but other reasons exist for the relatively smaller number of fe-

males who gain eminence in art. In a study of young talented female sculptors, Sloan and Sosniak (1985) found that it was most important to the parents of these sculptors that their daughters be happily married. Parents also hoped that their daughters would be able to do something in which they were interested, finish their education, and become financially secure. If parents primarily encourage their talented daughters in these areas, there is, perhaps, minimal encouragement given to their creative potential in art.

Runco (1991) has suggested that two broad personality and cognitive "transformations" occur in the development of high levels of eminence in persons of high ability. The first is the development of outstanding creative ability during the first two decades of life. The second begins in adolescence and involves the transformation of creative abilities into an integrated set of cognitive skills, career-focused interests and values, specific creative personality dispositions, and moderately high ambitions. Accordingly, if parental encouragement of art occurs only as coupled with the absolute need to marry and have children, a different set of priorities may be embedded in talented females.

Robert Kirshenbaum and I (1997) also investigated the relationships of these female artists with their husbands and partners. Ochse (1991) reported that an artist's first work of note often is produced in his/her 20s, with high productivity continuing well into his/her 40s. As noted earlier, it is during these years that most women bear and care for their children. Foley (1986) studied artists who were also mothers and found that these women experienced guilt and conflict between their roles as mothers and as artists. The extent to which female artists have uninterrupted time to work on their art, and the manner in which they find time to produce art, remains largely ignored in the research literature. The age at which women artists create art and find uninterrupted time for their work was also investigated in this study.

Little research has addressed the creative processes and personalities of women and whether gender stereotyping in childhood, education, marriage, and family has an impact on that process. We studied these artists to focus on perceptions of the impact of family, formal education, marriage, and motherhood on the development of their creativity and art. We hoped to gain insight about how this group of talented women combined their personal and professional lives.

We used the following criteria to select the female artists who had children for this study: (a) self-perception as artists as well as positive recognition of artwork by peers, (b) artistic production that has been sold and displayed outside the home at some time, (c) willingness to participate in the current study and to relate life history in detail.

The participants ranged in age from 39 to 51. Their children ranged in number from 1 to 5 and in age from preschool age to their late twenties. Six of the women were married and four divorced. All were college graduates with degrees in various areas including art, counseling, education, business, psychology, philosophy, microbiology, recreation therapy, and sociology. All had taken art classes in college, although only one participant had majored in art, and all had attended numerous art workshops after graduating from college. Their socioeconomic status ranged from low to upper middle, depending on combined income with their spouses, and the married women lived in better financial circumstances than those who were not married. The women came from all regions of the United States, and one participant had emigrated from Germany as a child.

The women produced different types of art: six painted, three made jewelry, and three sculpted. They also produced photography, poetry/screenplays, etched glass, and quilts, with many of the women working in more than one medium. The content of their visual art included such subjects as cave art, realistic images, and androgynous figures, along with abstract or archetypal shapes and symbols. One artist indicated that she stayed away from female-oriented images, but others included such images without focusing on them. Prices of their artwork ranged from a few dollars for greeting cards incorporating their art to about $1,600 for paintings. Art sales varied; some of the women were not interested in selling while a few sold regularly. One woman commented, "I sell a few things, probably [I could sell] a lot more if I managed to showcase them for the public, but I'm not a person who, at this point in time, is concerned about selling my art."

Most of the artists sold pieces on an irregular basis, and none relied exclusively on art sales as her primary income. Their main occupations included lab technician, counselor, Tai Chi instructor, jeweler, city art commission coordinator's assistant, beauty shop/gallery owner. Several women were homemakers who also gave art workshops for a small fee or did volunteer civic work. Evidence collected indicates that many are intellectually gifted and all are artistically talented. All reported that they were artistically inclined as children, and most were recognized by childhood peers as being talented in art. A range of artistic talent existed in the sample, and some of the artists may have been considered merely above average artists by their peers. However, all of the artists were recommended by their peers in an arts association because of the criteria specified earlier and the appeal and originality of their artwork. There is no way of knowing at this time, of course, if the artists we studied will ever be widely recognized as highly creative or as having made a significant impact in their fields. They all seem to have made an impact on their peers, in any case, and were considered to have achieved various levels of success in their communities and local areas.

We used several sources to learn more about these artists including questionnaires, interviews which document the women's perceptions about their accomplishments, primary source data including reviews of the artists' work, and interviews about the participants with colleagues and peers.

Our results indicated that most of the participants had good exposure to various art experiences as children and that their relationships with others, especially family, had a significant influence on their ability to do their work, their creative process and self-image as an artist, and their ability to express themselves creatively. The women's artistic productivity seemed to be dependent upon several factors, including family issues, early art experiences, influence of partners and teachers, creative process, and creative expression.

FAMILY ISSUES

Most of the women grew up in intact middle class families, although some of their parents were divorced. Three were first born and four were the last born. The number of siblings ranged from one to four, with most having one or two siblings. Fathers of the participants in this study had various careers, including involvement in the military, sales, store ownership, research psychology, and writing. Most of the mothers were homemakers, but some were also engaged in careers such as art, acting, teaching, accounting, hairdressing, managing a pharmacy, and bartending.

Parental support for their childrens' early interest in art varied greatly, but most of the parents ultimately tried to discourage their daughters from becoming artists, even if they supported their art production as a hobby. The women generally indicated they received little support from their families for their artistic activities during their childhood, either having their artistic attempts benignly ignored as "nice" or criticized for not being marketable (e.g., in the form of saleable portraits). Parents were much more encouraging when it came to schoolwork. All of the women usually received good grades in school or college, although several were underachievers for a few years in junior high or high school because they were bored or had other social interests. The majority were avid readers, especially those who described themselves as being introverted and shy as teenagers. Their fathers usually reacted negatively if they stated they wanted to become artists, as did those mothers who were not described as creative themselves. Only a few parents paid for art supplies and lessons; however, several relatives, particularly aunts, were considered supportive. This lack of parental support seems to have negatively affected the artists' past and current creative processes as reflected in the following comments:

~: *"My parents thought it was a phase I was going through. They kept telling me that I couldn't make a living as an artist, and I would argue with them."*

~: *"When I was young, I always liked to draw. When I was in school, I liked art classes, but I was never encouraged. In fact, I was discouraged by my family. My stepmother would say, "You can't do that. . . . You have to get married. You have to do this, you have to do that."*

Some parents subtly undermined their daughters' interests and pursuits by refusing to purchase art supplies or provide art lessons:

~: *"They were very practical people, so their encouragement was somewhat neutral. My mother wanted me to go to business school when I went to college."*

~: *"Sadly, my parents didn't buy me materials. I used my baby-sitting money to buy art pads, pencils, paints, and other supplies."*

As noted, half of the artists indicated that their fathers were not supportive and that these fathers perceived their devotion to their art in the following ways:

~: *"When I started to set up my studio, he gave me very negative feedback. He said, 'Yeah, we'll see. Why don't you get a real job?' When I took the computerized accounting class, he said good luck sarcastically. I asked him what he meant, and he said I couldn't count higher than the number of fingers and toes I had."*

~: *"My father's advice to me was that I might have a future in art if I could draw portraits accurately. 'If you can make a portrait look like a person, you may have a career.' Here I was, in the sixth or seventh grade, and if my people didn't come out looking like they were supposed to, he would say, 'Nah, this isn't it.' He was not very encouraging."*

~: *"Everything I brought home, unless it was a good representational drawing that looked like a phone, would get a negative reaction from my mother and father. Especially my dad would say, 'Why can't you paint things that we can tell what they are?' or 'That's all right, but can't you make it look more like a house or a person?' That's one reason I don't show my art.*

EARLY ART EXPERIENCES

A few of these artists mentioned that there was very little art in their home, but most commented on the availability of books. Only a few had gone to museums, and their earliest art experiences included being taught by a neighbor to draw horses, looking at statues in a town square (in Germany), drawing constantly (especially when lonely), playing music, dancing, finger-painting, making noodle pictures in kindergarten, gazing in wonder at Salvador Dali's picture of a melted clock, copying cartoon characters from a cereal box, and attending arts and crafts in school and at a Community Center.

Most were recognized in school as being artistic, although several women kept their interest in art to themselves because they were shy or afraid of peer disapproval. Some had friends who enjoyed drawing or writing with them, and several said that a friend or peer suggested they become an artist when they grew up. A majority of the women indicated that they had excellent art teachers in college, and some also had encouraging art teachers in public school. However, they also reported that their art teachers in public school discouraged them from becoming artists because of the poor financial prospects. Only a few were singled out by college teachers as being especially talented in art and specifically encouraged. Those who went back to school after having children developed positive relationships with instructors and were more strongly encouraged.

Influence of Partners and Teachers

A majority of the women married while in college or soon after. Those who worked held various jobs or pursued careers in education or sales, but most stayed home to raise families. Those who worked full-time reported that they were often too tired and distracted during the years they raised their families to engage in any serious artistic efforts. Over the years, the effect of children on their art forced the women to adjust their work schedules so that they did their most intensely creative work when the children were sleeping or at school. In a few cases, women worked on their art while their spouse looked after the children. Several commented that having children brought them back to art, since they were spending most of their time at home and needed some way to channel their creative needs. Although their children were a priority in their lives, these women enjoyed art both as a means of self-expression (which was vitally important to them) and as a means of "escaping" from the chores and mindset of motherhood without actually leaving their children. In one case, a woman separated from her family to return to school for a specialized degree in another part of the country.

According to the artists in this study, the majority of their husbands were not supportive of their art. Some husbands were not outwardly negative but were also not encouraging regarding their spouses' art. In general, those who were married to supportive husbands continued to stay married, and their husbands helped finance their art and raise the children. Husbands were most supportive of their wives' marketable art (e.g., jewelry), and some husbands pressured their wives to sell their art. Most did not regard their wives' art as serious, and 9 of the 10 artists in this study indicated that their husbands gave them either negative or extremely limited feedback. Some of the feedback they received from their husbands was similar to comments made by their fathers, who also wanted the art produced by these women to be more realistic, which would, in turn, make the art more marketable:

~: *"The one thing he won't give me is any feedback on my paintings. He won't tell me what he likes. It's led to some disagreements in the past, so I try not to ask him."*

~: *"He considers my painting a waste of time. I should be going over the books or doing something with the children. That is the reason I don't spend much time painting; I felt guilty."*

The women who had spouses who did not support their artwork are now divorced, although one has remarried. In the other marriages, spouses were neutral or supportive in some ways, such as helping to take care of children, providing financial support, and giving verbal encouragement, but the women indicated that their husbands often complained if their artwork was not being sold. Many of the women admitted that art sales were not their major concern, unless they were unable to afford necessary supplies and equipment.

Some women we studied had encountered wonderful art teachers who were supportive of their art. Limited opportunities existed for other participants to take art classes. Their teachers often recognized these artists for their interest and talent in the arts. Although they might have been recognized for their talent in art, they were not encouraged to pursue art as a career by their elementary teachers, who often indicated that it was difficult to have a successful art career. Several of their high school and college teachers recognized and were more supportive of these women. One of the artists described a teacher who was also a sculptor: "[that teacher] inspired me to notice the colors of nature." Another woman commented that "the teachers turned me on to art. They encouraged me to take everything one step further without suggesting what to do. They exposed me to a lot of work."

Although almost all of the participants had positive experiences with their high school teachers, many of their secondary art teachers also discouraged them from pursuing a career in art because it was not financially stable:

~: *"They acknowledged me with good grades, but I never was encouraged to pursue art as a career. What hit me in high school was that my high school counselor said, 'Major in art? That's stupid. You can't make that into a career.' I think he said that because I was a woman."*

~: *"When I became a senior, I told him that I planned to major in art. He suddenly became discouraging and told me that it was very hard to make it as an artist. He wanted me to know that it was a whole different situation being a working artist. It made me angry."*

The majority of the negative feedback provided to many of the artists by parents, husbands, and teachers revolved around the amount of money that could be earned as a professional artist. Money also had an impact on the amount of time that the women devoted to their art. As might be expected, the women who did not work outside of their home or studio had more time to create than those who also had jobs outside of their home:

~: *"I'm still considering going back to school to get my teacher's certification. I'd rather not have to do that. We are waiting to see if I can eke out*

enough money to satisfy my portion of the family
budget."

~: "I started out majoring in art when I went to
college. Then I realized that I might have to support myself, so I shifted my major to special education and kept art as a minor. I worked as a
special education teacher for three years."

The external factors identified by the artists in this study
indicated that they had a great deal to overcome in order to create their art. They overcame constant pressure from parents,
husbands, and teachers to pursue other work and to be financially successful, and they managed to persevere in creating art.

CREATIVE PROCESS AND SELF-IMAGE AS AN ARTIST

Although an art piece could be visualized and contemplated
for weeks, months, or sometimes years, most participants indicated that they completed most pieces in less than 20 hours
stretched out over several days or weeks. All of the women relied heavily on images and visualization as sources of ideas for
their artwork and sought archetypal images or received them in
dreams. Many women reported that those images that reap-
peared in their minds eventually "demanded" to be expressed. In
some cases and at some times, outside images and events affected them, especially for the woman who was a photographer.
For most, however, their art was drawn from within and trans-
formed as they worked in their medium. They usually used art
books to develop knowledge and ideas about technique and style.
Some of the women did sketches when considering a new work
or did studies of models or people in public if they included
realistic human figures in their art. Some used journal writing,
sometimes drawing in their journals, as part of the creative process. The relationship of the women to their medium and with
their children emerged as the most personal part of their creative process. They would reach a point at which the work would

start to emerge partly of its own volition, and they would follow the process without knowing where it would take them. Many commented that they were finished when either the piece started to bore them or it just "seemed to be done." They considered some pieces to be very special and these were not for sale, but their favorite pieces were not necessarily the type which sold well.

Combining the roles of parent and artist created the greatest challenges for these artists, who often stated that their children were a distraction from their art. The most financially successful artist of the group commented that having children was undoubtedly limiting if she compared herself to a woman who devoted her whole being to art. She also believed, however, that being a mother provided grounding in her life and may offer experiences that help the woman as artist to relate to humanity better through art. For her, it was a struggle to be a parent and spouse while retaining a strong sense of self, but art was her means for achieving that goal. While several of these artists indicated that art was an outlet for stress, they also said that devoting attention to art rather than children or friends sometimes made them feel guilty or ambivalent about work and parenting:

> ~: *"I time it so that my intense work is done when the weather's bad, the kids are away, or I have to be home for some reason."*

> ~: *"They're there and take up my time and energy, a lot of energy. I try to work at night after they are asleep. I work in the daytime if I think they are calm and won't interrupt me too much."*

> ~: *"I have trouble working when [my son] is around. I'm a loner and need silence. . . . When he was younger, I didn't even realize that I needed space away from him. I didn't do any work because I was exhausted from my life and my relationship with him."*

Although children were regarded by these artists as a source of distraction, many also believed they were a great source of inspiration:

> A mother may not be able to gain as much recognition as a woman who focuses on art early in life and does only that ... but a mother may experience more suffering that can be transformed into compassion for humanity that is expressed in her art.

These artists also indicated that their other family obligations distracted them from their work. In order to compensate for the time that both family and art consumed, many women performed fewer household chores than they believed were necessary.

Most of the women said they had wanted to be artists when they were young. Those who had always been called on to do art for peers and teachers considered themselves artists at a young age. Many thought of themselves as creative but did not consider themselves artists until after they had sold some artwork or had a show. Most commented that it took years of art production for them to feel the self-confidence necessary to call themselves artists:

> A real artist is a person who creates art, sells it, makes money, and supports himself in that manner. I'm beginning to realize that many artists create for the simple enjoyment of creating. Maybe one day their art will make them money. An artist has to keep creating art in order to discover the direction he or she wants to go with it. Artists study art until they find a niche, and then know what they do really well that satisfies them.

Many of the women distrusted the praise they received and were unsure of the quality of their art. In general, low self-esteem affected the creative process of these artists, who often felt guilty when they had to spend less time with their children to gain time to create. Some of the artists were shy, some were "loners" who had moved around a lot as children, and most had doubted their abilities and were somewhat apprehensive about their talent and artwork at some point in their careers. They were nervous about what others thought about their art and feared rejection of their very personal creations:

~: *"I don't trust what anyone says [about my quilts]."*

~: *"I'm afraid of what people are going to say when they see my paintings. My art is for me. I don't do it for anybody else anymore."*

These women were hesitant to show their art to others because they felt "it wasn't good enough" or feared rejection in some form. This low self-esteem might have affected their creative process and productivity. "Sometimes," one artist stated, "I make things and hide them because I don't think they're good enough. I'll bring them out and somebody will say they're pretty good and it surprises me. If I get enough positive feedback on a piece, I'll show it somewhere." Several of the women avoided the prospect of having their efforts (and, consequently, their self-confidence and self-esteem) diminished by either having their art rejected in art competitions or ignored by the buying public.

The Importance of Creative Expression

Most of the participants also commented about the process of creating art and how valuable this was for them. Especially for those involved in some aspect of sculpting, the visceral feeling of doing physical work as they created was very gratifying:

The process of doing art is often more important [than the product] to me because of my feeling that I have to get something out. . . . The act of welding, of fusing metal together, is very important to me. The passion I feel, the violence of creating something with an arc-welder as the sparks fly everywhere, watching the metal heat up, then manipulating it by bending, hammering, and cutting it, gives me feelings that are hard to describe. It's a rich feeling, one of power, I guess.

Several said they preferred making and selling things of their own design, for others' enjoyment, to working in a regular job. One woman, a counselor, said that art is a path to self-discovery and healing; this idea would appear to be true for all the participants in this study. Another woman commented, "I may not be in the mood to paint, but if I don't do something [artistic], it's like I'm suffering from drug withdrawal. If I don't take care of this creative urge, I feel like I'm going to blow up. I need that high of being creative." When asked about their futures, the goals mentioned by these female artists included being able to keep learning and doing their art, obtaining necessary equipment and materials when the money was available, and completing specific projects in the near future.

CONCLUSIONS

Robert Kirschenbaum and I drew the following conclusions from our research with these female artists:

1. Artistic productivity was dependent upon a number of factors including self-discipline, financial support and security, spousal encouragement and support, childrearing responsibilities, job demands, access to artistic materials or equipment, and workspace availability.

2. Art instruction was crucial to developing skills. This instruction could come informally, through workshops, or formally, in art courses.

3. When they were young, the artists considered themselves creative, artistic, or both. Access to art books and biographies helped give them direction in life.

4. Technical skills developed over time and were a means by which the artists discovered the nature of their talent as well as the genre and medium in which they preferred to work.

5. Vital to their development as both people and artists was the recognition of talent by a teacher or another significant person in their life.

6. Self-confidence as an artist was linked to sales and peer recognition.

7. Personal relationships were a major factor in their lives and emotional bonds with their children and husbands were as important to these artists as their art. Most indicated that their children were a higher priority than their art; however, the artists divorced spouses who were not supportive of their art.

8. The intensity of the involvement in their art as adults seemed to be directly related to the intensity of their interest in art as teenagers.

9. Children were both a distraction from and an inspiration for their art. Children were particularly inspiring if the subject the artist was exploring related to motherhood.

10. Outside approval affected these artists' beliefs about their own work, both positively and negatively. To avoid problems with low self-esteem, therefore, the mature, self-confident female artist should try to develop her own standards of excellence, both explicit and intuitive, that are true and appropriate for her art form and not susceptible to the vagaries of public opinion.

The artists who participated in this study were exposed to art as children and gradually became aware of their talents and aspirations as they grew older. They were creative in many areas. Despite limited encouragement from parents and, in some cases, from spouses, most of the artists persevered and continued to create. However, they had numerous external and internal obstacles to overcome, including lack of family support; absence of encouragement for art as a career from art teachers, parents and spouses; financial issues; caring for children; and low self-concepts. It is clear that these issues and obstacles had some negative effects on these female artists; however, they overcame them. This study indicated that these factors caused the artists to produce less art, have less time than they needed to create, and have diminished self-esteem regarding their products. The same factors also contributed to their creative process and the development of their identity as artist, their awareness and passion for their life and art, and their love of family and work.

Whether or not any of these artists will ever achieve the status of eminence cannot be determined at this time. What does seem clear is that because they are both artists and mothers, this label may not be of ultimate importance in their lives. These artists expressed their creativity not only in their art products, but also in their efforts in raising their children and nurturing their families. Though dividing creative energy frustrated all of the female artists in this study, none of the artists regretted having children, and all looked forward to time later in their lives in which they could devote additional hours to their art.

CHAPTER EIGHT

~:~

TALENTED WOMEN WHO CHOOSE A CONVENTIONAL CAREER

We can do no great things—only small things with great love.
—Mother Theresa

What factors are associated with women who want to achieve, who can achieve, and yet do not achieve in ways that were expected given their high potential during childhood? Is the absence of achievement caused by a fear of power, as Carolyn Heilbrun (1988) argued? She states that "Unfortunately, power is something that women abjure once they perceive the great difference between the lives possible to men and to women . . ." (p. 16) and defines power "as the ability to take one's place in whatever discourse is essential to action and the right to have one's part matter." She also believes that "ironically, women who acquire power are more likely to be criticized for it than are the men who have always had it." Perhaps, then, it is not fear of power that keeps women from taking their place, but rather fear of the impact of their decisions on those they love. Or perhaps other factors account for the underachievement that often characterizes the lives of gifted females.

In her discussion of the life of Dorothy L. Sayers, Heilbrun (1988) wrote of Sayer's unconscious decision to place her life" . . . outside of the bounds of society's restraints and ready-made narratives" (p. 50). By placing herself outside the social structure that demands " . . . not only that a woman marry but that the marriage and its progeny be her life's absolute and only center" (p. 51), Heilbrun believed that a vocation becomes possible, as does the fulfillment of talent.

I have always been interested in females of high potential who had done the opposite of what Sayers did—that is, selected the traditionally female career of education—and their perceptions of this choice. I wanted to explore the social forces, if any, that caused these women to become teachers and discover how they felt about their decisions. I administered a questionnaire to 67 gifted women and conducted follow-up interviews with 25 women who were purposely selected based on geographic location, marital status, and patterns of response on the initial questionnaire.

Participants

Sixty-seven gifted women participated in this study, selected from a larger group of 150 gifted females in graduate programs in education at the University of Connecticut. This group was selected because of a combination of their scores on graduate record examinations, high grades in graduate school, designation as an honors student, and/or other academic awards. One hundred and fifty females received the questionnaire, and 100 completed it. Of this number, 67 qualified for the designation as gifted based on information they provided indicating high achievement in a combination of areas: achievement test information, aptitude and intelligence scores, grades, rank in class, honor society designation, special accomplishments, and/or awards. Thirty percent of the final sample had been identified and placed in some type of gifted program during their academic years.

The questionnaire focused on the following six areas: (a) personal data (age, marital status, college or university attended, age of siblings and children, and information relating to the designation as gifted); (b) career (reasons career was selected, other career interests, parental acceptance of career, future career plans); (c) parental encouragement of academic abilities; (d) personal and professional achievements; (e) the effects of marriage and children on career or personal choices, free time, and housework; and (f) life satisfaction.

RESULTS

Four major areas had the greatest impact on these talented women: career choice, parental encouragement, effects of family on career or personal choices, and personal/professional achievement and life satisfaction.

CAREER CHOICE

In the area of career choice, participants answered questions about current career, the reasons for selecting this career, and retrospective beliefs about whether or not their career was the right choice. Approximately 60% of the women believed they had made a correct decision about their career choice, while 36% were unsure. Only 4% believed they had chosen the wrong career. However, 50% of the women who indicated they had made a correct decision about their career listed totally different career choices when asked what other field they would have chosen retrospectively. Fields included such diverse areas as environmental law, music composition, medicine, biology and other sciences, arts, and other areas. The most common retrospective career choice was medicine. Two respondents who indicated that they were satisfied with their careers in education provided insightful comments about why they were discouraged from careers in medicine. One respondent, a 43-year-old woman who had been identified for a gifted program because of an IQ score of 170, commented, "I was unable to pursue the career that I really wanted, to be a pediatrician. This was mainly because of my parent's divorce and financial problems. At the urging of my high school counselor, I chose an easier route—teaching." A

39-year-old female who had skipped a grade and excelled in school, said:

> I have taken many career inventories and on every single one, I was most interested in being a medical doctor. I believe I have a rather unusual skill of combining my talents in science with good interpersonal skills. I believe I would have been a compassionate and successful physician. Unfortunately, my family did not regard this as an appropriate career for a woman.

When asked to select the reasons for their current career choices, the respondents could rank 14 choices. These choices included influence or expectation of friend, teacher, or family member; interest in the career; enjoyment; prestige; chance; belief that the career would help people; financial reward; or another reason. The four most common responses by this group of gifted females were believing the career would help people, enjoyment of the field, interest in the career, and influence of a teacher. On both the questionnaires and in the interviews, however, two interesting trends emerged about career choice. First, many of these females in "traditional careers" were angry about the limited range of careers that they believed were available to them due to the social structure of their world. The second clear trend was that prestige and financial reward were *never* mentioned as one of the four most important criteria by any of the 67 women. The following comments are representative of approximately one third of this sample, who ranged in age from 25 to 58 years old:

> ~ "Societal influence—women could do three things—teacher, nurse, or secretary." (35-year-old, Massachusetts)

> ~ "Father said no daughter of his would be allowed to be anything except teacher, social worker, etc. He would not pay for me to 'learn how to be a

man.'" (36-year-old, Alabama)

~ "I had no idea of the realm of possibilities open to me. Being a female in a small rural Iowa town, my choice seemed to be limited to secretary, nurse, or teacher." (38-year-old, Iowa)

~ "I would have loved to go to law school, but my parents encouraged me to teach. My brother graduated from Yale Law School and my mother never forgets to mention this to anyone who will listen! What a commentary about parental influence!" (40-year-old, New York)

~ "Everyone laughed when I said I wanted to go to law school." (44-year-old, Maryland)

~ " [I] Could not get into veterinary school in 1959; [I] was told that they only take one woman per year and that woman had to be from a farm—I grew up in New York City!" (52-year-old, New York)

PARENTAL ENCOURAGEMENT TO PURSUE HIGHER EDUCATION AND CAREER ASPIRATIONS

The majority of respondents indicated that their parents encouraged them to go to college and pursue a career. However, three findings emerged regarding parental encouragement and they paint a contradictory picture. First, it was clear from both the questionnaires and the interviews that parents usually encouraged these gifted females to do well in school, but they offered little encouragement for their daughters' work beyond the college years. Approximately 20% of the participants said their parents reserved this encouragement solely for their sons. "I was told that my brother was smarter than I was and that it was probably a waste of time to send me to college because I'd just get married anyhow," wrote a 55-year-old from Maine.

241

Many participants also indicated that their parents had no idea how to encourage a specific career goal. Accordingly, these gifted females learned to do well in school, but had no idea how to focus their good grades and achievement scores into career aspirations:

> *My parents encouraged me totally but not toward a specific career. I was interested in medicine in high school but was never encouraged to seek out possible medical schools or investigate courses of study in that area. My guidance counselor completely dampened my interests and enthusiasm for this career. (39-year-old, New York)*

The second parent-related theme that emerged in the study involved parental expectations that these women would marry and have families. According to the respondents, parents encouraged education and establishing a career, but only when combined with having and caring for a family. Many were discouraged by their parents (especially their mothers) from pursuing careers after they had children. They were often encouraged to pursue a career only if it enabled them to "put their family first." Accordingly, many parents of women who had participated in this study considered teaching and nursing appropriate career choices for their daughters.

The third theme that emerged concerned the fact that parents of these women were often surprised when their daughters exceeded the plans their parents had held for them. One 39-year-old woman from Michigan explained, "I have exceeded my parents' personal aspirations for me and my family's dreams for both career and financial standing."

While 80% of the respondents indicated that their parents encouraged them, conditions were often attached to this encouragement. First, parents believed women should have a husband and children in addition to an education and a career. Second, parents encouraged their daughters to select a career that enabled them to devote themselves to a family.

Interaction Between Family and Career or Personal Life

The area that resulted in the most compelling disclosures about conflicts between ability and goals related to how the participants' marriages or relationships and/or the births of their children affected their careers or personal lives. Twenty-two percent of the respondents listed barriers or personal compromises that they faced during their lives. A higher percentage (36%) made statements indicating that both positive and negative occurrences resulted from marriage or childbirth, thereby affected their career and personal life:

> *My marriage and children have definitely been an obstacle in that they have limited the amount of time that I have had to pursue a career and dictated when I could or could not begin. Though not married now, I was married for five years and divorced four years ago. Presently, I am involved in a serious relationship. In both cases, I consistently find myself having to choose between furthering my interests and furthering the relationship. This has been difficult. (38-year-old, Florida)*

Some women were angry about the effects of their marriages: "My marriage has destroyed my self-image. I was totally 'put on hold' for 13 years in my own interest areas as my family always took priority. I put a tremendous amount of time into it and receive nothing. But my children are great!" remarked a 46-year-old woman from Connecticut.

The remaining third of the respondents were positive about the impact of marriage and/or children on their careers or personal lives:

> *I was married at 19 to a well-centered man of 20. My marriage has produced only positive effects. He supported me emotionally and financially while I finished college and switched careers. We delayed having children for 9 years until I found what I wanted*

to do. (34-year-old, New Jersey)

When asked how much free time each respondent had each day, the mean amount of time listed by respondents was slightly more than one hour each day. The most frequent response about the amount of free time these talented women had daily was 1/2 hour. The participants who listed the most hours (4 per day) were either single, divorced, or married with children who were out of the home. When asked what percentage of household work and chores respondents did as compared to spouse/partner and/or children, respondents indicated a larger percentage than might be expected. Deleting the responses of unmarried participants (who did 100% of their housework), the mean percentage of household work and chores undertaken by these gifted females was 71%. Only 31% of the sample did less than 75% of the household work, and 90% of this group attributed the lower percentage to their children's contributions rather than their spouse's.

The problems that these gifted females face in trying to combine a career and a personal life initially seemed to be no different than what all females face. The majority (80%) of questionnaire respondents made comments like this one:

> *I face two problems: 1. Chronic exhaustion—There are days I wouldn't get up if there was a million dollar check on my lawn. 2. Guilt—Cupcake Day in my daughter's first grade class conflicts with my 8:00 a.m. class. I can't go. (32-year-old, Connecticut)*

The major dilemma these gifted females faced was frustration that they simply did not have the time to pursue their own talents and/or interests; they were not satisfied by their current careers, their family responsibilities, and plans for their immediate future. Most wondered when their own self-actualization would occur and dreamed of acquiring the time needed to do something in their talent area. When asked to compare life today with their dreams for their future when they graduated from college, 60% of the respondents indicated they experienced a conflict between the real world and the cultivation and realization of their own talents. Societal expectations often led them *not* to plan a career that was personally satisfying, to put their talents and aspirations on hold while raising their families, and eventually to stop regarding themselves as capable of more than they are currently doing:

> ∾ *"My life is very different than the one I thought I'd have. When I graduated from college, I had no real direction, despite a degree. I had no idea what I wanted for a career."* (45-year-old, Texas)

> ∾ *"I never thought about my future when I graduated from college. (I'm saddened when I write this!) I believed the 'Prince Charming' propaganda."* (40-year-old, New York)

In other cases, respondents indicated that they had not been able to pursue their own talents because of the pressures of marriage and family. A 52-year-old from Michigan said of her life, "Let's put it this way . . . it's better than my mother's [life] but I want something more for my daughters."

Personal and Professional Accomplishments and Turning Points

The conflict between personal and professional lives was evident in this population of gifted females who often had a difficult time distinguishing between personal and professional accomplishments. Regarding personal accomplishments, the majority of the women listed either their family or the realization of their own potential as a personal achievement. A 40-year-old woman from New York wrote that her personal accomplishments were "getting to know my own talents and limitations and learning to live within these parameters; getting married; having my daughter."

It is interesting to note that the majority of these respondents listed or discussed professional accomplishments when asked about rewarding achievements in their personal development, thereby indicating that they believe professional experiences influenced their personal development. Accordingly, when asked to discuss their most rewarding achievements in their professional development, they often reiterated or expanded what had been listed as personal achievements.

The professional achievements listed might be considered modest when compared to those that are often considered important by either societal or male achievement standards (books written, awards won, prizes gained, etc.) However, each diverse achievement represents high levels of accomplishment for these women. The following examples of achievement represent the majority of talented women in this study across all age groups and geographic locations: "my teaching certificate," "an award for excellence in my college," "4.0 grade average," "a grant from my district," "a curriculum unit I developed," "my Master's degree," "developing an innovative program," "a workshop I gave," "going to a women's group," and "writing a book of poetry while teaching."

When interviewed, most of the respondents were apologetic when explaining their professional accomplishments. They indicated that they knew their achievements in this particular area might seem modest, but they were also often defensive, acknowledging how hard it was to accomplish anything given their work and family commitments. The other respondents were proud, without reservation, of what they had accomplished. Important turning points mentioned varied and included marriage and/or the birth of children, the death of a parent or child, divorce, or some professional event such as attaining a promotion. The majority of turning points, however, can be classified as personal and concerned marriage, children, or divorce:

> ~ *"When I had my first child I was not quite 22. I felt as though my world as I envisioned it had ended. I had always thought of myself as an independent career person and I was totally unprepared for motherhood. Most of my 20s remains a*

> mystery to me. I can barely dredge up a day in my memory." (43-year-old, Connecticut)

> ∻ "My divorce forced me to become responsible for myself, more focused and to use my time more efficiently and effectively." (45-year-old, New York)

Satisfaction with Current Circumstances of Life

The survey also asked questions concerning satisfaction with life, and the questionnaire included an open-ended request for comments. Forty-seven percent of the women who completed the questionnaire indicated that they were satisfied with their current lives, although over half of these women responded with a "Yes, but . . ." qualifying statement:

> ∻ "Yes, but I am still searching for a more meaningful, satisfying career that challenges me." (38-year-old, Florida)

> ∻ "Yes; however, there are times when I would like to get in the car and keep on driving." (40-year-old, Michigan)

Only 10% of these gifted females indicated that they were dissatisfied with the current circumstances of their lives, and in the majority of cases, the dissatisfaction related to marital status, and a fear of living independently. A 43-year-old, International Graduate Student commented:

> I have reached a very difficult stage in my life. I must make a decision about my 20-year-old marriage. I can't stand the thought of staying with the psychological abuse of my marriage nor am I confident enough to go it alone. I want to be married and have a partner, but at my age, I'll never find anyone else.

Participants who were divorced were satisfied with their lives and acknowledged the freedom resulting from a change in marital status. Most of these respondents were also, however, involved in another relationship. "I'm in good health. I'm fairly free to make my own decisions. I'm enjoying finding out more about myself without having to be responsible for others. I enjoy my work. And I'm loved by family, friends, and someone special," remarked a 45-year-old woman from Texas.

The remaining 43% of these talented females were unsure about whether or not they were generally satisfied with the current circumstances of their lives. Two categories of responses emerged from this group. The first category involved time to do what was required in life-work and family issues. Many women made comments such as this one by a 40-year-old woman from Florida: "I love my work and I love my family. Unfortunately, I can't have fulfillment in both and that takes a degree of satisfaction away from my life." Others mentioned problems that typically affect gifted females. A 38-year-old woman living in Missouri summarized the issues succinctly: "I feel: guilt over having a career, perfectionism about both my work and my home, the dilemma of layers and layers of attention to detail, and frustration about being responsible *to* and *for everyone!*"

A second category was found in the responses of women who indicated they were unsure about whether or not they were satisfied with their life. This category involved the continued struggle to realize their own potential and explore their talent areas more fully. Many eloquently discussed this dilemma:

> ∼ *"My life reflects my abilities, my decisions, choices, and the serendipity of fate. I rarely worry about the road not taken and tend to hold the optimist's view that most of my choices have turned out for the best given what I knew at the time. I have compromised." (37-year-old, Massachusetts)*

> ∼ *"I am constantly considering the ambiguity of my present status (personal/professional). Even though others view me as successful, I know I have not achieved what I am capable of doing. I am*

> plagued by the question of what would have hap-
> pened if . . ." (40-year-old, New York)

~ "I cannot generalize. Sections of my life are won-
> derful—my marriage, family, children—but per-
> sonally, I'm not satisfied. I now realize I have
> options, and this is both confusing and exciting.
> It's a lot of responsibility because my decisions af-
> fect other people." (38-year-old, Connecticut)

Many of these women were intensely emotional about not
having the time to pursue their own gifts and about the frustration that they felt in spite of personal happiness within their
marriage or family life. Many cried during the interviews and
discussed the guilt that they felt because they were not happy
themselves despite the fact that they believed they had created a
happy family environment. Others had given up their dreams
and goals because they consider them to be selfish or because
they have lost confidence in their own ability to achieve. A 40-
year-old from Iowa summarized her thoughts about her lost
dreams: "I did not have the drive or the focus in early adulthood
to accomplish all that I wanted. I know now that I could have
done anything. I didn't know, or didn't hear that soon enough."

CONCLUSIONS

The majority of the gifted women in this study (60%) were
satisfied with their career, although half of this group could immediately identify alternate careers they would retrospectively
select. The women who indicated unconditional satisfaction
(30%) believed their work made a difference and that their career mission in life was to work with those who needed them.
Many expressed optimism about their efforts. Yet, slightly less
than half of this group of "unconditionally satisfied" women also
indicated that they were unsure about their career choice or, in
the case of a few, believed that they made the wrong choice. The
majority of these respondents attributed this career choice to

parental discouragement of other careers or the societal forces that resulted in choosing a career that would also allow them to have a family. Parents gave encouragement more freely to and held different expectations for male siblings. Other research has discussed the effect of male siblings on the lives of women. In *Composing a Life*, an examination of the lives of five women of accomplishment, Mary Catherine Bateson (1989) notes that all five women did most of their growing up " . . . without competing brothers on the scene who might have been put in an implicit position of superiority" (p. 47).

The parents of some of the women in this study expected both males and females to do well in school, but upon completing college these gifted females were, in almost every case, expected to marry and have children. Parents gave more support and encouragement for additional studies and careers to male siblings. If marriage was not almost immediately forthcoming, a teaching or nursing career would suffice until that important event occurred. While parents expected male children to choose a career, they expected females only to finish college. For almost every woman in this study, parents and educators provided neither career guidance nor encouragement.

We may speculate that the limited career choices available to the women in this study when they entered college or pursued a career have certainly changed in the last decade or two. However, more recent longitudinal research explores the circumstances under which male and female high school valedictorians and salutatorians continue or discontinue top academic performance (Arnold & Denny, 1985; Arnold, 1995). The young women, but not the men in this study, displayed a sharp decline in self-estimated reports of their intelligence between high school and their sophomore year in college. The women also shifted their career expectations toward less demanding careers because of their concerns regarding work and future marriage and child-raising demands. In the seventh year of their ten-year longitudinal study, Arnold and Denny found that even though female valedictorians outperformed men in college, few of the women pursue doctoral degrees. These female valedictorians also performed at lower professional levels than males did.

The gifted women I studied who became teachers had a difficult time separating their personal and professional lives. They often considered their professional accomplishments personal victories—perhaps because given their limited amount of available time, these accomplishments are indeed a triumph of "found" time over responsibility. Most of these women had very little free time and did the majority of the housework, and most also indicated that they took the primary responsibility for raising their children. After working all day, they came home to what was, in reality, a second job. Little time existed for creative pursuits, yet most managed to involve themselves in projects of which they were proud. When measured by male standards or societal standards of professional achievement, creating a curriculum unit for classroom use or presenting a workshop at a local conference may seem to be a modest attainment. When measured by female views of the dual importance of family and work, these are accomplishments. And yet, are they the accomplishments which may have been realized if time, temperament, and devotion to their own early talents had been possible?

The greatest conflicts for this group of gifted women centered around the interaction of their careers and personal lives. This interaction, in turn, influenced their satisfaction in life. Their intensely personal struggles to develop their own talents, as opposed to nurturing the family, is firmly rooted in the lives of gifted females. So is the ideal in the following quotation by Mary Catherine Bateson (1989):

> The assumptions made about women and girls when we were children, which still linger today, are bound to leave wounds. Prosperity is not sufficient to remove these problems. The daughters of successful fathers may indeed incorporate that achievement

into their image of themselves, but they may
equally well receive the message that
achievement is not for girls. Devoted care
is not sufficient. Most women today have
grown up with mothers who, for all their
care and labor, were regarded as having
achieved little. Women with a deep desire
to be like their mothers are often faced with
the choice between accepting a beloved image that carried connotations of inferiority
or rejecting it and thereby losing an important sense of closeness. (p. 28)

The women in this study did not disclaim the label of giftedness, as other researchers have found in studies of gifted
women who have not achieved at levels they might have aspired
to when they were younger. Instead, these talented educators
often went to great lengths to document their abilities, and many
wrote and spoke with great pride of their accomplishments,
grades, scores and overall superior performance in most academic
settings. The women did not seem to be unaware of, ambivalent
about, or frightened by their potential. Yet many of these women
were unable to translate their superior performance in school
into what they considered success and productivity in their professional lives. About half of the women in this study were often perplexed about their own talent development and the cultural context of their giftedness. They knew that the realization
of their dreams and gifts affected others—their parents, their
spouses, their children. In most cases, where a spouse and children were involved, there was simply not the time or the energy
to pursue their own talents after working and taking care of their
families.

Carolyn Heilbrun (1988) defines a gifted individual as someone who is "not only talented but ... [has] a sense of great possibilities, great desires beyond the apparent possibility of fulfillment" (pp. 97-98). This characterization describes the other

half of the women involved in this study. Clearly frustrated about their current lives, these women tried to create a life that somehow connected their talents, their responsibilities, their families, their age, and their desires for fulfillment. The society in which these women were born and raised eliminated many possibilities that when they married and had children they could achieve at a similar level to their male counterparts. While the importance of maternal giftedness to our society cannot be underestimated, it is often not enough for women who want to do more. While our society has a critical need for those who excel in traditionally female careers such as teaching and nursing, decisions to pursue these careers should be considered by those who have been exposed to the full range of options available to them. Young gifted females should be encouraged to explore careers and advanced educational and professional opportunities that will challenge their intellect as well as fit into their personal plans for the future.

Over 50% of the women in the study were unsure about whether they were satisfied or not satisfied with their lives. Almost 70% of the women experienced frustration relating to their own talent development because of the demands of their personal lives. Given this ambivalence and frustration, we have much to accomplish as a society. We must ask what programs and strategies we can implement in our schools to ameliorate the societal effects of stereotyping. We must include parents in these programs and strategies, all of us attempting to work together to help expand career awareness. While many of these educators did work they considered to be important and meaningful, it was not often work they chose or in which they had a sincere interest.

As a society, we must offer an encouraging message to smart females: that ambition is not only an acceptable but also a desirable trait in females. A female model of productivity should include work that is personally exciting and stimulating beyond the work required to raise a family. Until we accomplish these goals, a negative societal message will continue to exist relating to the talent development, professional accomplishments, and the personal fulfillment of talented women.

CHAPTER NINE

~:~

OLDER TALENTED WOMEN WHO
ACHIEVED EMINENCE

*When my first wife was dying, I used to sit by her bed and I thought,
This is her true face. It was all hollowed and sharpened. In her youth
she'd been very pretty, but now I saw that her younger face had been
just a kind of rough draft. Old age was the completed form, the final
finished version she'd been aiming at from the start. The real thing at
last! I thought, and I can't tell you how that notion colored things for
me from then on. Attractive young people I saw on the street looked so
...temporary.*
—*Anne Tyler, Ladder of Years*

It's never too late to be what you might have been.
—*George Eliot*

Like most of the other women profiled in this study, determination and hard work characterize Claire Guardiani. President of a small, prominent liberal arts college in New England,
she is an intense and charismatic woman with a high energy level
and strong beliefs. A scholar in French language and literature,
Claire put her considerable energy into administration in a position at The University of Pennsylvania before being selected as
the president of her alma mater, a small highly selective private
college with a superlative reputation. At the time of our interview, she had been president for almost a decade and she had
made numerous changes at the college, improving its reputation,
financial standing, and national ranking. The college has tripled
its endowment under her presidency and embarked on a 22-
million-dollar building campaign. Since she has been president,
the salaries of faculty have risen while teaching loads have been
reduced. She has angered some of the faculty, while others rise
to her defense. Shared governance is a noble goal, but it is clear
that Claire makes most of the decisions at the college after lengthy

discussions with faculty, alumni, and a committed Board of Trustees.

While some college presidents call her a visionary, others call her impatient and a recent article about her in the major state newspaper labeled her a steamroller. As the female college president of her alma mater, she has determined a vision for her college that includes a continuous rise in the national rankings. Claire is an incredibly hard worker who gets up at 5:30 each morning to exercise and then is at her office each day by 7:30. Some of her days last 20 hours and she attributes her work ethic to the role modeling she experienced from her parents and grandparents. Both of her grandfathers were medical doctors, and her father was a West Point graduate who become a navy pilot and was shot down and captured during World War II. He later became a very successful businessman, and he had high expectations for all six of his children. Claire was the oldest child. Constant encouragement to achieve at higher and higher levels seems to have resulted in success for all of her siblings, who became doctors, teachers, engineers, and involved in other professions. Not to work at high levels all of the time is unthinkable to Claire, who has always dedicated her energy into every task she has undertaken. When she married, she worked hard at the marriage. When she had children, she worked hard at raising children, spending long hours with her son and daughter. She read to them, did science experiments, encouraged them, and had high expectations for them. She believes her children, who attended and graduated from Ivy League schools, are the most important work she and her husband have produced. She believes that nothing else in her life has been as significant or as rewarding as her children, who are currently in their twenties.

Claire knows that her work and ideas have been controversial, but she believes that controversy should exist when change is occurring. She also believes that if those who disagree with her feel strongly, they should fight back and continue to argue for their own beliefs. She scoffs at the idea that everyone should agree with her or like her and at the notion that those who are profoundly committed to ideals can be either passive or insist on being loved by everyone.

She believes that a major tenet of a small liberal arts college should be the obligation to provide service to those less fortunate, especially the poor, those whom most of society neglects, the schools that are not up to par, soup kitchens, shelters, and other countries which need our help the most. Accordingly, she has established internship programs at the college which are mandatory for all students, and she has been relentless in her encouragement of these internships that send students who are often brought up in privileged homes to locations in the poorest areas in the world: Mexico, India, China, and other areas. She believes in global responsibilities and indicated that "we are our brother's keepers," and so we exert extraordinary influence across the world. She also believes that many of the other small liberal arts colleges have abdicated their responsibilities in this regard. Too many of the Ivy League schools, she insists, have also ignored their responsibilities and instead are educating students whose major ambitions have to do with making money as opposed to improving society or the common good. In articles about her, other Ivy League presidents have called her the conscience of higher education.

Soon after reading Carolyn Heilbrun's 1988 book entitled *Writing a Woman's Life*, I began studying older women who had achieved eminence in their respective fields. In Heilbrun's analyses of women's biographies and autobiographies, she suggested that women may be incapable of writing their own stories because of their need to conform to what society says life should be rather than what life is. She also suggested that in their older age, women can take risks and use the freedom they have earned from fulfilling the needs of others " ... to make use of our security, our seniority, to take risks, to make noise, to be courageous, to become unpopular" (p. 131).

More recently, Friedan (1993) suggested that women grow older in a far more positive way than has been suggested by the popular press and that the later years may indeed be the most productive for women's development. A T-shirt recently given to me by one of my friends shares a similar sentiment: "These aren't hot flashes, they're just power surges." Anthropologists studying the Hadza hunter-gatherers of northern Tanzania reported that postmenopausal women are the serious breadwinners in that community. They work longer and harder hours out in the bushes and bring home the food. These findings certainly support my own work with talented women who achieved eminence after the age of 50. There are 37 million postmenopausal women in America already, and in another decade there will be 50 million. Research about this population of women seems critical for their development.

To understand the perspectives these women gained regarding their accomplishments and the cultural influences that affected their success, I studied older American women who gained eminence in their respective fields after the age of 50. Four sources were used in this research: (a) a questionnaire; (b) interviews which document perceptions of the women about their accomplishments; (c) primary source data including books, plays, articles, diaries, chapters written by the participants, or records, compact discs or recordings of their work; and (d) articles, chapters, dissertations, or interviews about the participants written by other researchers, journalists or writers.

The eighteen women in this study were between the ages of 51 and 92 and had each achieved recognition in a specific area of work, recognition being defined as either having books or articles written about them or receiving awards or special honors in their field. Each woman was either nominated by one or more persons such as university deans and presidents, journal editors, and others, or invited to participate because of major accomplishments documented by stories or articles in publications such as the *New York Times*, weekly news magazines, or journal articles. Each woman was recognized as a major contributor to her field, and several of these women had achieved the distinction of being a pioneer, or the first or one of the first in their respective fields, such as the first female forester in the country, one of the first female directors on Broadway, or one of the first successful female composers in the United States. Other participants in the study included a congresswoman, a famed poet, two authors, an artist, a mathematician, an entrepreneur, and three academics who conducted important research in diverse areas.

~: MARY HUNTER WOLF :~

Mary was born in Bakersfield, California in 1904 to a rancher and his wife, who died within two weeks of her daughter's birth. Within two years of his wife's death, Mary's father moved to Beverly Hills, an area that was still rural. Her father took a job in banking and remarried when Mary was four years old. Mary remembers her stepmother as someone who took good care of her, sewed dresses for her, and was always concerned and attentive to her needs. Mary had various interests as a child, but two major areas stand out: reading and debating. By the time she reached high school she had attended several different schools and had learned to love the theater, dance, and drama. Her father died when she was 12 years old, and Mary continued to live with her stepmother, although her father's sister, Mary Austin, became more involved in her life. Mary Austin was divorced, and her only child had been born mentally retarded and eventually died. An ardent feminist, Mary Austin was the author of numerous books, articles, and plays, including a play, *The Arrow Maker*, written in 1911, about the devaluation of women's talents. Austin also wrote *A Woman of Genius*, a novel which describes how traditional marriage can stifle women's creativity. According to Mary, her aunt was also interested in gifted students and wrote an unpublished book, "If I Had a Gifted Daughter." In addition to this manuscript, Austin also wrote *Greatness in Women* in 1923 and *A Woman Looks at Her World* in 1924.

It is apparent that Mary Austin had a significant impact on Mary Hunter's life, as did her childhood friend, Agnes de Mille, with whom she remained close friends throughout her lifetime. De Mille became Mary's friend when they attended the Hollywood School for Girls where they were involved in drama productions and theater games together. Agnes de Mille often asked Mary to accompany her to the theater where her father was a producer and director in the earliest Hollywood films, including *Four Horseman* with Rudolph Valentino. During summers while she was in high school, Mary worked in a Hollywood theater where Agnes de Mille's father produced films. After high school graduation, Mary left California to attend Wellesley, and Agnes de Mille remained to attend UCLA. They maintained close contact with each other for the remainder of their lives. Mary's father had hoped she would attend Wellesley, and although she followed his wishes, she was surprised at the "prep" school mentality she encountered at Wellesley and the lack of social consciousness of the student body in the 1920s. She continued to be involved in theater productions at Wellesley, but left college after her junior year because of health problems. She then spent the next few years with her aunt in New Mexico, where she lived, taught, and acted as a secretary for her aunt until moving to Chicago to finish her last year of college and begin her work in theater. She worked temporarily as a sales clerk, a radio talk show host, and eventually landed the part of "Marge" in *Easy Aces*, a radio comedy show that was almost as famous as the *Amos and Andy Show*.

Mary married a law student in Chicago and joined the socialist party, but moved to New York with the troupe involved in *Easy Aces*. This move occurred during the Great Depression, and while many of her friends were out of work, Mary was pleased to have a steady income. Her husband, who had just finished law school, remained in Chicago for about a year before joining Mary in New York. Unfortunately, as Mary's income continued to exceed her husband's, the marriage began to disintegrate, and eventually they divorced just as Mary's career began to peak. From 1938 to 1944, she directed six stage productions for the American Actors Company, a company she had helped found. From 1944 to 1955 she directed five Broadway productions and assisted with a sixth. She worked with Jerome Robbins on *Peter Pan* and helped nurture the careers of several choreographers and playwrights, including Tennessee Williams. She was one of the first group of nine female directors who directed but did not act in the United States. Interestingly, all of these female directors were single and childless.

At the height of her directing and theater career in New York City, two friends she had known from her years in Chicago reentered her life. The friends were married, lived in Connecticut, and had three young children. A tragedy left the husband widowed with a family to raise by himself. Mary recalls that considerable pressure was put upon her to marry her friend and become a stepmother to the three children who were aged eleven, eight and five. Mary left New York, moved to Connecticut, married her friend, and became a mother to the children who were, she recalls, in "terrible shape and needed me very much." She remembers this time as "fascinating, difficult, absorbing and interesting." Although her life changed drastically, she sought other creative challenges in the schools and the community, particularly working with disadvantaged youngsters in urban areas. Mary describes this period of her life as a time when she gave support and love to both her husband and the children that she came to love and who became an integral part of her life.

Her husband decided to end the marriage after ten years, when he fell in love with someone else. This decision devastated Mary, but what seemed even worse was that he also tried to end her relationship with the children, who by then regarded Mary as their mother. By this time, Mary had been away from the theater for so long that she could not simply return to Broadway as a director and producer. Additionally, as she empha-sized, she could not consider leaving Connecticut because her children were there and still needed her. When she was asked whether she missed the theater, she replied "Not especially," and when asked if she had any regrets about having left Broadway at the peak of her career, she looked surprised and exclaimed: "Re-grets? How could I have regrets? If I had not married him, I would not have had my children."

The impact of caring for three children and adjusting to a new husband at the age of fifty while simultaneously retiring from the theater presented Mary with many creative options. For the twenty-five years following her divorce, she remained close to her children and entered a new phase in her life, dedi-cating her talents and energies to the arts in her adopted state and becoming an educator and a political force for change in urban arts education. She was active in the Connecticut Com-mission on the Arts, eventually serving as its Chairperson. She was a producer for the American Shakespeare Festival Theater (ASFT) for which she developed education outreach programs for schools. She started an innovative counseling program which later became a model program in the country, using theater tech-niques with students who were economically disadvantaged. She also kept many of her New York connections, including her re-lationships with Agnes de Mille, Jerome Robbins, and many other actors, choreographers, directors, producers, and others associated with the theater. She moved to New Haven, which provided her easier access to New York City, and she embarked upon new challenges including starting innovative theater pro-grams at ASFT and for the New Haven Public Schools.

Her later interests involved starting programs for talented students in the arts and developing identification techniques for use with potentially talented students in drama. The schedule she kept during her eighties would have exhausted most teen-agers, and her list of commitments and various theatrical in-volvement is too long to be included in this chapter. In her late

80s she packed her bags, sold most of her furniture, and moved to Anchorage, Alaska with her youngest stepson and his family. She lived there for five years and became active in amateur theater, directing her last play when she turned 90. She returned to New Haven when she was 92, renewed many friendships, and moved into an assisted living facility for the elderly as her health began to decline. In our last interview, she was alert, active, and discussed a number of projects and work with which she was involved, including an attempt to have two "lost" O'Neill manuscripts, which had never been performed in the theater, produced by a local company.

When asked to discuss the creative cycles of her life, she paused and thought for a long period of time, and then held up her gracefully expressive hands which were covered with delicate webs of wrinkles and veins. She smiled and said, "I've given this a great deal of thought recently. I believe that women's creativity evolves in a different pattern than men's. Women spend their lives moving from one creative act to another and they can find both outlets and satisfaction from the creative expression of many different outlets." She then spread her hands and wove them in and out several times to illustrate the various creative acts some women undertake. "Men, on the other hand," she continued, "see an end goal and move toward the pursuit of that creative goal." To illustrate that point, she moved her hands in a straight upward path to a high point above her face and stopped. "That is why men are able to achieve goals and fame more quickly than women. But I think," she added, "that women have a richer creative journey, find joy in the diversity of their creative acts, and in the end, enjoy the creative process so much more."

❧ FRANCELIA BUTLER ❧

Francelia was slightly over 80 when I began interviewing her, with skin as delicate as porcelain and snowy white hair that she wears on top of her head in a network of curls. She is a wonderful storyteller who has a quick laugh and a determination that is evident in the first few minutes after meeting her. Her storytelling skills were obvious during one of our interviews, as she proudly displayed a photograph taken of Walter Cronkite and her during the 100th anniversary of the *International Herald Tribune* in Paris. The tale of how she and Cronkite started to talk and how he eventually told her how envious he was of her experiences in working for the newspaper in Paris immediately before World War II lasted almost two hours.

She was the oldest of four children born to a mother who was a Latin teacher and a father who was superintendent of schools. She spoke at great length about her parents, who were the subjects of a novel that she wrote. She clearly has ambivalent feelings about her mother, whom she describes as both cruel and kind. She reported that her parents abused both her and her siblings, and she recounted numerous scenes of parental neglect and cruelty both in interviews and in her novel. She remembers that her parents would tie her four- year-old sister naked to a post in the cellar and her mother would watch, laughing, while her father beat her with a rubber hose for the slightest infraction. Her younger sister became an alcoholic who committed suicide at 43; however, Francelia and her brothers seem to have survived their childhood abuse and excelled in their professional careers.

Francelia attended a private university lab school because her mother did not have a great deal of confidence in the public school system in which she taught. There was never a question in her parents' mind that she would attend college. At Oberlin, she majored in Latin and Greek and graduated at the height of the Depression. She ran away immediately following graduation because her parents had learned she was having an affair with her debate coach, who was married and had three children. She then held a series of low-paying jobs and barely made enough money to support herself before becoming the publicity director for the Raleigh Hotel in Washington D.C. Francelia was contacted by alumni at Oberlin and asked to arrange an alumni dinner at the hotel. Oberlin was the first college in the country to admit African Americans on an equal basis as white people and Francelia was determined that these alumni should also be invited to the event. She arranged to hold it in the basement of the hotel and conceived an elaborate plan to have guests enter the hotel through the back entrances. An older African American gentleman, however, misunderstood the directions, entered through the front lobby, and asked a white elevator operator to take him to the basement. The elevator operator reported the incident, and it created quite a scandal in the "whites only" hotel. Francelia was fired and according to her, "blacklisted" in Washington D. C. She was broke and had no chance of employment.

Seeing little future for herself in the area, she asked a friend to find her a place on a small ship headed for Europe, and she arrived in Paris just before the start of World War II. She had little money, no job prospects, and no place to live. Displaying her characteristic courage and nerve, she applied for a job at the *International Herald Tribune* and met her future husband, who worked as a copy editor. Posing as a drama critic, she was given the opportunity to review a new play and did so, composing an amateurish effort. The copy editor read her review and said, she recalled with a smile, "You have never written a review in your life, but you sure look as if you need work. Come back at six o'clock, and I'll try to teach you enough to help you get by in this job. If you watch what I do, maybe you will learn." She was a quick study and got the job, earning $5.00 a week and living at the YWCA.

She remembers this period of her life as very exciting. She lived in Paris for almost four years and eventually married the copy editor, a World War I Marine who had been injured when, at the age of eighteen, he was sprayed with mustard gas in the battle of Argonne. Francelia describes her years in France as exhilarating and remembers the day the American government put a notice in the *International Herald Tribune* for all U.S. citizens to leave Paris as soon as possible. She and her husband fled Paris on a refugee ship and arrived in New York where they got a small apartment. Her husband continued his work in journalism, and she took care of her baby daughter, who was born soon after their return to the states.

While her husband was alive, she did not continue her writing or pursue her career. "The chauvinism of males dictated that he would be the writer. He gave me the impression that I couldn't write—that is, until his death." Due to the injuries he had sustained in World War I, her husband died when their daughter was eight years old:

> Just before he died, he told me that I really could write and that I should go ahead and try. At Arlington Cemetery, where he was buried with full military honors, purple heart and all, I remember his funeral being the saddest day of my life. And yet, I also remember as his coffin was being lowered into the ground that I felt a sense of release, a certain feeling of release that now I could do what I wanted to do. You see, I had taken care of him for three years and he was so terribly ill.

After her husband's death she stayed in Virginia, where she held different jobs, eventually writing her first book about the history of cancer. The book sold well, according to Francelia, and she continued to write and do different types of work, including public relations work for the private school her daughter attended. Francelia's daughter entered college at the age of fifteen having skipped three grades because of her abilities. When her daughter began her senior year at William and Mary, she eloped with the man she was dating. On that day, Francelia decided to return to graduate school. She attended Georgetown for her Master's degree and then received two small fellowships that enabled her to attend The University of Virginia to pursue her Ph.D. in Renaissance literature.

After completing her degree, she worked as an assistant professor in the South but found the prejudice against female English professors to be stifling. She decided to try a larger eastern university, where she applied for a position exactly twenty-five years after the death of her husband. In her interview, the Chairman of the English department shook his head at her and said, "We have a rule in academia: fat, fifty, female, finished! And, you qualify in all respects. However, we are saddled with a subject that the School of Education has dumped on us and we must teach. If you are willing to teach Children's Literature, we may be able to give you a job." Francelia recalls that she responded, "But I don't know anything about that; I have two books out on the Renaissance already and that is what I want to teach." The Chairman returned, "the Renaissance is a field for young men."

As Francelia was something of a rebel or a "trickster," as she calls herself, she reluctantly accepted the position and with it, the assignment of Children's Literature. She set out to make the course the most popular on campus. Within two years, she had built the enrollment from 30 to 300 students and established a campuswide, then statewide, then regional, and finally a national reputation for herself. She published widely, continued to work on the Renaissance, wrote scholarly papers, poetry, fiction, and several books. One of her novels did quite well in the popular press and was favorably reviewed by the *New York Times*. Her list of publications is extensive and broad; she has published in *The Antioch Review, The New York Times Magazine, The New York Times, Shakespeare Quarterly, The Virginia Quarterly Review*, and many other highly regarded journals. Her books have been published by major publishers and her novel on child abuse is in its third printing. Her proudest accomplishment, she acknowledged in one interview, was the establishment of a scholarly journal in the area of Children's Literature, which is still published. Francelia became a feminist, she explained, after years of watching women being held back by males in academia, and she continues to protest the male-dominated system in her publications and frequent interviews with the press. Although she retired from her university position a few years ago when she learned she had cancer, Francelia has received numerous awards, honorary degrees, and prizes and continues to work.

As mentioned earlier, these women and those profiled in other chapters incorporated specific characteristics of talent, including above average ability and/or special talents, personality traits, environmental issues, and their belief in the perceived social importance of the use or manifestation of the talent. These factors resulted in a belief in self and a desire to contribute and enabled these talented women to actively develop their talents. Most also exhibited certain personality traits, including determination, motivation, creativity and patience, and the ability to take, and in some cases, thrive on risks. Every subject clearly exhibited determination throughout most of her life. The ability to strive for success and to continue to work hard, either with or without the love and support of one's family and/or partner, was evident in most cases.

Patience was also a characteristic of all the older women I studied. Some waited years to have the opportunity to invest considerable blocks of time in the development of their own talent, and some worked steadily over the years, only to be acknowledged for their specific talents later in life. Jeanne Kirkpatrick explained her success in her older years: "I never could have handled the job I am doing now when my children were growing up." A congresswoman who waited until her youngest daughter was ready for college, a composer who worked year after year to improve her art form, and the forester who sought work in her own field decade after decade all displayed this patience with the development of their own talent.

Another trait displayed by most of the talented women and *all* of the older eminent women was their willingness to take risks and to attempt tasks that others may not have the courage to pursue. How many women who are almost 50 years old and who are not financially secure would choose to return to graduate school to pursue a Ph.D. in Renaissance literature?

The most diverse factors that emerged in the talent manifestation of the women in this study were the environmental issues that contributed to or detracted from their success. Some came from upper middle class families, some were born into poor families. Most had nurturing families, but some had families who were abusive or distant. Almost all had siblings and about half were the first born. Most married or had long-term relationships and almost all of those who married had children.

A few delayed placing primary emphasis on their career because their children needed them, and some labored constantly on their journey to accomplishment. Most found some way to do both. The congresswoman I studied kept up a steady record of community, civic, and other responsibilities that all contributed to an eventual overwhelming victory in her election bid to the House of Representatives. However, it is important to note that she did not initially realize how qualified she had become to run for public office until she sought help from her college career office. That help was vital to her:

> I don't know how I got the idea that I should go back to the career office at my college. Somebody suggested it to me when I applied to law school and didn't get in because I applied late. You see, I didn't know what to do with my life so I applied to law school and school for Social Work. My career office helped me to arrange all of the volunteer stuff I had done and to put it into professional terms. Then I began to see that all of the programs that I'd developed and marketed, all of the leadership that I'd provided in the PTA to get parents more involved, and all of the other stuff that I'd done could be marketed in professional terms. And I can remember saying, 'Look at all the things I've done.' The career office counselor helped me re-

> *alize that all of the things I've done fit into the real
> world of business and after that, I said I'm not going
> to do volunteer work any more, I'm not going to re-
> peat this phase of my life. I'm going to move forward.*

While this woman accomplished much on her own, the help she sought was integral to her success. This help was not due to chance; rather, she, like most participants in this study, actively sought support, help, further education, more knowledge, and increasing levels of sophistication in her work.

PERCEIVED SOCIAL IMPORTANCE OF TALENT MANIFESTATION

Most of the older eminent women had gained throughout their lives a strong desire to use their talents in ways that were personally satisfying to them and which would benefit society. They did not simply have a drive to succeed, but rather they also defined success in their own unique, feminist way. The congresswoman in this study had been asked to be the first woman in her geographic area to chair the United Way Fund Drive and to be the first president of The League of Women Voters. However, she wanted to take a different path than did most women who have successfully raised three children and are married to doctors. She had personal ambitions about doing what she really wanted to do with her life and consciously decided that volunteer work would no longer help her achieve her personal goals. Instead, she ran for Congress.

Each of these women developed, from a combination of factors, a belief in themselves and a desire to make a difference or a creative contribution. They all had high self-esteem and believed their self-concept and self-esteem came both from their own successes and from the love and support they received from family and friends. Each also wanted to contribute to make a positive difference in the world. For these women there was no choice—they were simply not satisfied with their lives unless they could actively develop their talents. Most of them, when asked, discussed friends and siblings who were just as smart or even smarter (if one uses school performance as the basis for assessment), but who were content to lead lives that did not involve the constant work and energy needed to develop their talents.

Why did these older talented women continue to strive? Why did they work so hard when their friends and colleagues were content to live different lives? Some of them explained eloquently that their talents evolved over many years and that they used their diverse life experiences as background and preparation for their future accomplishments. An award-winning children's writer included in this study waited until her five children were older and then she began to write, weaving all of her life experiences into her literary work, including her Hispanic heritage and the insights she gained as a mother. She believes that the years she spent taking care of her small children contributed to her tapestry of life experiences and led her to acquire the wisdom and understanding that enabled her to make contributions at a later time in her life. The essential question remains: Why did these women need to achieve, and why were they willing, indeed, why did they feel *obligated* to pursue their talents in an active way when so many equally talented women are content to use their talents differently? They felt obligated because they believed in themselves and wanted to develop their talents in an area of personal importance to them.

Lehman (1953), in his study of men in almost all fields of intellectual achievement, has shown that the most creative period for the quality of achievement is between 30 and 45 years. He also acknowledged, however, that one's quantity of productivity is often greater after the age of 40. The women in this study believe that they reached both the highest quality and quantity of intellectual development after the age of 50.

This finding suggests that for these women, a different pattern of peak creative accomplishment may occur in some fields at a later time in their lives than it does for men. However, differences also exist between productivity at 55 and productivity at 90. The oldest women in this study, those in their eighties and nineties, have slowed down considerably and miss the energy level they had when they were in their sixties and seventies. In fact, they often indicated that if the acquired wisdom of their eighties and nineties could be coupled with the energy they had at 70, they could do anything! Mihaly Csikszentmihalyi (1997), in an analysis of 91 creative individuals who had made creative contributions and who continued to be active in their work well into their sixties, found similar results. The individuals he interviewed were robust and involved and seemed to be happy and productive.

However, we must use caution must in generalizing the finding about a later pattern of peak creative accomplish for women across all fields. Sharon Bertsch McGrayne (1993), in a study of fourteen Nobel Prize women in science, clearly found a pattern of consistent work resulting in early discoveries for many of the scientists she profiled. The commonalities she found in her subjects differ in some ways from those found in the subjects in my study. McGrayne found that the women she studied adored science, had sympathetic and influential parents and relatives, strong religious values, a supportive man in their lives, and they had good luck and good timing . Of course, McGrayne could not interview the majority of the women profiled in her book, and, as Heilbrun (1988) pointed out, biographies and autobiographies do not always portray an accurate description of the female experience since women seem to consistently negate their own accomplishments. The older women I studied did not acknowledge the importance of luck and timing, but rather emphasized the results of their own hard work and active efforts to be successful.

As noted earlier, Simonton (1978) suggested several external factors that affect creative development, including a set of philosophical beliefs essential to the development of creative potential. But how does a woman acquire or develop this philosophical belief about her own right to create and use her talents in a society in which the overwhelming majority of leaders, artists, scientists, historians, and inventors are men? Gerda Lerner (1993), in *The Creation of Feminist Consciousness*, examines this question from an historical perspective. Noting the long history of extraordinary women traced in her book, she raises a similar concern about women with special talents:

> Their individual achievements are awesome and inspire respect, yet it must be noted that their individual effort could not lead to a collective advancement in consciousness. The women of talent existed, they struggled valiantly, they achieved and they were forgotten. The women coming after them had to start all over again, repeating the process." (p. 274)

Perhaps the women described in this chapter, who are able to achieve at higher levels now than at any time in our society, will break this cycle. And perhaps younger talented women, who struggle with decisions about relationships, having children, and pursuing their own talents, can gain some understanding from the women in this study. These women have demonstrated that talent development is a lifelong process that, for them, culminated later in life. And many of them, when asked, advise younger women to make peace with whatever decisions are necessary during their twenties and thirties, continue to develop, and realize that time is on their side.

PART THREE

~:~

SOLUTIONS &
RECOMMENDATIONS

CHAPTER TEN

⁓⁓

RECOMMENDATIONS FOR DEVELOPING TALENTS & GIFTS IN FEMALES

A finished person is a boring person.
—*Anna Quindlen*

A successful life for a man or for a woman seems to me to lie in the knowledge that one has developed to the limit the capacities with which one was endowed; that one has contributed something constructive to family and friends and to a home community; that one has brought happiness wherever it was possible; that one has earned one's way in the world, has kept some friends, and need not be ashamed to face oneself honestly.
—*Eleanor Roosevelt*

The recommendations in this chapter have emerged from my 25 years of working with gifted and talented girls and women across the lifespan while teaching in gifted programs and classrooms and at the University of Connecticut. Each has proven helpful with parents, teachers, and gifted and talented females of all ages. Parents and teachers working with gifted and talented girls and women should understand, however, that each individual has unique personality characteristics, environmental issues, interests, learning styles, and abilities.

RECOMMENDATION ONE: CHANGE PERCEPTIONS

❧ HELP CHANGE THE IMAGE THAT SOME GIRLS AND WOMEN HAVE OF THEMSELVES

One need not look very far to find how negative stereotypes influence females' self-perceptions. As Mary Catherine Bateson (1989) has indicated, women have experiences which consistently undermine their confidence and aspirations: "Most women today have grown up with mothers who, for all their care and labor, were regarded as having achieved little" (p. 28). Home, school and society abound with these stereotypes, and we all have a responsibility to help females realize that the internalization of stereotypes has hurt us all. Women who have provided devoted care to their children and worked to create homes filled with love, care, and attention have *not* achieved little. They may not have made choices that were best for themselves either. Rather, they simply may have been caught up in the expectations of the times in which they lived.

I remember a touching conversation with one of my favorite people, my great aunt Dorothy Barrett, who lived to be 96 years old and taught me a great deal about life. As I grew older, I realized how much I had learned from her. One of hundreds of conversations we had replays regularly in my mind. We were having lunch in her apartment, which was next door to the middle school in which I was teaching. I had returned to graduate school, had far too many commitments, and was tired and feeling overworked. After listening to me discuss these feelings for a few minutes, my aunt said quietly, "Oh, how I used to love my work. It broke my heart to have to quit."

"Why did you have to quit?" I asked.

"Well, my mother became very ill. It was breast cancer and very debilitating. The doctors had opened her up, and she never really healed after that. Bandages had to be changed and she was in pain. I had to take care of her. We couldn't have a stranger do what she needed. After she died, I wanted to go back to my office job. I was only in my early thirties, still unmarried and I enjoyed my job so much. But my father was home alone and someone needed to take care of the household."

"Couldn't you just hire someone?" I asked.

My great aunt smiled at me before she replied. "Sally, duty was a concept that we all were raised to understand and follow. It was my responsibility to take care of my father, to cook, and keep the house. It was the early 1900s. Women who were needed at home did not work out of the home. I never did again." She paused and smiled at me again. "How fortunate you are to be able to have the choice to work, my dear. Choices were so very limited when I was your age."

After that conversation, I don't think I ever complained to her again about being too busy at work. My great aunt took care of her mother until her death and lovingly cared for her father for over 35 more years, until his death at 96. Her life had great meaning and touched many in our family. I like to think that the time she spent caring for her father, as well as the time she spent with her family, contributed to the confidence that many in my family had in their abilities and in the success they have had in their careers.

❦ REALIZE THAT MANY WOMEN HAVE UNCONSCIOUSLY INTERNALIZED FEELINGS ABOUT THEIR OWN AND OTHER WOMEN'S ACCOMPLISHMENTS

Stephanie, one of my graduate students, listened to an evening lecture in a graduate class I taught on gender issues in which I discussed the impact of internalized views of women's accomplishments on other women's perceptions. She later told me that as she was walking to her car that evening, she reflected on what I had said. She told me she really believed that she was different, perhaps because she was younger, and she did not believe that she had internalized stereotypical beliefs about women. As she was driving home later that night, Stephanie had a flat tire. Because she was pregnant, she put on her emergency flashers and waited for help rather than try to change the tire herself. Twenty minutes later, a state trooper's car pulled up and she watched as the police officer walked over to her car window. Looking up, she noticed that the trooper was a woman; she later told me, "My very first thought was 'Oh Gosh, what good is she going to do?'" Within 20 minutes, Stephanie's tire was fixed and she was on her way home. She did not forget, however, about her own thoughts and continued to remember how she did indeed internalize negative or ambivalent thoughts about women and their different types of accomplishments. In her teaching, she faced some difficult realizations as she began to honestly consider her own prejudices. She understood she did have internalized views about young boys being better in math and science, and she also realized that she allowed the male students in her class to interrupt her while she remediated the same behavior from her female students.

In 1987, I wrote an article on gifted females subtitled "You Can't Change What You Don't Recognize." In too many situations, women do not recognize the obvious and subtle ways in which they demean their own accomplishments as well as those of other women. We must help gifted girls and women understand the ways in which subtle and not-so-subtle stereotypes and messages from home, school, and the environment in general affect them. One of my favorite cartoons depicts two women sitting at a table in a restaurant while a waiter looks down at them and says, "I'm sorry, we only serve men here." One of the women responds, "Great, bring us two!" Changing the images we have of ourselves and other women can be accomplished in many ways. We can teach ourselves, our students, and our children to look carefully for stereotyping and to examine their environment for instances in which women's accomplishments are undermined.

At a recent dinner party, my husband and I listened to a woman who looked at her husband after every statement she made and asked, "Isn't that right, John?" She seemed afraid to voice any opinion without getting permission from her husband. Other women I know glance surreptitiously at their partners after they speak, as if they need approval for merely having said something. What happens to the confidence of girls and women? It is obvious that women's talents will not be developed to their fullest if their self-confidence continues to erode.

❦ TEACH GIFTED GIRLS AND WOMEN TO QUESTION AND SPEAK OUT

Parents and anyone in contact with girls and women should encourage them to display their strengths and be strong, com-

petent, and proud of their accomplishments. In order to eliminate the Great Impostor Syndrome described earlier, females of
all ages need to learn to say "thank you" when complemented on
their successes and accomplishments. Parents, especially, need
to understand that talented girls must realize the link between
ability and success, and they should praise their daughters for
their ability, not just their effort. Girls and women need to learn
to speak out against what they believe is wrong and to question
issues and policies about which they have doubts. They should
learn to understand and handle some of their own problems. A
grade perceived as unfair in elementary or secondary should be
questioned by the girl, not the parent. Girls themselves, not
their parents, should resolve problems in school so that they gain
experience and confidence in resolving problems in life.

Renzulli (1978, 1986) has discussed the differences between
schoolhouse giftedness and creative productive giftedness, indicating that while we should nurture and develop both, individuals who make important creative accomplishments in the world
display creative productive giftedness, as opposed to schoolhouse
giftedness. All too often, parents and teachers encourage smart
girls to do well in school, be quiet and studious, and work to get
good grades in all content areas—in other words, develop schoolhouse giftedness. According to the gifted women I have studied, young girls who will make a difference in our society are
those who learn to speak out, challenge authority and have the
courage to create and produce new ideas and products. They
should begin this cycle in elementary and middle school and
parents and teachers should encourage these traits.

❧ IDENTIFY THE STRENGTHS AND INTERESTS OF GIRLS AND
WOMEN; SPEND TIME LEARNING MORE ABOUT AREAS OF
INTEREST

The congresswomen in my study of older women spent almost 20 years raising her children while being involved in both
local politics and volunteer efforts. She had so much trouble

identifying what she did well that she had to see an employment counselor at her alma mater to help her. Gifted females must learn to know themselves—to identify their strengths and interests and what is important for them to achieve. In her biography, the famous physicist Fay Ajzenberg-Selove (1994) paraphrased Hillel: "If you are not for yourself, who will be? And if not, when?" (p. 223). An equally strong argument can be made for having talented girls and women identify what they do not do well. As Lucille Ball once said, "I think knowing what you cannot do is more important than knowing what you can do." Many methods can be used to identify strengths and interests including formal assessment instruments such as the *Interest-A-Lyzer* (Renzulli, 1997), and informal methods such as conversations, interviews, and discussions in which girls and women are urged to think about what they like and what they are interested in pursuing.

Questions such as the following included in the *Interest-A-Lyzer* (Renzulli, 1997) can help to identify enjoyable areas: "If you could write a book, what would the subject be? If you had an hour or two of spare time, what would you choose to do? What kinds of activities do you like? If you could choose what you would learn about in school, what would be selected? Why?" An analysis of these responses and replies to other questions like them can help talented girls begin to think about their life's work. Encouraging them to reflect on their talents and style preferences, such as whether they like to do things alone or with others, will also help them to consider choices in work. Exposure to different types of careers can enable young girls to find challenging, fulfilling work in the future based on their interests and what they enjoy doing.

❧ Understand that Women's Ways of Leadership Should Emerge as Being Distinct and Different from Those of Men

Women must evolve new feminist models of leadership by being themselves and understanding styles that work best for them. Female leaders whom I have interviewed favored cooperation with colleagues over competition and believe in encouraging their subordinates rather than discouraging them or acting in a dictatorial way. As we still have far too few women in leadership positions in nearly every profession, we must work harder to create new female conceptions of leadership. These new conceptions must evolve from the characteristics of effective females as opposed to the characteristics of males which some women sometimes emulate after they have achieved success.

❧ Realize that Women Must Fully Share Home Responsibilities with Partners and Children

Roberta Katz, Netscape Communications' general counsel, refused to accept the burden of being a Supermom, which she defined as a full-time executive and full-time mother rolled into one: "I told my husband, 'I can't do two jobs with you doing only one. We each have to do one and a half.'" This statement should become a mantra for every working woman and parent. We must raise children, both males and females, who clearly expect to share household responsibilities equally, especially daily ones. When we accomplish this equality, Betty Friedans well-known statement "equality in work, without domestic equality, leave women doubly burdened" will no longer be applicable.

❧ Discuss the Negative Impact of Continued Emphasis on Appearance

Too many women are affected by the continued stress of worrying about appearance and weight as opposed to concentrating on their education, talents and character development. Encouraging gifted and talented women to be less concerned about appearance and more concerned about developing their talents will help as will the societal changes discussed earlier. Parents should raise and encourage girls who separate who they are and want to become from what they look like. Young and adult women must stop their obsession with weight and appearance and lobby for changes in media and television to present more realistic portrayals of women.

❧ Provide a Forum in Which Older Women can Discuss Their Experiences, Triumphs, and Failures and Younger Women Can Develop Plans for Their Future

In the *Ladies Home Journal* ("American Women," 1997) survey of 1,000 women discussed earlier, 60% said they wouldn't want their daughters to follow in their footsteps because they have regrets about their own life choices. Many of the women's regrets focused on marrying too young and not going to college despite having high potential. Enabling older women to discuss these types of decisions with younger women can be helpful in encouraging younger women to develop a plan of action for their lives—a plan essential for their talent development. Women who have been successful should share strategies they have used to create success. If a clear plan to finish college and graduate school and pursue a specific career is present, chances are increased that these women will achieve their goals.

❧ Discuss Issues about Work, Including the Pleasures Gained from Meaningful Work

We must also work to change the views women have internalized about themselves and work. A few years ago, one of my daughters became frustrated and angry with me because I could not attend a school function scheduled on an evening when I was to give a speech in another state. She looked at me and asked in anger, "Why don't you just quit your job?"

I looked at her in amazement and replied, "Quit my job? I don't consider what I do each day a job, Sara. I love my work, and I am happy that I have found work that makes me feel that I can make a difference." When she began to understand that I love my work, it was interesting to watch her reactions change to be much more positive about my career.

The working world is changing quickly and drastically. New careers are being created each month and some of them involve skills and talents that women could only have dreamed about a decade ago. Those of us who grew up in the 1950s did not really understand the types of choices we had then, and many of us believed that we would have one job or one career in our lives. Girls, at that time, were especially wrong in thinking that our choices were limited and that we would only work for part of our adult lives. The reality is that very few of us have had the opportunity to take time off to raise our families, and some of us didn't want to be forced to make that choice. Once we started working and found work we loved, the last thing that some of us ever considered was giving up our work.

The difference between simply having a job and finding meaningful work , however, is enormous, and helping gifted and talented girls explore the world of work can make a profound difference in their future. Talented young girls should learn that there are many connections between love and work. In my research, the happiest women I studied were those who had both meaningful work and people they loved in their lives. When I compared the women who worked outside their home to those who did not, those who worked outside their home were happier. What they had in common was their belief in themselves, the knowledge that their work made a difference, and joy in their accomplishments.

❦ Understand that While Work May Change, Most Girls Will Work Outside of the Home.

Futurists predict that most teenage girls will work for at least 45 years of their lifetime and have several different careers. If girls believe that in the future, many women will stay home and take care of their children on a full-time basis for many years, they are probably mistaken, unless circumstances change drastically in the next two or three decades. Some parents who have children may want to take care of them full-time for a few years after they are born. If they do, society should support their choice. However, many young parents will not be able to stay at home with their children because they will need to support themselves and their families financially. Many will not want to stop working for a block of time because of the profound effect this decision may have on their careers. These realities point to the importance of excellent child care in the future, as well as the role government both at the national and local level should play in formulating national childcare policies and establishing a federal initiative on safe, affordable, high-quality day care centers in our country.

Changes in the work force are happening at a faster rate than ever before in our nation's history, and it is clear that we will not stay in the same positions for most of our lives, as did many of our parents and grandparents. If someone initially works at something she or he does not like, it is not a lifelong mistake. Changes are more possible now than ever. Young women should learn how to plan for future careers that may change and spend time planning with parents and teachers. Planning is essential, as is finding the right college or program to help learn necessary skills. Parents and educators should encourage young women to take as many math, computer, and science courses as possible in order to have more options in the future. They should understand that as they learn more about themselves and their interests and talents, they may change careers several times during their lifetime.

❦ CONSIDER PERSONAL DEFINITIONS OF SUCCESS

Wally Lamb, a well-known author and creative writing teacher, spent nine years working on his first novel, *She's Come Undone*. Lamb achieved high levels of success, as his book made the *New York Times Bestseller List*, and he was on the *David Letterman Show* and the pages of *People* and *Glamour*. When Oprah picked his book for her monthly book club, sales skyrocketed. Recently, Lamb gave a speech in which he discussed success, explaining that "Success isn't measured in limo rides or stock portfolios or book sales or brushes with celebrity.... Success grows from love and from the joy and the terror and the challenge of worthwhile work. It's the process, not the product. The unglamorous journey, not the flashy arrival."

Having potential can be a real dilemma because we never really know when we have realized our potential, and working to be a success is illusory at best. We should encourage gifted females to choose their own road to success by finding what they love to learn about and doing it. A futurist once said that we all have three visions for the future: one that is possible, one that is probable and one that is preferable. Women should be urged to find future work that is preferable, for my research has found that preferable work is what brings both fulfillment and joy.

❦ ENCOURAGE PERSONALITY CHARACTERISTICS SUCH AS INDEPENDENCE, SMART RISK-TAKING, AND SELF-CONFIDENCE

"Remember," said Lily Tomlin, "we're all in this alone." Independence in girls in both learning and affective issues guarantees more options. We all want our children to love us and want to spend time with us. However, we also need to understand that we must raise gifted females to be independent. Young girls must learn to pursue opportunities without parental support, to ask questions, plan their own learning, and not be afraid to pursue their dreams and further their own knowledge in an independent and self-directed manner. In most of the adult gifted females I studied, independence was one of the first characteristics which enabled these women to have the courage to pursue their own ideas, understand their own ambitions, and have the strength of character necessary to overcome the conditions which threatened to interfere with their aspirations.

In the lives of women of extremely high levels of productivity, certain traits are repeatedly mentioned; those included in every case study are risk taking and self-confidence. Pioneering astronomer Margaret Geller, professor of astronomy at Harvard and winner of a MacArthur foundation genius award, explained:

> If you don't take any risks, you'll never do anything having real impact. Never. That's very hard to learn because people always advise you to take the more secure job position, for example. It's not good advice because security doesn't really matter. If you're going to do creative things, you have to be secure in the idea that you can create. That's the only kind of security that actually matters. If you don't have that you don't have anything. (Ames, 1997, p. 83).

Geller believes risk taking is enormously important, as is having a deep internal confidence. Some people develop confidence when they are young, but for others confidence can take a much longer time to develop. Confidence in oneself begins in childhood, and its absence can thwart many ambitions. My research with gifted females has repeatedly indicated the importance of smart risk-taking, self-confidence, belief in self, and self-discipline—all traits that parents and teachers should strive to develop in all children.

Recommendation Two: Re-educate Society

❧ Make Sweeping Curricular Changes in All Content Areas in School and at Home

Equality in schools has improved greatly since the passage of federal legislation ensuring gender equity in our schools, but we still have a long way to go. Our children still rarely study women in history or science, and we still see an absence of female contributors and role models in every content area. Girls continue to read more books about male characters at home and in school. Parents still read nursery rhymes and fairy tales that reinforce outmoded versions of females. Reading different types of books and rhymes to young girls can begin to make a difference, including two I taught my daughters:

> Jack and Jill went up the hill to fetch a pail of water.
> Jack fell down and broke his crown, and . . . Jill as-
> sumed the throne.
>
> And he did whatever it is that handsome princes
> do while she went back to school, got her doctorate,
> and pursued important work, and they lived happily
> ever after.

Researchers and practitioners in the field of curriculum development and programming options for gifted students have
generally paid little attention to theory development or research
regarding gifted females. Consider, for example, the most common goal of gifted programs and gifted curriculum—the development of critical thinking skills. Lists of specific critical thinking skills found in curricular documents reveal a set of reasoning skills which are predominantly based on pure "logical reasoning" or male orientations to what is fact, what is logical reasoning and what is justifiable conclusion. Some researchers
(Belenky, Clinchy, Goldberger, & Tarule, 1986) agree:

> Nowhere is the pattern of using male experience
> to divine the human experience seen more clearly
> than in the model of intellectual development. The
> mental processes that are involved in considering
> the abstract and the impersonal have been labeled
> 'thinking' and are attributed primarily to men
> while those that deal with personal and interper-
> sonal fall under the rubric of 'emotions' and are
> largely relegated to women" (p. 71).

We need to realize that current curricula may be based on
the assumption that giftedness is associated with certain skills
developed from research on gifted males, not gifted females.
These are not important skills, but where is there room for
Women's Ways of Knowing (Belenky, Clinchy, Goldberger, & Tarule,
1986) in classroom curricula? Where is there even a suggestion
that the patterns of women's thinking are an important concern

or one that merits serious research?

There is an absence of serious examination of programming considerations given to the developmental differences between boys and girls and to learning conditions which favor female achievement. Some research has pointed out that young girls do better in math if they have a female teacher and are in predominantly female classes. As indicated earlier, contradictory research shows a need for further studies to address these issues, and public schools have made few attempts for change. In one study of the achievement of females in single-sex and coeducational schools (Lee & Bryk, 1986), females in single-sex schools demonstrated greater gain than females in coeducational schools. What have we done to explore the implications of these findings on the achievement of gifted girls?

Making a greater, systematic impact on stereotyping of literàture and textbooks will only be accomplished when we both find and create opportunities to infuse women's contributions throughout the entire curriculum of our schools. Ask a young girl how many women artists she can name or how many females she can identify who have made great contributions in science or history in the United States. Her answers, or lack thereof, will create a clearer picture of the problems we face in providing female role models in school and home. Parents and teachers need to provide books, videotapes, and other resources to address this deficit (see Chapter 11).

❧ Lobby for Media and Television Changes

Some would argue that we have come a long way from the television days of "Dukes of Hazzard" and "I Dream of Jeannie." However, we need only watch contemporary shows such as "Bay Watch," "Melrose Place," and Saturday morning cartoon shows to remember how far we still have to go. It is still difficult to find credible female heroines or role models for young girls on television. Parents should monitor television and commercial watching, discuss stereotyping with sons and daughters, and point out obvious examples of stereotyping in both television and in reading materials. Print media, as noted earlier, provides a multitude of stereotypical experiences for all young people. Both the magazines and many popular book series provide negative stereotypes of women and young girls. Fortunately, many excellent resources (see Chapter 11) are also available to help provide positive role models. Parents, schools, and librarians should purchase these resources and use them so that all young people become initially aware of them and able to use and benefit from them independently.

✿ Provide More Awareness Programs for Both Males and Females.

A representative number of programs for providing science opportunities, role modeling experiences, and career expansions are profiled and included in Chapter 11. Several of these are particularly beneficial to talented young women, providing excellent experiences in science, math, literature, and the social sciences. Programs should provide talented girls and women with the opportunities they need to gain awareness of the environmental issues they will face. Women also must learn that if the environment is not right, they should feel confident enough to try to change it. Fay Ajzenberg-Selove (1994) recommends that young future female scientists not accept admission to graduate departments which do not have at least two women faculty members, preferably tenured, and several female graduate students. She has found, as have several of her female colleagues, that a woman is less likely to succeed if these support systems are not present:

> Science department heads must also tell male teaching assistants and male graduate students that civility and respect toward women students is expected, and that their demonstrated absence is cause for dismissal. This may be particularly important with foreign male students

from male-dominated societies. In some science departments, the majority of graduate students are foreign. (p. 221)

Schools and other concerned adults should also provide programs and resources to help boys understand that stereotyping can have a negative impact on their dreams and aspirations as well as their ability to help nurture and encourage the dreams and aspirations of their mothers, wives, sisters, and daughters.

❦ Carefully Consider Encouraging Girls to Participate in Single-sex Classes, Clubs, and Activities and Attend Girls' Schools and Women's Colleges.

When Oberlin college was first established by a group of men in Ohio, they considered their goal to be enabling a group of smart young men to earn their education by doing farm labor for tuition waivers. Later they remembered that someone needs to do the cooking, cleaning, and laundry and decided to admit women to Oberlin to accomplish these tasks. Women's classes were not scheduled on Monday, a day when all female students at Oberlin did laundry, mending, and cleaning for the male students at Oberlin to whom they were assigned. I was told this story in 1968 when I visited one of a number of women's colleges to which I had applied for admission. I attended an excellent women's college, Chatham College, in Pittsburgh.

My own experiences and research support the notion of talented girls attending women's colleges and also becoming involved in single-sex opportunities whenever possible before their college years. In girl's schools, 80% of girls take four years of science and math as compared with the national average of two years in a coed environment. Elizabeth Tidball (1973), a George Washington University researcher whose name is synonymous with research about single-sex education, found that graduates of women's colleges did better than female graduates of coed colleges in terms of test scores, graduate school admissions, number of earned doctorates, salaries, and personal satisfaction. Tidball also found that one-third of the female board members of Fortune 1000 companies are graduates of women's colleges, even though those women colleges contribute less than 4% of the total college graduates. Forty-three percent of the math doctorates and 50% of engineering doctorates earned by female liberal arts college students are awarded to graduates of Barnard, Bryn Mawr, Mount Holyoke, Smith, or Wellesley, all women's colleges. Tidball demonstrated a statistically significant, positive correlation between the number of women students who go to graduate school, objectively determined career, or intellectual accomplishment, and the number of women faculty present in their environments when they were students. She determined that women faculty are important to women students in all kinds of settings. Tidball also found that women faculty at all types of institutions report greater concern for women-related issues than do male faculty. She believed that the smaller proportion of women faculty present in most coeducational institutions suggest that it may be difficult for women's voices to be heard and have a positive influence on the institutional climate for women.

Tidball (1980) raised provocative and fascinating questions about talented women who attend women's colleges. She determined that the proportion of accomplished women who graduate from coeducational institutions is far smaller than is warranted according to the quantities of students who entered and those who graduate. She has further found that the brightest and most motivated women do not necessarily gravitate disproportionately to women's colleges. In one study of career accomplished women, the most selective coeducational institutions were less likely to be represented by their female graduates in *Who's Who of American Women* than less selective women's colleges. She believes that the problem is related to a lower climate of expectation for women at many coeducational colleges and universities.

"Separated by Sex" (AAUW, 1998) raises questions about

the achievement of girls in single-sex schools. After reviewing dozens of studies on single-sex education, the AAUW team summarized research which shows increases in achievement in some single-sex schools and classes and no increases in others. Their analysis of current research indicates the following: evidence is mixed regarding whether single-sex education works, the components of a good education are difficult to identify, some single-sex educational programs produce positive results, the long-term impact of these programs is unknown, and sexism can be found in any learning environment. Some of the differences occurring in programs may be explained by the time periods in which the studies were conducted (in more recent studies the achievement advantages are lessened) or the area in which the studies are conducted (as societal attitudes in certain cultures interact with achievement). The new AAUW (1998) study raises provocative questions while summarizing current research about single-sex classes: Something about single-sex classes makes them preferable to coed classes by many girls; single-sex classes can be alternately empowering (because they are a safe place for learning or discussion) or oppressing (because they may reinforce sex stereotypes); single-sex classes have effects on other classrooms in coed schools.

This current review of research (AAUW, 1998) indicates that girls in single-sex schools may not show increased improvement in academic skills, although they do seem to show both increased confidence and positive attitudes about math and science. This new study may have elucidated the most important finding regarding single-sex education. Achievement gains may be less important than attitudinal changes.

A variety of studies conducted at the elementary and secondary school level indicate some academic advantages for girls attending single-sex schools (Lee & Bryk, 1986; Marsh, 1989; Riordan, 1985; 1990). Other comprehensive studies (Lee, 1997) suggest, however, that while female classes in all girl's schools were more equitable regarding gender, they were not as academically rigorous. This finding is, of course, problematic for gifted girls. These mixed results indicate that the right environment combined with both academic challenge and personal and environmental support ultimately makes the difference. New research must focus on investigating not simply achievement, but also the development of leadership skills and career plans in girls and women.

Writing about the benefits of her single-sex education at Wellesley, Susan Estrich, a professor of law and political science at the University of Southern California, recalled a conversation she once had with a Harvard Law Professor. At Harvard, she explained, men vastly outnumbered women, and sexism was the rule. After one male professor told her that women didn't do very well at Harvard Law, she commented, "I laughed and decided to prove he was wrong. That's a Wellesley education."

Jill ker Conway (1994), writing in her second autobiographical book *True North*, describes her first impressions when she visited Smith College for an interview for the presidency of the college which she later assumed:

> A campus ablaze with crocus, daffodils, scilla, and rich strawberry and cream magnolias. Brighter than the spring flowers were the faces of the young women I saw everywhere. I could spend months at a time at the University of Toronto without ever hearing a female voice raised. Here the women were rowdy, physically freewheeling, joshing one another loudly, their laughter deep-belly laughter, not propitiatory giggles. The muddy afternoon games on the playing fields produced full-throated barracking. I was entranced (p. 244).

She further described her tour of the campus, given by an undergraduate student who planned to major in economics, but who also had interests in religion and philosophy and who was considering choosing a double major. The entire environment caused ker Conway (1994) to realize that "this was a real alternative society, a place of true female sociability, where women ran things for themselves." (p. 244). And when the trustees and faculty worried about whether Smith could survive as a women's college, she remembers her eloquent argument for all-female education:

> One had only to explain the historical trends which had confined middle-class women to domesticity, unravel the ambiguous motivations which inspired coeducation, push people to think whether the classroom experience for young women and young men was really the same, and point to the outcomes in the careers of graduates from women's colleges. In any event, one could also point out that women's colleges were the only truly coeducational ones so far as faculty were concerned. It was the Harvards and Yales which were single-sex institutions in that dimension" (p. 245).

Ker Conway (1994) cited a letter written to a friend by an early student at Mount Holyoke College. In the letter, the young woman wrote that Miss Lyon wanted to produce hard marble women, not soft marble, which was easy to shape but quickly crumbled before the forces of the elements. Hard marble was more difficult to shape, but it could take a brilliant polish which would last and was impervious to wind and weather:

> The gripping image came from the cemeteries of New England, places everyone visited. The young women who hung on her [Miss Lyon's] words would have known how one had to brush the moss and lichens away from soft marble to read the fading inscription, and how the polished headstones retained their luster, and their message, undimmed. The luster and the imperviousness to external circumstances were

dynamizing images for women's self-directing will" (p. 237).

Mary Lyon, the founder of Mount Holyoke, wanted to educate women about their intellectual and moral lives. Jill ker Conway believed that Lyon's initiatives were aimed at the women's capacity for future action, for a purpose in life that went beyond marriage and domesticity. Opportunities for single-sex classes and for girls to become involved with other girls in Girl Scouts, girls' clubs, or after-school science classes can enable parents and teachers to help girls understand the necessity of having a purpose and a dream in life as well as a plan to realize that purpose.

❧ ENCOURAGE GIRLS TO BE ACTIVELY INVOLVED IN SPORTS, ATHLETICS, AND ACADEMIC COMPETITIONS

My research with gifted females in high school strongly suggests the importance of athletics in a number of areas. The majority of the high achieving students I studied were involved in athletics, even if they were not particularly athletic themselves. Some served as managers, others as trainers or scorekeepers, but all of the girls participated in athletics after school. Most participated in at least two or three sports during the time that they were in high school. They learned valuable lessons, in particular, that it was all right to lose. Losing teaches talented females to realize there will be another game. As Maureen O'Connor, the mayor of San Diego, explained:

> The thing that helped me most in political defeat was competitive sport. If you compete in a race and swim well but lose, you're satisfied that you did everything possible and you try again. In 1983, I ran a good race, but I lost by about 2 percent of the vote. I knew there would be another time and that I would like to run again. As it turned out, it happened.

Marian Wright Edelman concurs, stating "failure is just another way to learn how to do something right." My research with high achieving gifted girls in high school indicated that high school athletics and extracurricular activities were of critical importance to achievement in this population for several reasons. First, it taught girls that they could take risks, lose, and still survive. Second, it provided them with a peer group of other active high energy girls, many of whom were committed to achievement both in school and in sports. Thirty years ago, only one in 27 girls played high school sports; today that number is one in three. In 1972, the year in which Title IX was passed, approximately 4% of girls in high school in the United States participated in interscholastic sports. According to a study done by the National Federation of State High School Associations, in 1994-95, high school participation for girls was 39% to 61% for boys, In the NCAA, in 1993-94, female participation was at 36% (up from 29% in 1992) as compared to 64% for males (Whittaker, 1997). Unfortunately, researchers estimate that boys still participate at almost twice the rate of girls, and Isaac and Shafer (1989) report that the percentage of women coaching secondary school teams has decreased since 1972.

Competition in other areas is also consistently mentioned in autobiographies and biographies of women of accomplishment as being something young girls should be exposed to in their formative years. Consider the thoughtful comments of nuclear physicist Fay Ajzenberg-Selove (1994), whose career was interwoven with incidents of discrimination as well as successes:

> Boys and young men are traditionally and repeatedly placed in competitive situations, and they learn to be judged individually, as well as in groups of teams. Fewer young women have this opportunity. Competition, both intellectual and athletic, prepares young people for real life. It is good when a young person learns repeatedly to try hard and both to lose and to win with a measure of grace, and some equanimity. One does not help young women if one

> shields them from competition; one makes
> them less able to achieve. (p. 220)

Some theorists indicate that gifted girls prefer noncompetitive environments in which cooperative learning is used. But as indicated earlier, some talented girls also enjoy competition (Hernandez Garduño, 1997; Gavin, 1996), and since competition exists in the world outside of school, it seems to make sense that we expose girls to situations in which they learn to be active, competitive, and sometimes victorious.

❦ Encourage Gifted and Talented Females to Participate Fully in Extracurricular Activities While in School and in Clubs and Associations Which Support Their Talent Development

In the three-year research study that my colleagues and I conducted with gifted high school students who either achieved or underachieved, one of the major factors associated with achievement was the positive use of time and student involvement in sports and in extracurricular activities of all types (Reis, Hébert, Diaz, Maxfield, & Ratley, 1995). The differences were obvious, as all of the achievers were involved in clubs and extracurricular activities. Clubs such as Latin Club, Chess Club, National Honor Society, and Russian Club (in which students worked for three years to save money for a trip to Russia) were critical in teaching these young women how to accomplish tasks, how to use time wisely, and how to be young leaders. These clubs and activities provided opportunities for many types of interactions, such as interaction with adults who could support their goals in a small group setting. Second, the clubs enabled them to spend time with other students who were involved in pursuing intense interest areas and working toward positive action. These peers also became support systems for other students who wanted to achieve.

Participation in programs such as Girl Scouts also seem to make a difference to talented girls. In a 1991 National Outcomes Study of the Girl Scouts that included over 5,000 Girl Scouts and a nonmember control group, the benefits of this organization appeared clear (Girl Scouts of the United States, 1991). Overall, when Girl Scouts were compared to nonmembers, they reported significantly greater opportunities to achieve most in self-reliance, self-competence, social skills, respect for others, feelings of belonging, concern for the community, leadership, values and decision making. Other research on Girl Scouts has indicated that when girls experience these outcomes, they are less likely to make choices that will hurt their physical health and more likely to make choices which promote healthy development (Girl Scouts of the United States, 1997).

In a study of the influence of scouting on American women of distinction, 64% of a random sample of American women of accomplishment had participated in Girls Scouts as compared to 42% of a random sample of all American women. The women of distinction indicated that Girls Scouts had provided a positive influence in their lives, and 72% made a firm connection between their later success and their Scout experiences. The longer they stayed in scouting, the more profound and lasting the impact seemed to be, as 91% of the women with five years or more of Scouting experience believed that their self-confidence was enhanced by scouting. Belonging to Girl Scouts provided these women of distinction with the kinds of experiences that help women attain success, enabling them to learn how to express themselves and providing them with leadership opportunities that they did not receive elsewhere, and encouraging them to set and keep high aspirations throughout their lives.

❧ Provide Counseling Forums, Discussion Groups, and Seminars for Girls' Support in Elementary, Middle, and High School

Opportunities for female peer support groups as well as weekly or monthly seminars for gifted girls with teachers and others who have an interest in gender equity issues can also make a difference in the lives of girls. These seminars, possibly held during time set aside for gifted programs, can provide role models through speakers, books, films, videotapes, the Internet, and through independent study opportunities. Groups can read and discuss fiction and nonfiction books about female heroines. Opportunities for girls to discuss conflicts they may face or are currently undergoing and programs which use peer mediators are particularly helpful. These seminars can provide time to discuss and plan career opportunities, college and graduate schools, and financial aid. For girls from lower socioeconomic situations, these groups can be an invaluable source of support to help equalize the opportunities provided for talented girls from higher socioeconomic families. Topics for gifted girls' seminars can vary widely, from the external and internal barriers faced by talented girls and women to bibliotherapy sessions using some of the resources cited in Chapter 11. Groups can discuss issues related to underachievement in school, transitions from elementary to middle school and from middle to high school, as well as any decline in belief in ability. The major purpose of these forums is to provide an environment in which girls' voices can be encouraged and heard, and in which young women will learn to understand the issues which may confront them and develop action plans for their futures with firm goals and specific timelines.

❧ ESTABLISH WOMEN'S SUPPORT GROUPS AND PROFESSIONAL OPPORTUNITIES GROUPS TO NURTURE AND PROVIDE SUPPORT FOR GIFTS AND TALENTS

In the *Ladies Home Journal* ("American Women," 1997) survey on women's attitudes mentioned in Chapter Three, 66% of the respondents indicated that they were lonely. Most were too busy to have the time or the opportunity for friendships. Unlike their mothers, who could get together regularly for coffee or to chat on a daily basis with their neighbors, today's women indicate they have no sense of community or belonging. "There is no cohesion of family and friends," explained one woman. Another said, "I work full-time and don't really have the chance to get to know my neighbors because I'm gone all the time. Friendships with other women have to be the last thing—after family, kids, husband and the job."

Support networks can help many successful talented women persevere and be successful. The American Woman's Economic Development Corp. (AWED) is a nonprofit Manhattan center which offers courses in marketing, finance, and other business basics. Women who attend these classes learn the basics of starting a business and find mentors to help support their efforts. Another group, The National Association of Women Business Owners, successfully lobbied a House of Representatives Committee to hold hearings on female entrepreneurs, resulting in legislation providing incentives and low-interest loans for this group. Females of all ages should be encourage to find groups that will help nurture and develop their talents.

❧ Provide Career Counseling for Gifted Females

My research has consistently indicated that women who have achieved at the highest levels discuss their work in terms of the joy they have found and the fun they have had in their careers. Autobiographies, biographies and interviews with women of accomplishment tell the same story: "Science is not a dead cathedral, it is live and it is fun, and it is full of passion" said Fay Ajzenberg-Selove (1994, p. 225). I have found that parents often give gifted girls less help and advice regarding careers than their male siblings.

Teachers and counselors may also neglect opportunities to provide gifted girls the encouragement they need to consider a full range of career options. Parents, teachers and counselors should concentrate on interests and make sure that girls do not avoid taking courses in math, science, and technology which, if not taken, will severely limit their future choices. Finding a career which enables a woman to capitalize on her interests and help do what is enjoyable is crucial.

❦ Discuss the Importance of Peers and Loved Ones Who Support Women's Aspirations

Discussions about the importance of putting one's education first are critical, as is the need to understand and plan for the future, particularly if females want to pursue advanced degrees. As research discussed earlier (Arnold, 1995; Holland & Eisenhart, 1990; Reis, 1995) indicates, some talented women defer their own dreams. It is critical that young women enter college with firm goals and a strong sense of self so that if they fall in love or become involved in a relationship, they will continue to pursue their academic and career goals and not allow their ambitions to be diminished. Having a peer group or set of friends to support and nurture these hopes has been demonstrated to be essential. The group of supportive peers does not have to be large as we have found that one or two friends can make a critical difference in helping gifted females realize their dreams (Reis, Hébert, Diaz, Maxfield, & Ratley, 1995). Likewise, family support and the support of loved ones who nurture dreams is also critical.

❦ Encourage Role Models and Mentors to Be Actively Involved in Developing Talent in Young Women

Almost every biography and autobiography about gifted women indicates the importance of some type of mentor, role model, or the presence of an adult who provides support and advice during school, college, or early adult life. Scientists who have written about their lives consistently mention the importance of individuals who reach out to mentor and support young women in this regard. The mentoring can be long-term, as in the case of a doctoral advisor who helps a young Ph.D. to start her publishing career, or who includes a young professional on panels at important conferences and in a host of other professional opportunities over decades. Mentoring can also be short term, as in the case of a high school mathematics teacher who reaches out and tries to encourage one or two young female students who have extremely high potential in a math class.

Teachers in gifted programs can be extremely helpful as mentors, as many of them have years of involvement with young women through elementary, middle, and high school. In this role, they can be active, assertive advocates for the girls' academic development, as well as help meet their social and emotional needs.

❦ ENCOURAGE PARENTAL AWARENESS OF THE SPECIAL NEEDS OF GIFTED GIRLS AND WOMEN.

Parents play an enormous role in helping gifted girls realize their potential. Research on gifted girls indicates that they may try different kinds of behavior at school and at home in an effort to explore and understand their own styles. Some gifted girls speak out, fight for attention, challenge authority, and are regarded as troublemakers by their peers. Other gifted girls are quiet, studious, and seem sure to be continuously successful in school. Neither group is guaranteed to be successful in life, however. In fact, as has been repeatedly mentioned in this book, being successful in school does not often guarantee success in life. Understanding how school success translates into leadership and career opportunities is critical to the development of gifted females.

Time spent with daughters is also critical for parents to help gifted girls develop their talents. Psychologist Mary Pipher (1994), who discussed the problems facing adolescent girls in *Reviving Ophelia: Saving the Selves of Adolescent Girls* convincingly documents that because girls live in a society obsessed with superficial appearances and which is often hostile to females, they are highly vulnerable to depression, suicide, eating disorders, and addictions. Pipher believes their energy, curiosity, and spirits are crushed. Spending time with daughters can help reverse these problems. Unfortunately, the total time that American children spend with their parents has decreased by one third in the last 30 years (U.S. News and World Report, 1995). Parents need to understand that if gifted girls are to overcome both the external and internal barriers which threaten their potential to become fulfilled adults who work to make a difference in this world, it will take both time and effort on their parts.

❦ Realize that Culturally and Linguistically Diverse Gifted Girls Face Unique Issues

Some of the same issues as well as other unique issues confront gifted females who are culturally and linguistically diverse. We cannot generalize, for example, what has been found about Mexican American gifted females to all Hispanic gifted females. It is clear that more research must be conducted among these diverse cultural groups. In our research with Hispanic students who were primarily from Puerto Rico and the Caribbean, we found that some girls were held back by parental stereotyping and cultural beliefs about the role of women. We have also found that parents of girls from these cultural groups were usually very loving and protective of their daughters and were often fearful of having them leave home or be far away. These young women received unique support and love from their families and the network of love which encircled them enabled some to realize their potential. Support systems were sometimes unique to their culture. The diversity of all cultural groups should be celebrated and understood, as should the premise that there is not one kind of success or one path to accomplishment, while simultaneously understanding that success needs to be guided by sound advice and ongoing support.

❦ Develop an Awareness of Personal Dilemmas and Personality Differences

We must encourage and help young gifted girls develop particular personal characteristics and personality traits which have been consistently identified in successful gifted adult females, including determination, independence, risk taking, and the ability to solve problems. None of these characteristics will be manifested in the same way, as individual personalities affect how they are displayed. Teachers and parents should encourage young girls and women to be aware of these characteristics and their different manifestations. Parents should encourage their daughters to take advantage of opportunities for study away from home and programs such as Space Camp or Talent Search. (I discuss several opportunities in Chapter 11.) Sending girls to leadership programs away from home can encourage both the exploration and the development of these personality characteristics, as can helping girls learn to be independent and learn at an early age to make their own phone calls, use the computer to find information, and be assertive in learning about and pursuing interest areas.

Liza, our youngest daughter, has several favorite children's books. She particularly likes *The Fourth Little Pig* by Teresa Celsi (1992) in which the three little pigs are saved by their sister, Pig Four, an independent free spirit who cannot understand why her brothers are hiding from a wolf. After saving them, her brothers stay home, but she chooses to travel because she realizes, "there are worlds to explore, if only you're willing to open the door." Books like this one encourage positive characteristics such as independence.

Gloria Steinem once said, "A woman without a man is like a fish without a bicycle." Although difficult to discuss, relationships often conflict with female talent development. Helping young women understand the criteria they should use to make decisions about relationships, whether or not they should commit to a relationship, and at what time in their lives can be critical to their talent development. We should help young girls understand that friends are essential, but romantic relationships may be problematic during a time that education should be first. They must also learn that choosing the right partner is essential if they are to develop their own talents.

Using children's literature as a way to discuss this difficult decision can help encourage young girls to think about their future partners. In the wonderful children's book *The Paper Bag Princess*, Robert Munsch (1980) created a heroine I often discuss with young girls. Her name is Elizabeth and she is engaged to Prince Ronald. Unfortunately, a terrible dragon steals Ronald after burning down their castle with his fiery breath. Dressed in a paper bag she salvages, Elizabeth uses her brains and wits to outsmart the dragon and rescue Ronald. Prince Ronald looks at her with distaste and tells Elizabeth that she looks like a mess. He suggests that she return when she is dressed like a real princess. Elizabeth responds, "Ronald, your clothes are really pretty and your hair is very neat. You look like a real prince, but you are a bum." The last line in this wonderful book is "And they didn't get married after all." Reading this book with gifted females of all ages provides an avenue for some fascinating discussions. Young girls can talk about the type of person they want to marry as well as the type of partners they do not want to marry.

When I discuss this issue with parents, some become angry and ask if I am trying to tell talented young girls not to marry. On the contrary, I try to stress that I have found that *early* marriages often have a negative impact on the development of both belief in self and talent in young women. Friendships are wonderful during this critical time of life, but young women need to understand that a partner in life is someone who cares about the other person's hopes, aspirations, and dreams and who will support them emotionally.

It often takes a young woman many years to develop a unique sense of herself and a belief in her abilities. For many of the gifted women I have studied, this development only occurs during their late twenties—a far better time to choose a partner and a lifestyle. This later timeline may produce far better relationships, allowing time for women to gain both a sense of self and a belief in self. However, some women who were influenced by the women's movement and believed their career should be established before thinking about children realized later that they waited too long to have children. It is more difficult to conceive children after 30, and after 40 this difficulty increases, as does the chance of birth defects in children. Some of the gifted women I interviewed who have not had children are angry that they had to make a choice and waited too long. One extremely successful commercial writer told me, "I believed the rhetoric and thought I could control my career and my biological clock. I was wrong. My clock ran out." Usually, however, if a woman waits to marry and have children until she has finished graduate school and attained a better sense of self, it should not interfere with her ability to conceive and bear a child.

To have children or not is a critical issue facing talented girls and women. Once a woman has had a child, the way she looks at the rest of her life changes. She often puts her own dreams and plans on hold, and there are seldom large blocks of time in which to pursue her own work. I am not advocating that talented women should not have children, rather that they should plan carefully. Many gifted women raise children successfully while also pursuing their own talents, but many do not. Consider Carolyn Heilbrun's (1997) commentary on the life of Clara Wieck:

> I am reminded how for many years we have heard how Clara Wieck's wicked father actually tried to stop her from marrying Robert Schumann, fearing it would be the end of her career as a highly regarded pianist and composer. Foolish, antiromantic Papa, standing in the way of true love. So Clara married Robert, bore eight children, nursed Robert through his breakdowns, and spent the years after he was institutionalized playing his music (some of which she may have written) all over Europe to keep his name before the public. She had no time for her own musical ambitions, but a woman's professional life is always considered

well lost for love. But need we always mourn
the lack of enduring love when, in hindsight,
we consider the life of an accomplished woman?
(p. 105)

Other critical issues facing gifted females are perfectionism,
well-roundedness, and trying to do everything well. Gifted females cannot do everything well and should not try to accomplish this foolish and elusive goal. E. Paul Torrance (1997), in
Manifesto for Children, provides excellent advice for talented girls
and women when he encourages them to identify a passion area,
find a mentor, and avoid worrying about being well-rounded and
trying to achieve perfection in all areas.

We must also help girls maintain their own personality, know
who they currently are and who they want to become. They
need to learn to be cautious when other girls' personalities begin
to change. My daughter, firmly entrenched in adolescence, often talks to me about how silly some of the girls in her school
have become in their interactions with boys. She, on the other
hand, has maintained her confidence and seems to be headed
for a secure future. Girls need to be wary of advice from parents
and teachers about being "good," advice which results in many
girls who don't speak out in class and who never ask questions.

RECOMMENDATION THREE: EXPAND OPTIONS AND ELIMINATE MISSED OPPORTUNITIES

Marcelene Cox once said that "Life is like a camel; you can
make it do anything except back up." Too many gifted women
look back with great regret at missed opportunities. We must
provide encouragement to help gifted girls pursue their dreams,
hopes, and ambitions, and encourage young girls to enjoy solitary learning and feel comfortable in accepting their uniqueness.
Learning to work and produce alone and understanding the benefits of independent work will help some gifted girls understand
that they can produce in life. Helping them to understand that

they are not different and they are not alone will also help enable them to achieve their goals and realize their dreams.

❧ Reconsider Our Research Agenda

The reports of a shrinking gap between male and female scores on standardized tests may lead some teachers and parents to unwarranted complacency. Consider reports of research by Feingold (1988). Using the norms from the four standardizations of the Differential Aptitude Tests given between 1947 and 1980 and from the Preliminary Scholastic Aptitude Test, and the Scholastic Aptitude Tests given between 1970 and 1983, he examined patterns of differences. He found that on tests of language, spelling, and clerical skills, girls still outperform boys by a small margin. Boys outperform girls on measures of spatial visualization, high school mathematics, and mechanical aptitude. In addition, according to this research, gender differences, except at the upper levels of performance in high school mathematics, have "declined precipitously over the years surveyed, and the increases in these differences [in high school mathematics] over the high school grades have diminished" (p. 95). Feingold found no gender differences on tests of verbal reasoning, arithmetic and figural reasoning.

While some educators may consider this good news, a more careful analysis is necessary. Certainly it is encouraging that overall differences are decreasing. Yet it is still evident that equal ability and achievement do not guarantee equal opportunity to attain success and satisfaction with career choice. If the gender gap between standardized test scores has been minimal in the past and continues to close, we might reasonably expect to see the performance gaps in careers, professional accomplishments, and consequent financial benefits also closing. However, the career gap has not closed.

Although nearly half of the work force in the country is female and advertisements, television shows, and statistics of women entering graduate school all seem to indicate that females have come a long way since the 1950s, a more careful analysis of current statistics indicates that the struggle for equity has far to go. Evidence suggests that there is no reason that successful professional, wife, and mother must be mutually exclusive categories. A recent study of marriage, motherhood, and research performance in science indicates that married women with children publish as much as their single colleagues (Cole & Zuckerman, 1987). Many bright women choose alternatives to homemaking and many more will enter the workforce in the future. Married women's workforce participation has converged with that of their divorced and widowed counterparts. It considerably exceeds that of single mothers with children under six as 55.1% of single women with children under six work, 62.7% of married women with a husband present and children under six work, and 69.2% of widowed, divorced, or separated women with children under six work (Bureau of Labor Statistics, 1998). If we believe that each individual should have the opportunity to make choices about how best to develop their full potential, and how to accomplish personal fulfillment, we must seek to better understand and provide opportunities for gifted females.

All of this discussion suggests that we must reconsider our research agenda and our interpretation of results of gender differences (or increasing similarities) as we plan for school and life experiences to enable each young girl or woman to make appropriate decisions. Among the first issues we must consider are the importance of sex differences and the importance of gender differences and be very clear on the distinctions between the two. Sex differences are those differences generally attributed to a biological basis; gender differences are a result of socially attributed categorizations. Our interpretations of the sources of sex or gender differences, the size and meaningfulness of these differences, and the degree to which these differences really illuminate differences in performance are also of crucial importance, as is some consideration of the potential bias in our research and practices based on the historical dominance of men in the fields of psychology and higher education.

❦ IN THE FUTURE, CONDUCT NECESSARY CRITICAL RESEARCH ABOUT GIFTED FEMALES AND FOLLOW IT WITH ACTION

Although research related to talented females is more prevalent than it was a decade ago, it is certainly not being carried on to the degree that it might. What Callahan stated in 1979 is still true today, "Underlying the problems of achievement and motivation of gifted and talented females lie hypotheses yet to be tested and perhaps untestable in the experimental tradition" (p. 412). A major concern related to research in the area is lack of control over the environmental and societal factors that influence young girls. Since we will not radically change the cultural or environmental factors in our society within the next few years, research related to talented females should be concentrated in three areas.

The first area is the identification of the degree to which cultural, societal, and environmental factors impact the educational experiences of students and how the impact, if negative, can be lessened or eliminated. We know, for example, that teachers need training to establish equity in classroom interactions. Some teachers who have received this type of training have succeeded in eliminating classroom bias as well as improving overall teaching effectiveness, enabling them to initiate a higher level of intellectual discussion.

The second area of research currently being considered relates to the internal barriers experienced by females that might have an impact on their ability to realize their potential. Research of this type has been conducted by Hollinger and Fleming (1984), who studied the effects of the internal barriers of underachievement, non-assertiveness, fear of success, social competence, and self-esteem on the realization of potential, and Kramer (1985) who studied the effects of social interactions and perceptions of ability. In both of these studies, no treatment was offered to assist the subjects in overcoming their internal barriers. If a counseling program had been initiated, successful female role models introduced, and teacher/counselor/parent training provided, results of the posttreatment analysis might have yielded different findings. One problem with research on high school-age females which is not longitudinal is that differences in motivation, fear of success, and other personality variables may not surface until college years.

The third type of research relates to longitudinal/developmental studies of both gifted females and males. This type of research will be influenced by changes in the culture that occur between the beginning and ending years of the study. However, longitudinal research can provide valuable information related to the time in life at which various blocks to achievement occur.

Future efforts in longitudinal research should concentrate on treatments that can alleviate the problems that have been identified by prior research. In order to provide a gauge by which we can measure the impact of the women's movement and history upon societal changes, longitudinal research on the social and emotional development of talented females must continue. Longitudinal research is also needed on the effect of single-sex advanced math and science classes coupled with counseling and the presence of female role models over a prolonged period of time. If, as some researchers believe, young girls do better in math if they have a female teacher and are in predominately female classes, we need to examine the effects that an early and prolonged program might have on attitudes and the pursuit of scientific and mathematical careers. This type of intervention might also be extremely beneficial for females from low socioeconomic circumstances.

Additional research relating to the attributes of women who have achieved is also needed, such as the studies about female artists with families and older women who have achieved eminence discussed in this book. If we can continue to identify the personality and societal factors that enable some talented women to become successful, we can share this information with parents and educators and provide the advice, guidance, and insights needed for young females to successfully embark upon their road to self-fulfillment.

In considering research that still needs to be done, we must begin to construct a sound theoretical framework of the development of gifted women. The study of abilities, attitudes, and values must accompany a theoretical framework or empirical evidence of the relationship between those characteristics and women's achievement. Further, our research should be designed to allow for maximum understanding of the processes of learning and development in order for all individuals to have maximum choice in career and life decisions. This research on learning and development of gifted females should provide direction for translating theory into practice in appropriate educational strategies to enable this population to realize its potential.

Most important, we must not allow the findings of sex or gender differences to lull us into categorization or stereotyping of any individual. To find that males and females differ on a variable as a group is not a basis to assume that all males share more or less of a given characteristic while all females are on the opposite end of the continuum on that same characteristic.

A Plan for Success for Gifted Females

The following plan for success for gifted girls and women has emerged from my research with successful gifted women who have attained their personal and professional goals.

1. Work hard, set specific goals, take safe risks, be aware of the reasons failure occurs, and don't give up on important goals or issues. Develop determination while simultaneously learning flexibility and understanding how to adapt in a changing world.
2. Identify your priorities and creative interests early, have the courage of your convictions, and use your academic abilities

and projects to help you to pursue interests. Don't try to do everything well; it's a silly goal. The honor roll is not critical and it is certainly all right to get lower grades in some subjects—as long as you learn to work and identify the subjects and content areas you love.

3. Realize that there are time periods in which priorities shift and maintain your dreams and plan carefully for the next phase of your life.

4. Understand the need for support and friendship and find peers who will support your academic and personal goals. You don't have to give up friends who do not share your interest in academic excellence. Many gifted females exist comfortably within two spheres—their childhood friends, family, and neighborhood sphere as well as another sphere of academic peers who support their academic dreams and goals.

5. Develop a plan for your education and personal life enabling you pursue your dreams. Don't be too concerned about specific careers; discover your interests and what you enjoy. Careers are rapidly changing, so adapt your interests to new career areas.

6. Become involved in as many diverse extracurricular and sport activities and experiences as possible—travel, museums, clubs, etc. Keep exposing yourself to experiences outside of school that enable you to "stretch."

7. Put yourself first during the time you are in school. If you can, postpone dating. Choose a partner wisely, don't commit to a serious relationship until after your education is completed unless you develop a relationship with someone who completely supports your ambitions and dreams. Ask hard questions of someone with whom you are considering a future life, especially about sharing commitments and responsibilities for home and family. Remember Oscar Wilde's comment that marriage is the triumph of hope over experience and the current divorce rate of almost 50% in our soci-

ety. Take your time and choose a partner wisely. If you have
children, raise them in a gender-fair environment with an
understanding of how all people should nurture each others' talents.

8. Have fun with learning and with the interests you select.

9. Don't worry about things that are not terribly important
and don't be critical of or a perfectionist about yourself. As
Chekhov wrote, "Wisdom is knowing the difference between
tragedy and burned potatoes."

10. Continue to work on developing a sense of self and a belief
in your own abilities. As you mature, take time to examine
your own sense of self and to work on continuing to understand your talents and how you can best realize your potential. Take time for your own accomplishments and talent
development each day.

Strategies for Helping Gifted and Talented Females Succeed

Many people who have studied the area of gifted girls have
discussed similar suggestions for helping girls to realize their
potential. The commonality of the suggestions for ameliorating
some of the adverse social and cultural factors may be indicative
of the soundness of the advice (Bell, 1989; Callahan, 1979; Grau,
1985, Kerr, 1985; Noble, 1989; Olshen & Matthews, 1987; Reis,
1987; Wells, 1985). We know that teachers, beginning at the
preschool level, should screen books and curricular materials for
sexist statements, attitudes, and illustrations. Teachers and parents, from preschool through college, should monitor class language for bias and use creative questioning to help achieve necessary attitudinal changes. Callahan (1979) also suggested a
number of curriculum changes including providing role models
of gifted women engaging in successful problem solving activities, providing activities to teach girls the impact they can have
on their own destinies in order to help them develop an internal
locus of control, and providing opportunities for gifted females

to interact with successful female role models.

Specific Strategies to Help Educators Encourage Girls in Mathematics and Science

According to the National Research Council (1989) which published a national report on mathematics, by the year 2000 the need for workers in fields requiring mathematics and science backgrounds will have increased by 36% from the 1986 level. We must encourage more females to enter the field of mathematics, as we have failed in our past efforts. Research has consistently demonstrated that teachers can affect how girls perceive and relate to mathematics. In fact, many female mathematicians cite teachers as the primary persons who encouraged them in math as children. Some even attribute their career choice or research interests to one teacher who introduced them to the topic and encouraged them to become more involved in the area. Based on these findings, my colleague Katherine Gavin and I have found the following strategies to be extremely helpful in our efforts to encourage girls in mathematics classes. Most can be implemented fairly easily and quickly, and have been suggested by experts and/or proven to be effective in encouraging young girls in mathematics (Campbell, 1992; Hanson, 1992) and in science. Although these suggestions were written with specific reference to females, most of them can apply to improving and equalizing the classroom environment for students of either gender.

1. Use Specific Strategies to Provide a Safe and Supportive Classroom Environment.
    All girls, especially adolescents, need a mathematics classroom in which they will be heard and understood and in which they can discuss ideas before coming to conclusions. The teacher should provide a setting where students are not permitted to call out answers randomly and where students have plenty of "think time." A period of uncontested silence for females may

encourage them to share their thoughts with others. Teachers should not rush to provide closure to a lesson, for a "mulling period" is often essential for talented girls studying advanced topics. A very effective strategy is the "Think-Pair-Share" technique in which, after time for private thought, students share their answers with a neighbor and then with the entire class. The paired discussion lends credibility to their thinking, fosters mathematical communication, and leads to the development of a sense of confidence.

Teachers should also become personally aware of the additional attention they sometimes give to boys. It is hard to deny a waving hand or someone calling out, but increased attention, even negative attention, can reinforce behaviors. Girls need equal attention, and to ensure that teachers provide it, teachers can establish peer observations with colleagues. A teacher observes a peer's class and tallies the number of times girls and boys are called upon. One way that some teachers address the issue of classroom equality is simply to alternate between calling on males and females in class.

A safe and supportive class can provide opportunities for students to reflect in writing about their ideas and fears about mathematics and/or science. A "comment box" enables students to drop a note about their feelings or their understanding of the content of the daily lesson, including questions they have and related topics they would like to pursue. Students can also address feelings in creative journal assignments, including mathematics metaphors as suggested by Buerk and Gibson (1994). A sample assignment might be the following: If mathematics were a food (color, animal, etc.), it would be and why? The results can quickly foster communication and provide information about personal feelings. Consider the following entries written by mathematically talented adolescent girls:

> ~: *If math were a food it would be a pineapple. On the outside it appears to be all rough, tough, and prickly. But on the inside, it's soft—sometimes*

sweet, sometimes sour.

~: If math were a food, it would be a lobster. It takes
a while to get to learn how to eat it, but once you
learn, it can be kind of fun.

Teachers can also use journals to encourage communication about mathematical concepts and offer talented students a way to bring deeper understanding and/or new insight to areas they wish to pursue. They can stimulate creative writing assignments focusing on feelings about math and science. Girls often enjoy the intimate student-teacher dialogue created by the journal-writing process. An outgrowth of this experience could be to create discussion groups at lunch or in after-school clubs in which girls can discuss their feelings and explore interesting mathematics and science topics.

2. Assume Personal Responsibility to Encourage Talented Females

Adolescent girls who are talented in mathematics and in science may receive mixed messages from their parents, teachers, peer group, and society in general. They need specific encouragement to help them believe that they are truly talented in these areas and to encourage them to continue to pursue math and science in high school, college, and beyond. Teachers need to tell gifted girls of their talents and encourage them in their present study of mathematics as well as to continue in mathematics.

In the classroom, teachers who try to encourage talented girls may believe that they should help their students solve problems and issues that emerge in science and in math. However, merely giving them extra help may be detrimental to females' sense of self-confidence. Teachers must establish an environment in which students persist in seeking solutions for themselves and in which teachers answer questions with a question, giving hints but not solutions. They must have high expectations for girls, let them know it, and praise them for being able to solve challenging problems.

Teachers must also be aware that females who are talented in mathematics and science are often talented in other academic areas as well. Without encouragement to pursue their talents, they often choose other more traditionally female-oriented fields. Teachers must make parents aware of the need to support their daughters' talents in mathematics and science. In school, teachers should ask older girls taking Advanced Placement courses to talk to younger students to encourage increased participation in these courses. And in every stage, parents and teachers should encourage girls to take and remain in advanced mathematics classes so that opportunities remain open to them. Teachers who find outstanding talent in science or mathematics may want to consider taking on the challenge of becoming a long-term mentor to a talented student, staying in touch for several years to continue encouraging the talents in this area.

3. Employ Instructional Strategies that Address the Characteristics of Females

During middle school and usually continuing through their adolescent years, mathematically talented females exhibit great attention to detail in their work, strong organizational skills, and for some, a sophisticated level of maturity. Educators can use these skills to motivate girls' interest in mathematics. For example, teachers can encourage girls gifted in math to organize a Family Mathematics Night (EQUALS, 1986) or Family Science Night (EQUALS, 1989) at the elementary school for parents and children to engage in enjoyable mathematics and science activities together. A book published by EQUALS has a variety of activities specifically designed for such an event. The girls choose activities for the evening, issue invitations, set up, and actually run the entire event (under the auspices of a teacher-mentor).

Tutoring younger children and organizing mathematics or science clubs or Saturday enrichment math and science programs also encourages and empowers talented adolescent females. Some current research indicates that some girls tend to thrive in small group work, especially all-female groups. In coed groups, boys may dominate, becoming the leaders in the group and monopolizing the discussion, while girls become the recorders of the discussions. This tendency is especially true with computer work. If students work in pairs or small groups, boys often demand and get to use the keyboard far more often than girls. Encouraging girls to work together usually resolves this problem. Because some girls have been socialized to play more often with dolls rather than blocks and to read books rather than tinker with their bicycles, they may need more time to work with manipulatives and hands-on science experiments or assignments. They may also need in-class time to build models, see how things work, and develop their sense of spatial relationships. The activity "Cooperative Geometry" (EQUALS, 1986) is an excellent example of group work with manipulatives which develops spatial thinking as well as encourages a true cooperative problem-solving spirit. The extensions are especially challenging for talented elementary and middle school students.

4. Use Language, Problems, and Activities Relevant to Girls
    Suzanne Damarin (1990) examined traditional mathematics vocabulary and found that it reflects a strong male influence. The language contains goals of mastery and mathematical power. Students attack problems, and instructional strategies include drill and competitions. She believes that instead of talking about working toward mastery, teachers should talk about internalization of concepts. Instead of attacking problems, students should interact with them, sharing problems and working cooperatively toward solutions. Rather than focusing on activities relating to football yardage, baseball statistics, and housing construction, teachers should also consciously incorporate problems and activities that girls enjoy. Problems dealing with endangered species, recycling, the spread of disease, population growth, and

quilting have proven to be excellent suggestions. Activities involving patterns including tangrams, paper folding, and tessellations, and those involving art such as making mobiles, computer graphics, and scale drawings appeal to many girls. Some favorite teacher resource materials with activities that encourage girls in mathematics are listed in Chapter 11.

5. Create a Challenging Curriculum That Promotes Deep Mathematical and Scientific Thinking

Teachers must encourage talented females to feel comfortable with, and even seek, a state of challenge when studying mathematics and science. Challenging the familiar with ideas that stretch the mind should be a major goal of a program for talented students. By providing the safe and supportive environment discussed earlier, teachers can nurture this spirit of risk-taking in girls. From elementary school exposure to such topics as different numeration systems, the Fibonacci Numbers, LEGO-Logo, and non-routine problem solving to secondary school study of non-Euclidean geometry, fractals, chaos theory, and combinatorics, students need to struggle with a change of mindset and relish this struggle, for it fosters a deep, intimate, and broadened understanding of mathematics. NCTM has published a series of Addenda books that are an excellent source of ideas for topics. Several science ideas are also presented in Chapter 11.

In designing curriculum for talented females, teachers should include a variety of alternative assessments. Research indicates that females may not do their best thinking during timed tests. Independent and/or small group projects provide an ideal medium for these students to showcase their talent. These projects should go beyond a typical term paper and should focus on investigative activities in which students assume the role of first-hand inquirers—thinking, feeling, and acting like a practicing professional.

In an enrichment program model called *The Enrichment Triad*

Model (Renzulli, 1977) and *The Schoolwide Enrichment Model* (Renzulli & Reis, 1997) Renzulli has advocated creating student products to develop research skills and provide an opportunity to use authentic methodology. These projects are most effective when they are primarily directed toward bringing about a desired impact on an audience, whether it be fellow students, administrators, town officials, mathematicians, or senior citizens. The teacher functions as a facilitator, pointing the student in the direction of resource persons and materials as needed or providing direction in learning methodology to conduct the investigation. Some examples of these projects might include investigating real scientific problems in the community or contacting local community officials for needed surveying or design projects, such as a population survey or a statistical analysis on the use of current library facilities, or an energy audit of town hall using mathematical analysis with recommendations to the town council for improved efficiency. The NCTM addenda series book, *Data Analysis and Statistics Across the Curriculum* (1992), is also an excellent resource for such projects and outlines guidelines for both long and short term projects with time lines and evaluation criteria.

With the increased use of block scheduling at the middle and high school level, enrichment clusters provide challenging and interesting mathematics and science offerings to students. Enrichment clusters combine groups of students who share common interests to come together during designated time blocks to pursue these interests (Renzulli, 1994; Renzulli & Reis, 1997). Single-sex enrichment groups, if possible, could provide an increased sense of confidence for females. During these extended time periods, students can pursue mutual mathematical interests together. For example, they might study fractals using computer models and decide to create programs which generate original fractal pieces. Or, they might gather to start a Young Architects' Guild focusing on learning about architectural design and using this knowledge to create a play space for children at a local preschool or redesigning a veterinarian's office space. Again, the teacher acts as a guide and the students are empowered to discover the joy of mathematics and see the relevance of mathematics in the real world. They learn to value mathematics and, hopefully, become inspired to continue study and pursue a mathematically related career.

6. Provide Female Role Models and Mentors for Girls

Many teachers understand that some girls have a unique connectedness to people. Teachers should capitalize on this characteristic and include an historical perspective in their mathematics curriculum to help students become aware of both the people and the creative processes behind mathematics. The lives of mathematicians and scientists, their interests in the subject and how they created their mathematical discoveries will help young female students appreciate the creative process as well as the difficulties faced in getting new theories accepted. Concepts as basic as the notion of zero, irrational numbers, and negative numbers were quite controversial when first presented and were adopted only after great difficulty.

The names of the following female mathematicians from previous generations are usually not recognized by boys or girls: Hypatia, Marie Agnesi, Sophie Germain, Evelyn Boyd Granville, Sonya Kovalevskaya, and Mary Somerville. Nor are an entire new generation of mathematicians. These famous women made distinguishing contributions, and teachers can make these women come alive by celebrating their birthdays, hanging their portraits in bulletin board displays, and encouraging females to perform autobiographical skits dressed in period costumes. Videotaped interviews conducted between student reporters and a remarkable woman who has suddenly come back to life in the twenty-first century can also be effective. These dramatic monologues or skits provide a creative twist to the historical perspective that appeals to some talented females.

Role models need not all be historical; students can learn

about women currently working in the fields of mathematics and science—astronauts, engineers, physicists, astronomers, etc. Some modern women who have made important contributions to their fields include Rita Levi-Montelcini, a Nobel Laureate biologist; Reatha Clark King, chemist; Shirley Jackson, theoretical physicist; Edna Paisano, statistician; Gertrude Elion, a Nobel Laureate pharmacologist; Maya Lin, architect; and Judith Ressnick, astronaut. Some excellent resources on the lives of female mathematicians and scientists with interesting anecdotal family and personal stories are also listed in Chapter 11.

A rewarding experience for teachers as well as girls is organizing and participating in a career day for girls that focuses on mathematics, science, and technology. At these conferences, generally held for girls in middle or high school, female professionals conduct hands-on workshop sessions with girls, interacting with them, and exposing them to actual on-the-job activities which spark career interest in girls. It is exciting and rewarding to visit these sessions and observe girls listening to a dog's heartbeat with a veterinarian, performing a chemical test on local river water with an environmental engineer, or trying to determine car insurance rates for teenage girls with an actuary. Teachers can contact the following associations for help planning these days:

1. **Multiply Your Options**, PIMMS, Wesleyan University, Middletown, CT 06457
2. **Expanding Your Horizons**, Math-Science Network, 2727 College Avenue, Berkeley, CA 94705
3. **Girls + Math + Science = Choices**, Rose Arbanas, c/o Calhoun ISD, 17111 G Drive N., Marshall, MI 49068.

We have conducted several of these career days at the University of Connecticut and found that in addition to the hands-on workshops, panels of professional women are also effective and can offer a greater variety of careers. To enliven these panels and encourage interaction between the women and the often shy female students, we highly recommend the "Tool Clues" activity (Family Science, 1989). In this activity, female professionals provide bags of "tools" used in their careers, Students working in groups try to guess their profession using a twenty-question format.

One of the greatest benefits from these interactions with professional women is the opportunity for establishing mentorship and internship programs. Participating in these programs gives mathematically talented females the opportunity to work directly with a female role model in a high level mathematics-related career position. As Sheffield (1994) points out, "we especially need to encourage girls and other traditionally underrepresented groups to consider careers in highly technical fields that involve strong mathematical backgrounds, and mentorships are an effective means of doing this" (p. 25).

General Recommendations

In addition to the recommendations about math and science discussed in this chapter, the following specific strategies have emerged from my work and from the research discussed in this book for girls, families, parents, teachers, and counselors. It is, of course, unrealistic to expect that all of these suggestions can be implemented, but implementing several should be a goal for each group.

Gifted and Talented Girls Should:

1. be exposed through personal contact and the media to female role models and mentors who have successfully balanced career and family;
2. develop independence and intellectual risk-taking, as well as an understanding of sex-role stereotyping/cultural biases/gender prejudices and high social-self perceptions;
3. be involved in career counseling at an early age and be exposed to a wide variety of career options;

4. become involved in leadership roles and extracurricular activities;
5. participate in sports, athletics and multiple extracurricular activities;
6. learn to question, speak out, and take action;
7. learn from mistakes and try again;
8. discuss issues related to gender and success in supportive settings with other girls;
9. learn various communication styles and the value of planning for the future;
10. delay becoming involved in romantic relationships until formal education is completed;
11. find peers and friends who support their academic goals and help them identify interests; and
12. identify a dream for important work and develop a plan to make that dream come true.

PARENTS, TEACHERS, AND COUNSELORS SHOULD:

1. form task forces to advocate for programming and equal opportunities and to investigate opportunities for talented girls;
2. spotlight achievements of gifted females in a variety of different areas, encourage girls and young women to become involved in as many different types of activities, travel opportunities, and clubs as possible;
3. show sensitivity to the different nonverbal ways girls express themselves;
4. encourage girls to take math/science courses and reinforce successes in these and all areas of endeavor;
5. understand some of the personal characteristics of gifted females which may impede their success (see Chapter Three);
6. encourage relationships with other gifted girls who want to achieve;

7. maintain options for gifted girls in specific groups such as self-contained classes, groups of girls within heterogeneous classes, science and math clubs, or support groups;

8. ensure equal representation of girls in advanced science and math classes;

9. constantly point out options for careers and encourage future choices but help girls focus on specific careers;

10. stress self-reliance, independence, and decision making;

11. educate and raise males to assume equal partnership in relationships and support the talent development of those they love;

12. express a positive attitude about talents in girls in all areas and be a constant source of support, avoiding criticism as much as possible;

13. not attempt to remediate all behaviors which show spirit, passion, resiliency, or anger since some of these characteristics are essential to adult creative productivity;

14. consciously discuss and actively challenge obstacles and barriers to success by pointing out negative stereotypes in all environments; and

15. foster a secure sense of self by helping talented girls understand and develop a belief in self and their talents and abilities.

PARENTS SHOULD:

1. become assertive advocates for the development of their daughter's interests and talents;

2. maintain a proactive, supportive role to support their daughter's interests;

3. provide career encouragement and planning;

4. provide extensive experiences in museums, travel, and interaction with adults;

5. develop independence and an inclination for creative action;

6. encourage interests but not insist that their daughter achieve the honor roll;

7. not criticize too much and never make fun of appearance or weight—do not focus on their daughter's appearance as it sends negative messages about what is most important;

8. encourage humor and positive risk taking;

9. encourage their daughters' decision making and allow their daughters to make her own decisions;

10. encourage participation in sports, competition, and extracurricular activities—teach their daughters that everybody loses sometime; and

11. monitor television viewing and media exposure—watch out for magazines such as *YM*, *Cosmopolitan*, and many other teen magazines which primarily stress appearance and beauty.

Teachers Should:

1. provide equal treatment in a non-stereotyped environment and in particular, provide encouragement in math/science classes;

2. reduce sexism in classrooms and create an avenue for girls to report and discuss examples of stereotyping in schools;

3. help gifted females appreciate and understand healthy competition;

4. group gifted females homogeneously in math/science or within cluster groups of high ability students in heterogeneous groups;

5. use practical problems in assignments and reduce the use of timed tests and timed assignments within class periods; rather, provide options for untimed work within a reasonable time frame;

6. expose girls to other gifted females through direct and curricular experiences—field trips, guest speakers, seminars, role models, books, videotapes, articles, movies, etc.;

7. provide educational interventions compatible with cognitive development and styles of learning (independent study projects, small group learning opportunities, etc.) and use a

variety of authentic assessment tools such as projects and learning centers instead of just using tests; and

8. establish equity in classroom interactions.

COUNSELORS SHOULD:

1. provide individualized, goal-oriented career counseling and maintain an interest in talented girls with high potential who need help to develop their talents;
2. provide group counseling sessions for gifted and talented girls who share issues such as multipotentiality, under-achievement, or absence of belief in ability;
3. encourage participation in honors and advanced placement courses, and in extracurricular activities and summer and out-of school programs such as college science and math classes;
4. sponsor conferences, workshops, and symposia for and about gifted women for talented girls and their parents;
5. provide bibliotherapy and videotherapy in small group sessions; provide readings in a wide variety of excellent resources and view films such as *The Joy Luck Club* based on the novel by Amy Tan about the struggle of talented women;
6. establish support groups with a network of same-sex peers;
7. contact parents when gifted girls begin to underachieve or seem confused about abilities, aspirations, or careers;
8. provide a variety of career counseling and exposure opportunities; and
9. provide information about societies, web pages, and resources which encourage and support gifted girls and women.

CONCLUSIONS AND ENDINGS

As the next chapter is primarily a listing of curricular materials, programs and resources to encourage girls and women, I conclude here with some general thoughts about lessons learned in the last two decades. Studying gifted females across the lifespan is a complicated and fuzzy problem. Carolyn Heilbrun (1988), in her beautiful book, *Writing a Woman's Life*, explained:

> Endings—the kind that Austen tacked onto her novels—are for romance or for daydreams, but not for life. One hands in the long-worked-on manuscript only to find that another struggle begins. One gets a job to find new worries previously unimagined. One achieves fame only to discover its profound price. (p. 130)

Endings, of course, are not endings at all, but rather new beginnings. As I conclude this book, I begin a new one about the older gifted women I have been studying for ten years whom I only briefly introduced in this book.

The unique pattern of the lives of talented and gifted women seems almost to defy theories of development, yet, in my work, several findings have emerged. There is no clear path for any of us, as our lives and creativity are both more connected with our love for our family and our friends and are more diffused than the lives and creativity of our male counterparts. Because relationships are so central to women's lives, they cannot be secondary to their work and individual attainment. Relationships to talented women are parallel to their work. Yet, without meaningful work, women are simply not as happy. Over and over again, in the hundreds of interviews I have conducted with women at various stages in their lives, they echoed their desire for meaningful work which made a difference. Most also understood that the individual ways in which they defined their life's quest would differ from the ways that other talented women defined their goals. There is no one way to be a gifted female; giftedness rather is defined in these women by a variety of accomplishments, work options, and by the diverse ways they matured and developed a unique sense of an adult self.

Academically gifted girls and women often search for a way to combine their gender and their academic gifts so that they achieve a balance and fit. This struggle seems to continue throughout school and into adulthood. I have found that most women resolved this struggle when they neared the age of 50. It was at this time that they achieved a balance of family and work, an understanding of their unique sense of self and a belief in their ability to accomplish their goals. And of course, many also found time—the most precious gift for realizing one's dream. Their understanding of self lead to a belief in accomplishment which was not present in some of the younger women I studied. The younger women still struggled with the need to balance self and relationship and self and personal ambition. Younger women have much to learn from their older sisters. Too many make solitary journeys without seeking the support and guidance of those who have gone before. My interviews with older women taught me much about how to better live my life and accomplish my goals.

This book took longer to write than I thought because my family is of primary importance to me. However, my work is also important, and if I had not consistently found time for it, I would not have been as happy as I am today. Some time each day for my *own* work, not teaching my classes or attending meetings, not the laundry or housework or chauffeuring to lessons, but rather my own creative work was necessary for me to be content. This time, so precious to me, contributed to my own well-being as well as to the well-being of those I love. When I could take some time each day for my own work, I was a happier, more relaxed person and was more able to give to those I love. When I could not, I was frustrated and it showed. By giving voice to this dilemma, I solved it. My family looked for opportunities to give me time to do my work. When they had long-term projects and work to accomplish, I found time for them.

It seems that more women can realize their talents with the reciprocal support of family and friends. I am proud that my family, friends, and colleagues helped me create the time to complete this book. I think that martyrdom and selfless sacrifice has been too long the domain of many talented women, who by doing too much themselves, deny the joy that their partners, children, and friends feel in freely giving support and help.

It is time to help both young girls and adult women realize their abilities and potential. This goal will be accomplished by appropriate planning, careful selection of choices, partners, and work environments, and by developing personalities that take risks, question authority, and ask "why" more often. Virginia Woolf wrote that we must slay the angel in the house, the censor within us. Speaking out, asking why, and developing the courage to create are all essential to the emergence of our talents. But these talents will not emerge in a singular voice or form, but rather in a multitude of voices and forms—those displaying gifts across many domains and in many areas. A celebration of these and a realization of the need for meaningful work that makes a difference will help each talented woman create her own unique voice and form.

CHAPTER ELEVEN

~:~

CURRICULAR MATERIALS, PROGRAMS, & RESOURCES

Life is either a daring adventure or nothing. To keep our faces toward change and behave like free spirits in the presence of fate is strength indefatigable.
—Helen Keller

As noted throughout this book, parents and teachers have become increasingly aware of the range of problems facing gifted females which include sex-role stereotyping from infancy to adulthood, lack of inclusion of women's accomplishments in literature or textbooks, lower teacher and parent expectations for gifted females than gifted males, and the absence of available adult female role models in both nontraditional and traditional professional roles. We know that gifted females listen to the advice they receive from counselors, teachers, and parents more than their male counterparts, are more critical of themselves at an early age, and have lower confidence about their abilities and diminished career choices than gifted males in college (Arnold & Denny, 1985; Callahan, 1979; Eccles, 1985; Fox, 1977; Grau, 1985; Hollinger & Fleming, 1984; Kerr, 1985; Noble, 1989; Reis, 1987; Rodenstein & Glickhauf-Hughes, 1979; Schwartz, 1980).

I made suggestions for ameliorating some of the social and cultural factors affecting gifted females in Chapter 10. Teachers and parents should take an active role in screening books and curricular materials for sexist statements, attitudes, and illustrations. Teachers should make a variety of curriculum changes to provide role models of gifted women engaging in successful problem-solving activities, activities that teach girls the impact they can have on their own destinies, and opportunities for gifted girls to interact with female role models. Few would disagree with these suggestions, yet, for many teachers and gifted education coordinators, time is a factor. Finding appropriate female role models, for example, is a difficult process in any location and an almost impossible task in some geographically remote or rural areas. Arranging for mentors takes time and training before an interactive student relationship can begin. These difficulties do not provide a sufficient rationale for failing to initiate these steps, but they indicate a need to provide practical suggestions for ways to begin the process of breaking down gender stereotypes. The following resources, materials, and programs have been especially helpful in encouraging gifted girls in specific content areas as well as in general areas. Other educators have also compiled excellent annotated bibliographies for encouraging talented females (Kolloff, 1996).

The annotated bibliography contains selected references that have been used in a variety of ways: as textbooks in mini-courses, as enrichment exposure activities (see Renzulli, 1977), as both "role-models" and "mentors in print," and as a starting point for ordering texts and other non-stereotypic resources for bright youngsters. Some of the references are also extremely useful in helping gifted girls make personal, educational, and career choices that are appropriate for the multipotentiality of their talents and the sometimes overwhelming number of options available to them.

Of course, the day that this list is completed, it is also obsolete. It continues to be the responsibility of all of us to look for new materials, share them with teachers, colleagues, and friends, and continue to work for the inclusion of materials for girls in the curriculum across all content areas, in our homes, and in the media.

ANNOTATED LIST OF RESOURCES

General Programs, Projects & Information Centers

The AAUW Equity Library

Helping to make a difference for today's girls and tomorrow's leaders, the AAUW Educational Foundation offers ground-breaking works on gender bias in education. The following are available: *Shortchanging Girls, Shortchanging America* (results of a national poll on girls and self-esteem in print or video form), AAUW Issue Briefs (package of five briefs with strategies for change), *The AAUW Report: How Schools Shortchange Girls* (a report documenting girls' second-class treatment in American schools).

AAUW Educational Foundation, Dept. T, 1111 Sixteenth Street N.W., Washington, DC 20036-4873
Phone: (800) 225-9998 Ext. 246

Girls Can! Community Coalitions Project

Providing gender-fair educational opportunities for girls in grades K-12 at locations across the country, these model programs stress working with diverse community groups to develop innovative projects.

Program Director, AAUW Educational Foundation, 1111 16th St. NW, Washington, DC 20036
Phone: (202) 728-7602
www.aauw.org/4000/programs

Girl Scouts of the USA

The Girl Scouts offer numerous programs and suggestions for girls ages 5 through 17 involving computers and technology, careers, the environment, personal finance, and sports.

Girl Scouts of the USA, 420 Fifth Avenue, New York, NY 10018-2702
Phone: (212) 852-6512
www.girlscouts.org

Institute for the Academic Advancement of Youth
Promoting academic ability in math, science, and the humanities, the Institute has developed a variety of programs and services including a summer and academic year program, distance learning, writing tutorials, a center for talent identification, publications, and conferences.

IAAY, John Hopkins University, 3400 North Charles Street, Baltimore, MD 21218
Phone: (410) 516-0337   *Fax: (410) 516 0804.*
www.jhu.edu   *iaay.programsinfo@jhu.edu*

LEAD *Leadership Experience and Development: A Summer Program at the University of South Carolina*
Examining leadership areas in government, law, business, communications, medicine, education, the arts, athletics, and public service this week-long residential program brings together young women and some of South Carolina's most prominent female leaders. Activities include classroom work, projects, community service, recreational and social events and lectures.

LEAD, University of South Carolina, 937 Assembly Street, Suite 108, Columbia, SC 29208
Phone: (803) 777-9444/(803) 777-CAMP   *Fax: (803) 777-2663*
            patp@rcce.sc.edu

National 4-H Council
Educating young people and adults through hands-on approaches, this organization focuses on life skills—acquiring knowledge, using the scientific method, mastering technology, making career decisions, managing resources, communicating well, and working productively.

National 4-H Council, 7100 Connecticut Avenue, Chevy Chase, MD 20815
Phone: (301) 961-2840   *Fax: (301) 961-2894*

National Women's History Project.
This nonprofit educational organization provides opportunities for women to redesign museums, discover women's historical sites, document the lives of women and celebrate women's contri-

butions through their Women's History Network. Their catalog features books, posters, and gift items honoring history, diversity, the workplace, and contributions in math, science and technology, as well as information about a summer program for teachers.

Phone: (707) 838-6000   *Fax: (707) 838-0478*
                                           NWHP@aol.com

The Program for the Exceptionally Gifted (PEG)

PEG offers young, academically talented women the opportunity to begin college one to four years early within a supportive community of their peers.

Mary Baldwin College, Staunton, VA 24401
Phone: (540) 887-7039   *Fax (540) 887-7187*
www.mbc.edu   *peg@cit.mbc.edu*

Single Sex Schooling Information

Women's colleges throughout the country focus on developing skills and leadership in girls and women. They offer specific strategies and suggest options for middle and high school girls in math, science, and leadership.

Women's College Coalition, 125 Michigan Avenue, NE, Washington, DC 20017
Phone: (202) 234-0443
National Coalition of Girls' Schools, 228 Main Street, Concord, MA 01742
Phone: (978) 287-4485
www.ncgs.org

The Summer Institute for the Gifted

Offering a three week residential, coeducational academic camping program for talented students in grades 4-11 at various sites throughout the country, this institute combines a full spectrum of challenging courses with opportunities for cultural experiences, social growth, traditional camp activities, and off-campus trips.

College Gifted Programs, 120 Littleton Road, Suite 201, Parsippany, NJ 07054-1803
Phone: (201) 334-6991   *Fax: (201) 334-9756*
www.cgp-sig.com   *info@cgp-sig.com*

Take Our Daughters to Work Day
Giving girls positive messages about work and self-worth, this annual event aims to raise girls' self-esteem and career aspirations. What can boys do on this day? A curriculum guide suggests discussions about what they can do to show their support for girls, what it will take for women to be equal in society, and what will be the benefits to them when girls and women gain equity. Numerous other resources are also available at the MS Foundation office.
Ms. Foundation for Women, 120 Wall St., 33rd Floor, New York, NY 10005
Phone: (800)676-7780
www.ms.foundation.org/

UCONN Mentor Connection: A Real-World Experience
Bringing high school juniors and seniors together with university mentors to create a community of scholars, this program provides challenging work involving authentic methods and research on problems of interest on the cutting edge of various fields of study.
UConn Mentor Connection, University of Connecticut, 362 Fairfield Road U-7, Storrs, CT 06269-2007
Phone: (860) 486-0283   *Fax (860) 486-2900.*
epsadm07@uconnvm.uconn.edu

The Windows Project
This project was created to promote girls' computer skills and confidence through research, creating a database on notable women, and training in multimedia technology.
Gayle Beland, Project Director, 5 Tsienneto Road #74, Derry, NH 03038
Phone: (603) 624-6356   *Fax: (603) 623-7625*

Women's Educational Equity Act (WEEA) Resource Center
Advancing gender equity in educating girls and women, this program aids in meeting the requirements of Title IX and publishes the Resources for Educational Excellence Catalog and WEEA Digest. The catalog provides materials on violence prevention, teacher training and professional develop-

ment, school to career, language, math, science and technology.
Phone: (800) 225-4276x2304
www.edc.org/CEEC/WEEA

Resources for Adults

GENERAL

Boys and girls together: Non-sexist activities for elementary schools.
(1980). Holmes Beach, Fl.: Learning Publications.
Activities for establishing sex equity in the classroom use the present curriculum and materials already found in the classroom.
Phone: (941) 778-6651

National Black Child Development Institute. (1989). *Beyond the stereotypes: A guide to resources for black girls and young girls.* Washington, DC.
This reference book provides lists of books, sound recordings and videos, annotated and classified by age group (3-7, 8-11, 12-15 and up).
Phone: (202) 387-1281

HISTORY

The times and triumphs of American women. (1986). Seneca Falls, NY: National Women's Hall of Fame.
This educational kit features women from the past and present: women who have contributed to the development of the country through outstanding achievements in the arts, athletics, education, government, humanitarianism and science. Exercises and activities relate directly to material covered in the book.
Phone: (315) 568-8060

Women's journeys, women's stories: In search of our multicultural future. (1997). Newton, MA: WEEA Equity Resources Center

Beginning where other history texts leave off and updating previous accounts, this new women's history curriculum fills critical gaps in our nation's history. It addresses the women's rights movement, native women, women of the south, and immigrant women.

Phone: (800)225-4276x2304

www.edc.org/CEEC/WEEA

LITERATURE

Books for today's young readers. (1981). New York: Feminist Press. This annotated bibliography offers recommended fiction for ages 10-14.

Phone: (212) 650-8890

MATHEMATICS AND SCIENCE (SEE PP. 367-377)

MENTORING

Bluestein, J. (1995.) *Mentors, masters and Mrs. Macgregor.* Deerfield Beach, FL.: Health Communication

A collection of entertaining and inspiring stories written by both famous and ordinary folks describe favorite teachers, mentors, and other special people and includes 4-22-year-olds' comments on their criteria for what makes a really great teacher.

Cowen, L., & Wexler, J. (1998). *Daughters & mothers: A celebration.* Philadelphia, PA: Running Press Book Publishers.

Celebrating the powerful, enduring and multifaceted relationship between mothers and daughters through essay and photography, this book shares the stories of artists, athletes, celebrities, politicians, toddlers, teenagers, moms, and grandmoms.

Hughes, K. W. & Wolf, L. (1997). *Daughters of the moon sisters of the sun.* Stoney Creek, CT: New Society Publishers.
This book captures remarkably candid and compelling stories gathered from 21 teenage girls and the mentors with whom they talked during a weekly two-year long focus group. The idea for this unique program was founded on the pioneering work of Carol Gilligan.

PARENTING

Parenting for high potential. Washington, D.C.: National Association for Gifted Children.
This quarterly publication is filled with practical information and sensible advice and includes special features, a consumer column, resource roundup, parenting Q&A, home/school report, and kids' section.
Phone: (202) 785-4268
www.nagc.org

"Raising confident competent daughters: Strategies for parents." (1995). Concord, MA: National Coalition of Girls' Schools
This booklet offers information on how parents can increase their daughters' self-confidence and appreciation of math and science.
Phone and Fax: (978) 287-4485

PERSONAL DEVELOPMENT ACROSS THE LIFESPAN

Brown, L. M., & Gilligan, C. (1992.) *Meeting at the crossroads: Women's psychology and girls' development.* New York: Ballantine Books.
Compelling stories told by young adolescent girls whose feelings of disconnection, dissociation, and repression provide readers with a better understanding of what they may have left behind at their own crossroads.

Bukovinsky, J. (Ed.). (1996.) *Women of words: A personal introduction to thirty-five important writers.* Philadelphia: Courage Books.

Through biography and original portraits by artist Jenny Powell, this anthology features the best of women's literature in English from the last two centuries.

Carmack, S. D. (1998). *A genealogist's guide to discovering your female ancestors.* Cincinnati, OH: Better Books.

This book contains special strategies for discovering hard-to-find information about female lineages; valuable research techniques for uncovering historical facts, personal accounts, and recorded events; and a multitude of uncommon resources.

Carpenter, D., & Winfree, W. (1996.) *I am beautiful: A celebration of women in their own words.* Bridgeport, CT: Rose Communications, LLC.

These powerful and inspirational stories of real women from all walks of life across America tell what it means to be beautiful. Each photograph and essay reveal a sense of self and the link between personal history and outer appearance.

Choices. (1993). Santa Barbara, CA: Girls Incorporated of Greater Santa Barbara/Advocacy Press.

This handbooks helps preteen and teenage girls with decision making.
Phone: (800) 676-1480.

Ealy, C. D. (1995). *The woman's book of creativity.* Hillsboro, OR: Beyond Words Publishing, Inc.

Examining and expanding the definition of the creative process, this book offers women guidance in accepting and nurturing their inherent ability to express their talents. It goes beyond the traditional creativity models based only on men to focus on a holistic "spiral" process.

Garbor, A. (1995). *Einstein's wife: Work and marriage in the lives of five great twentieth-century women.* New York: Viking/ Penguin Books.
Going beyond the Superwoman stereotype, this book explores the intimate portraits of five eminent females who successfully combined ambition and love.

Goldberger, N. R., Tarule, J. M., Clinchy, B. M., & Belenky, M. F. (Eds.). (1996). *Knowledge, difference and power: Essays inspired by women's ways of knowing.* New York: Basic Books.
Posing new, complex questions, these essays go to the heart of current conversations about gender, culture, reality and truth.

I'll Take Charge. St. Paul, MN: Center for 4-H Youth Development.
This life-planning and career development curriculum designed to help young people gain a sense of competency in their lives. *Phone: (612) 625-3107*

Ireland, P. (1997). *What women want: A journey to personal and political power.* New York: Penguin Books.
Exploring her own empowering journey, the current President of NOW shares her mistakes, triumphs, and hopes for the future.

Josselson, R. (1998). *Revising herself: The story of women's identity from college to midlife.* New York: Oxford University Press, Inc.
Among the first to confront many contemporary issues not faced by their mothers or their grandmothers, the women in this study show how they have forged identities through the ongoing balancing of their need for self-assertion and relationships.

Nelson, M. B. (1998). *Embracing victory: Life lessons in competition and compassion.* New York, NY: William Morrow and Co., Inc.
The author of *Embracing Victory* teaches women how to compete without losing dignity and a sense of humor and tells how it can enhance both intimacy and success at work, home, and in sports.

Poulton, T. (1997). *No fat chicks: How business profits by making women hate their bodies—and how to fight back.* Secaucus, NJ: Carol Publishing Group.
Exposing the real reason—money—many women spend their lives chasing the "perfect" body, this book focuses on how the glorification of emaciation feeds beauty, fitness, fashion, diet, food, and health-care industries.

Sark. (1997). *Succulent wild woman.* New York: Simon & Schuster, Inc.
This colorful, unique volume is an invitation to live a rich, succulent life, exploring love, sexuality, romance, money, fat, fear, healing, adventure and creativity.

"Take action for girls (TAG) newsletter." St. Paul, MN: TAG at UMWHC-TAG
This newsletter offers information and action tips on relevant topics for girls.
Phone: (612) 644-1727   *umwhc@piper.hamline.edu*

Resources for Girls

ARTS

Epstein, V. S. (1987). *History of women artists for children.* Denver, CO: VSE Publisher.
Epstein tells the history of women in art through brief biographies of 29 women artists of distinction and includes examples

of each artist's work.

Nechita, A. (1996). *Outside the lines.* Marietta, GA: Longstreet Press.
This artist prodigy whose large abstract paintings are reminiscent of Picasso's work shows us fifty of her paintings with a commentary on each. Her subjects range from family to harmony, nature, and peace.

Turner, R. M. (1991). *Rosa Bonheur.* Boston, MA: Little, Brown and Co.
Part of the series *Portraits of Women Artists for Children*, this biography recounts the development of an artist in the nineteenth-century when it was difficult for women to gain recognition in this field. Other biographies in this series include Faith Ringgold, Frida Kahlo and Georgia O'Keeffe.

HISTORY AND SOCIAL SCIENCES

Ashby, R. & Gore Ohrn, D. (Eds.). (1995). *History: Women who changed the world.* New York: Viking.
Organized into three historical periods (prehistory to 1750, 1750 to 1850, and 1890 to the present), short biographical portraits introduce readers to the lives and accomplishments of 120 influential and brilliant women. Each section has a summary describing the typical life of women and the status of women's rights in that period. The editors have included a bibliography, a list of books for further reading, and three indexes.

Brown, D. (1997). *Ruth law thrills a nation.* Boston: Houghton Mifflin.
Cartoon-style illustrations and fascinating descriptions recount Ruth Law's daring attempt in 1916 to fly from Chicago to New York City in one day.

Casey, S. (1997). *Women invent! Two centuries of discoveries that have shaped the world.* Chicago: Chicago Review Press.
Inspirational stories about women inventors take readers on a fascinating journey through the process of inventing, from idea generation and creation of models to obtaining a patent and marketing and selling the invention.

Chang, I. (1996). *A separate battle: Women and the civil war.* New York: Puffin Books.
This stirring volume from the *Young Readers History of the Civil War* series presents a survey of women's many roles and contributions before, during, and after the Civil War and includes archival photographs, engravings, maps, illustrations, and cartoons.

Colman, P. (1998). *Rosie the riveter: Women working on the home front in world war II.* New York: Crown Books.
An award-winning overview of the role women played in the wartime workplace from 1942-1945, Coleman uses black and white photographs, magazine quotes from the period, and descriptive text to illustrate the jobs women took, the impact they had on the workplace, and the effects this participation had on the United States after World War II.

Fireside, B. J. (1994). *Is there a woman in the house . . . or senate?* Morton Grove, IL: Albert Whitman & Company.
Based on archival research and interviews with nine living subjects, Fireside focuses on the amazing contributions of the following women who served in the House or Senate from 1916 to the present: Jeannette Rankin, Margaret Chase Smith, Shirley Chisholm, Bella Abzug, Barbara Jordan, Millicent Fenwick, Geraldine Ferraro, Nancy Kassebaum, Barbara Mikulski, and Patricia Schroeder.

Freedman, R. (1998). *Martha Graham: A dancer's life.* New York: Clarion Books.
Martha Graham, the American dancer, teacher, and choreogra-

pher revolutionized the world of modern dance. This stunning volume documents Graham's life from birth in 1894 to her final dance performance at the age of seventy-five and continued career as a choreographer until her death in 1991.

Gormley, B. (1997). *First ladies: Women who called the white house home.* New York: Scholastic, Inc.
From Martha Washington to Hillary Rodham Clinton, this introductory text examines the lives of America's First Ladies. Each profile focuses on one First Lady with special emphasis on her time in the White House.

Great Women. (1992). Ann Arbor, MI: Aristoplay.
Three terrific biographical card games (played like rummy) introduce players to outstanding American women—an aspect of America's heritage often missing from history books.
Phone: (800) 634-7738

Johnston, N. (1995). *Remember the ladies: The first women's rights convention.* New York: Scholastic, Inc.
This carefully researched book examines the key participants and events of the 1848 Women's Rights Convention in Seneca Falls, New York.

Leon, V. (1998). *Outrageous women of the middle ages.* New York: John Wiley & Sons.
Covering cultures from around the world during 500 A.D. to 1400 A.D., enlightening profiles introduce readers to fifteen fascinating women from Middle Ages who defied the conventions of the times.

Lunardini, C. (1994). *What every American should know about women's history: 200 events that shaped our destiny.* Holbrook, MA: Adams Media Corporation.
Focusing on significant contributions made by American women

from early seventeenth century to the present, brief essays highlight women's accomplishments in the areas of education, social and labor reform, family life, and equal rights from Harriet Tubman and Elizabeth Cady Stanton to Toni Morrison and Maya Angelou.

Macy, S. (1998). *Winning ways: A photohistory of American women in sports.* New York: Scholastic, Inc.
From bicyclists in the 1880s to today's track stars, this highly readable resource surveys the achievements of female athletes and teams who have had an impact on the world of sports.

San Souci, R. D. (1993). *Cut from the same cloth: American women of myth, legend, and tall tale.* New York: Philomel Books.
Arranged geographically from Northeast to West, fifteen stories feature legendary American women from folktales, popular stories, and ballads. Some of the heroines include Bess Call, Annie Christmas, Sal Fink, Pohaha, and Hekeke.

Stanley, D. & Vennema, P. (1997). *Cleopatra.* New York: William Morrow.
This captivating pictorial biography describes the life of Cleopatra, her reign as the Queen of Egypt, her passionate desire to unite the world under Egyptian rule, and her relationship with legendary leaders who risked their lives and kingdoms to win her heart.

Sullivan, G. (1994). *The day women got the vote: A photo history of the women's rights movement.* New York: Scholastic, Inc.
Appealing to young readers, this meticulously researched introduction to the Women's Rights Movement contains dozens of dramatic photographs and fascinating facts organized into twenty-four photo essays on subjects ranging from dress reform to women in war.

Sullivan, G. (1996). *In the line of fire: Eight women war spies.* New York: Scholastic, Inc.

This captivating volume recounts the stories of female war spies who risked their own lives to obtain information for the military. Ranging from ordinary wives to thrill-seeking adventurers, the author describes the motives, activities, and sometimes tragic ventures of eight courageous spies.

Welden, A. (1998). *Girls who rocked the world: Heroines from Sacajawea to Sheryl Swoopes.* Hillsboro, OR: Beyond Words Publishing.

Illustrated with photographs and drawings, thirty-five biographies of thirty-five girls, past and present, from all around the world who have achieved amazing feats and changed history before reaching their twenties.

Winegarten, R., & Kahn, S. (1997). *Brave black women: From slavery to the space shuttle.* Austin, TX: University of Texas Press.

Tracing the history of black women from slavery to the present, this resource celebrates the achievements of famous and lesser-known female African Americans including Bessie Coleman, Mae Jemison, Barbara Conrad, Debbie Allen, and Barbara Jordan.

Zeinert, K. (1996). *Those remarkable women of the American revolution.* Brookfield, CT: Millbrook Press.

Readers examine the changing role of women during the American Revolutionary War and documents the marks these colonial women left on the battlefields, on the homefront, in print, and in the political arena.

MATHEMATICS AND SCIENCE (SEE PP. 367-377)

PERSONAL DEVELOPMENT

A girl's world. (1995). Ridgefield, CT: Laurie Hepburn Productions
Featuring real life female role models—jet pilot, horse veterinarian and glass artist—paired with preadolescent girls, this video about career choices can inspire dreams and help give direction in girls' lives. It received the Parents' Choice Foundation 1995 Gold Award in children's video category.
Phone: (800) 275-9101

Auerbacher, I. (1995.) *Beyond the yellow star to America.*
Unionville, NY: Royal Fireworks Publishing Co.
Dealing with group acceptance, self-esteem, and peer pressure, a young immigrant child of the Holocaust succeeds with relentless drive and the support of her parents.
Phone: (914) 726-4444

Berkin, C., & Norton, M. (1979). *Women of America: A history.* Boston: Houghton Mifflin.
This book traces the circumstances of women in America from 1600 and looks at the future of women. Topics covered include the Protestant and Quaker views of women, Irish working women, Chinese immigrant women in 19th century California, the feminization of academe, and the role of women in World War II. The book also provides extensive suggestions for further reading.

Blue jean magazine. Victor, NY: Sherry Handel.
A new magazine for young girls by young girls provides excellent role models and articles for young girls.
Phone: 888-4-BLU-JEAN

Dee, C. (1997). *The girl's guide to life.* New York: Little Brown & Co.
Helping girls strengthen their self-esteem, handle gender bias,

and set exciting career goals, *The Girl's Guide to Life* provides background on a variety of issues, empowering activities, historical facts, and first person stories.

Dyer, W. W. (1979). *Pulling your own strings*. Dresden, TX: Avon Books.
This "how-to" book focuses on how to be a decision-maker and action oriented person and contains sample dialogues, strategies, and checklists. It is a great resource for planning activities for bright females.

Epstein, V. S. (1980). *The ABC's of what a girl can be*. Denver, CO: VSE Publisher.
From Architect to Zookeeper, this illustrated resource presents nontraditional career possibilities to young girls.

Gourley, C. (1997). *Beryl Markham: Never turn back*. Berkeley, CA: Conari Press.
The journey of an aviator and adventurer growing up in Africa explores how a young girl survives abandonment by her mother and never being quite able to please her father.

Griffin, L. & McCann, K. (1995). *The book of women: 300 notable women history passed by*. Holbrook, MA: Adams Publishing, Inc.
Overlooked in history books and not a part of our common knowledge, the women in this small volume were risk-takers, courageous, infamous, defiant, resilient, creative, and brilliant.

Haven, K. (1995). *Amazing American women*. Englewood, CO.: Teacher Ideas Press.
A collection of quick read stories celebrates the lives of 40 American women who contributed to the shaping of our country. Each story explores a significant time in each of the women's lives and is followed by questions to explore and additional reading suggestions.

Higa, T. (1991). *The girls with the white flag.* New York: Kodansha International.
A spellbinding story of love, courage, and the resilience of the human spirit during WWII in Okinawa, Japan, depicts a child's will to live and her determination never to give up hope.

Johnston, A. (1997). *Girls speak out: Finding your true self.* New York: Scholastic Press.
Readers take a rare journey to discover the strengths of being female, how to stay powerful and find their true selves.

Johnston, J., (1987). *They led the way: Fourteen American women.* New York: Scholastic, Inc.
Brief biographies of American women reveal how they were instrumental in American history.

Karnes, F. A., & Bean, S. M. (1997). *Girls and young women entrepreneurs: True stories about starting and running a business plus how you can do it yourself.* Minneapolis, MN: Free Spirit Publishing.
Stories about twenty girls and young women whose dreams would not be stopped offer inspiring advice, tips, and resources to help girls realize their business potential for profit and nonprofit.
Phone: (612) 338-2068   *Fax: (612) 337-5050*
                                 help4kids@freespirit.com

ker Conway, J. (1990). *The road from coorain.* New York: Alfred A. Knopf.
Describing her early years in Australia and the path that brought her to America and, eventually, the presidency of Smith College, this is an extraordinary account of one highly gifted woman's development. The sequel, *True North*, reflects on her education, marriage, and career.

Kessler-Harris, A. (1981). *Women have always worked: An historical overview*. New York: Feminist Press.
This overview of women's work experiences in America focuses on the tension between women's work inside and outside the home and weaves together material about diverse groups of women—immigrant, African American, wealthy, poor, and middle-class.

New moon: The magazine for girls and their dreams. Duluth, MN: New Moon Publishing Co.
Celebrating girls, exploring the passage from girl to woman, and building healthy resistance to gender inequity, this international magazine is a model of girls' self-expression. Girls from all over the world contribute to the content of this magazine.
Phone: (218) 728-5507   *newmoon@newmoon.duluth.mn.us.*

Shannon, J. (1994). *Why it's great to be a girl: 50 eye-opening things you can tell your daughter to increase her pride in being female*. New York: Warner Books.
These fascinating facts will make girls aware that being born female offers an astounding variety of benefits, from females' committing fewer crimes and snoring less than men to their superior communication skills and unique talents.

Thomas, M., Steinem, G., & Pogrebin, L. C. (1987). *Free to be . . . you and me*. New York: Bantam Press.
This collection of stories and songs designed to expand children's horizons includes "The Story of X" about stereotypes and expectations and "Atalanta," a fairy tale about a princess who is a winner and decides her own future.

WRITING AND LITERATURE

Lowry, L. (Ed.). (1995). *Dear Author: Children write about books that changed their lives*. Berkeley, CA: Conari Press.
Collected by Weekly Reader's *READ* magazine with an intro-

duction by Lois Lowry, these 75 eloquent and touching letters are written by students and intended for young people. The children write about the books that changed their lives, and the letters affirm the power of literature to affect us.

Gilbert, S.M., & Gubar, S. (Eds.). (1996). *The Norton anthology of literature by women: The tradition in English.* New York: W.W. Norton.

This collection brings together in a single volume major works by over 150 women authors from all the world's English-speaking countries. Authors include Jane Austen, Ann Bradstreet, Phyllis Wheatley, Sojourner Truth, Shirley Jackson, Toni Morrison, Grace Paley, Maya Angelou, Margaret Atwood, and Alice Walker.

ker Conway, J. (1992). *Written by herself: Autobiographies of American women: An anthology.* New York: Random House, Inc.

From brief biographical sketches of twenty-five American women accompanied by autobiographical pieces written by each, readers learn about these women in their own words.

Kirschner, L., & Folsom, M. (1976). *By women: An anthology of literature.* Boston: Houghton Mifflin.

Eighty-eight selections, classical to contemporary, represent the creative energies of women. The anthology presents the works of more than seventy writers, including Willa Cather, Colette, Emily Dickinson, Isak Dinesen, Anais Nin, Flannery O'Connor, Katherine Anne Porter, Adrienne Rich, and Virginia Woolf.

Krull, K. (1994). *Lives of the writers: Comedies, tragedies (and what the neighbors thought).* San Diego, CA: Harcourt Brace & Co.

Briefly presenting the lives of twenty noteworthy female and male writers, this book is an inspiration to girls who enjoy and appreciate literature and writing. It includes stories of Frances Hodgson

Burnett, Jane Austen, Emily Dickinson, Zora Neale Hurston, the Bronte Sisters, Louisa May Alcott and Murasaki Shikibu.

L'Engle, M. (1971). *A circle of quiet.* San Francisco: Harper & Row.
L'Engle, M. (1984, 1996). *The summer of the great grandmother.* New York: Harper & Row.
L'Engle, M. (1988). *Two-part invention: The story of marriage.* New York: Harper & Row.
This beloved author of children's books writes of her life, recounting her childhood precocity, her beginnings as a writer and her most fulfilling role as a wife and mother.

Lyons, M. E. (1995). *Keeping secrets: The girlhood diaries of seven women writers.* New York: Henry Holt & Co.
By keeping diaries these women discovered themselves and crafted bold public lives as authors and activists. As they continued to write in new forms, their private journals illustrated their journey from self to diary to printed page and back again.

Meigs, C. (1995). *Invincible Louisa: The story of the author of Little Women.* New York: Little Brown and Co.
This book offers the full story of the brave and loving Alcott family and the real-life story behind *Little Women.*

Current Fiction for Girls

Barnes, J. A. (1997). *Promise me the moon.* New York: Dial Books for Young Readers.
A young girl's dream of becoming an astronaut is nurtured by her family, boyfriend, and teachers. As she grows up she learns that achieving a goal can bring pain and loss as well as fulfillment.

Cooney, B. (1996). *Eleanor.* New York: Viking Penguin.
Leading a lonely and sad life surrounded by wealth as a child, this

story of Eleanor Roosevelt, who became one of our nation's most compassionate and beloved first ladies, helps readers understand why she fought for the rights of disenfranchised people as an adult.

Creech, S. (1997). *Chasing redbird.* New York: Harper Collins. A young thirteen-year-old girl sets out in search of her place in the world. She discovers it in her own backyard, uncovering family secrets and truths about herself.

Dear America [series]. New York: Scholastic Inc. The books in this fictional series are written as diaries of young girls in early America. Some events and characters are based on actual historical events and real people. Each book, authored by different writers, tells about the longings, hardships and confusing times they faced. Titles include: *A Journey to the New World— Patience Whipple; The Winter of Red Snow—Revolutionary War; When will this Cruel War be Over?—Civil War; I Thought my Soul Would Rise and Fly—Slavery; So Far From Home—Irish Mill Girl in Lowell, MA; The Diary of Clotee, a Slave Girl; Across the Wide and Lonesome Prairie—Oregon Trail.*

Lansky, B. (Ed.). *Girls to the rescue: Tales of clever, courageous girls from around the world.* Deephaven, MN: Meadowbrook Press. In these entertaining and inspiring stories there's no waiting around for Prince Charming; these girls are too busy saving the day! Ten tales empower girls to believe in themselves and their abilities. Also from the editor: *Ten more tales* (1996) and *Ten more!!* (1997).

Evetts-Secker, J. (1996). *Mother and daughter tales.* New York: Abbeville Publishing Group. These folktales of many world cultures explore the special bond between mothers and their daughters.

Fenner, C. (1997). *Yolanda's genius.* New York: Simon and
Schuster for Young Readers.
A nurturing, spirited and humorous big sister finds a way to
recognize and develop her younger brother's talent. She helps
him to understand and develop his gifts.

Gaglang, M. E. (1996). *Her wild American self.* St. Paul, MN:
Coffee House Press.
Appealing to adolescent readers, Filipino-American stories confront issues of assimilation, friendship, conformity, and self-de-
termination.

Hamilton, V. (1995). *Her stories: African american folktales,
fairy tales, and true tales.* New York: Blue Sky Press.
Broadening readers' understanding of themselves, this collection
focuses on the magical lore and wondrous imaginings of African American women.

Hearne, B. (1997). *Seven brave women.* New York: Greenwillow
Books.
A young narrator recounts the brave exploits of her female ancestors, including her great-great-great-grandmother, Elizabeth,
who came to America on a wooden sailboat. As readers explore
the narrator's family history, they also witness different chapters
of American history from the Revolutionary War to the present.

Hurwin, D. W. (1997). *A time for dancing.* New York: Viking
Penguin Books.
What do you do when your best friend is dying? Two seven-
teen-year-old friends tell their story after one of them is diag-
nosed with incurable cancer.

Kehert, P. (1993). *Cages.* New York: Pocket Books.
Upset about problems in her life, a young girl steals and is caught.
She risks losing a scholarship, and her relationship with her best

friend is strained. The only good thing about the situation turns out to be her sentence—20 hours of volunteer work at the humane society where she finds out about her own potential.

Keiller, G., & Nilsson, J. L. (1996). *The sandy bottom orchestra.* New York: Hyperion Books.

Fourteen-year-old Rachel comes to terms with her eccentric family while taking refuge in her violin playing.

Kindl, P. (1997). *The woman in the wall.* Boston: Houghton Mifflin.

Anna is fourteen and painfully shy. She disappears into the woodwork of her family's house and hides until a message gives her a reason to emerge.

Krantz, H. (1997). *Walks in beauty.* Flagstaff, AZ: Northland Publishing.

Describing the life of a young Navajo teenage girl during her last year of junior high school, this novel recounts her school experiences, a first boyfriend, traditional rites of passage, and a self-examination of cultural values. It tells of her growth and how she learns to define and accept herself.

Krisher, T. (1994). *Spite fences.* New York: Bantam Doubleday Dell Publishing Group, Inc.

Growing up in the South just before the Civil Rights' Movement in the 1960s, a thirteen-year-old white girl in a black community has friendships that threaten the town's way of life. With her camera she finds a way to independence and a different kind of truth.

Koller, J. F. (1997). *A place called home.* New York: Simon & Schuster.

Learning that making decisions takes more than courage, fifteen-year-old Anna is determined to protect her brother and sister while keeping everyone else from finding out about her mother's disappearance.

Levine, G. C. (1997). *Ella enchanted.* New York: Harper Collins.
This spirited account of spunky, intelligent, funny Ella's tells of her quest to break the curse laid on her and her determination to be herself.

MacLachlan, P. (1993). *Baby.* New York: Bantam Doubleday Dell Publishing Group, Inc.
Discovering a baby girl in a basket outside her home, a twelve-year-old girl and her family come to love her, knowing that some-day the real mother will return to take the child away.

Naylor, P. R. (1998). *Ice.* New York: Simon and Schuster for Young Readers.
Thirteen-year-old Chrissa moves to her grandmother's farm to live. She learns more about her absent father and some of the reasons for her distant relationship with her mother.

Nolan, H. (1997). *Dancing on the edge.* New York: Harcourt Brace.
A young girl from a dysfunctional family creates an alternative world that nearly results in her death, but ultimately leads her to reality.

Pfitsch, P. C. (1997). *Keeper of the light.* New York: Simon & Schuster.
Faith Sutton, a young woman in the 1870s, takes over her father's job as lighthouse keeper on Lake Superior after he dies in a daring rescue attempt. When the new inexperienced keeper arrives, Faith reluctantly moves to town with her mother who, along with society, does not approve of Faith's lighthouse duties. Despite a promise made to her mother, Faith returns to the light-

house when an unexpected storm threatens the ship on which her mother is a passenger.

Richmond, M.A. (1992). *Phillis Wheatley (American women of achievement).* New York: Chelsea House Publishing.
Narrating the life of the first African American published poet, this historical novel recounts the life in early colonial America for a young, gifted enslaved girl. Her efforts to define self, develop literary talents and fight for freedom are highlighted against the background of the Revolutionary War and slavery.

Schroeder, A. (1993). *Ragtime tumpie.* New York: Little, Brown & Co.
A young black girl who will later become famous as the dancer, Josephine Baker, longs to find the opportunity to dance amid the poverty and vivacious street life of St. Louis in the early 1900s.

Web Sites

General Sites

Advancing Women in Leadership
An on-line journal for women in leadership; publishes manuscripts that report, synthesize, review or analyze scholarly inquiries focusing on women's issues.
www.advancingwomen.com/index.html

A Girl's World Online Clubhouse
A chat room, pen-pals, book list for parents and teachers and much more— written for girls by girls, with the help of caring grown-ups; a fun way to help girls develop comfort levels in using computers.
www.agirlsworld.com/info/parents.html

Blue Jean Magazine
Samplings from the popular paper magazine for young women.
www.bluejeanmag.com

Empowered Young Females
An attractive web edition of the print magazine (updated monthly).
www.girlpower.com

Hues Magazine
For girls of every background and culture, an awesome online magazine.
www.hues.net/

Teen Voices Online
Poetry, articles, and advice columns, written by young teen women, that challenge today's media images of women.
www.teenvoices.com

Womenspace
Online quarterly sponsored by the Women's Pharmacy dedicated to young women introduces important topics which are sometimes neglected by other publications.
www.womenspace.com

Gifted/Talented Sites

Gifted Resources Homepage
Links to on-line gifted resources, programs, talent searches, mailing lists, associations and much, much more.
www.eskimo.com/~user/kids.html

IAAY at Johns Hopkins University
Promoting the academic ability of children and youth through challenging programs in math, the sciences, and humanities.
www.jhu.edu/~gifted

Kidsource Online
Information on gifted children, the college process, discussion list addresses, and many valuable links.
www.kidsource.com/kidsource/content2/Help_My_gifted_child.html

GT World
Online support community for parents of gifted/talented children offering different electronic venues where people can gather.
www.gtworld.org/

Women and Talent: To Encourage More Expression of the Multiple Talents of All Gifted Women
Articles, interviews, topics, quotes, awareness, book lists, lists of films and television shows with gifted/talented characters and more.
www.rocamora.org/womentalent.html

Parenting

Expect the Best for a Girl. That's What You'll Get
What parents can do—resources, programs, institutions, publications.
www.academic.org./programs.html

Personal Development

An Income of Her Own
Supporting female entrepreneurship through articles, activities, and resources.
www.aioho.com

Dare to Dream Foundation
Exposing middle school girls to successful female role models from every walk of life and across every profession.
www.daretodream.org

Girl Power
Features excerpts from the *Girl Power* book, list of resources for meeting other girls with similar interests, and a "speak out!" area.
www.girlpower.com

Girl Power
Sponsored by the Department of the Health and Human Services to encourage and empower girls ages 9-14 to make the most of their lives.
www.health.org/gpower/index.htm

G.I.R.L.S Conference Homepage
Growing Individuals Reacting to Life Struggles, sponsored by Simmons College.
www.gis.net/~adena/girls.htm

UNICEF'S Voices of Youth: The Girl Child
Explore the path of a girls life, dangers, stories of girls around the world, girls' education; discuss, give opinions, and write others; take action—learn how to understand your actions.
www.unicef.org/voy/meeting/gir/girhome.html

Programs

Action without Borders
Links people and organizations in 120 countries to find solutions to social and environmental problems.
www.idealist.org

Expect the Best from a Girl
A sampling of programs for girls in the arts, writing, math, ecology, leadership, entrepreneurship, science, athletics, theater, and much more to encourage girls, ages 11-14, to spend time with the computer in a friendly, interactive way.
www.academic.org/index.htm/#1ndex

The Girls' Middle School
An innovative curriculum to prepare 6th-8th grade girls for leadership roles.
www.girlsms.org/index.html

The National Museum of Women in the Arts
Celebration of the achievements of women artists.
www.nmwa.org

Technology

Children's Software Review
All kids can go on adventures, make things, explore and learn with good software that doesn't necessarily have a "girlish" theme.
www.childrenssoftware.com

Cybergrrl, Inc.
Webgrrls networking and resources for learning about the Internet and exploring job opportunities; Fencina search engine of women-oriented web sites.
www.cybergrrl.com/

Girl Games, Inc.
Encourages girls ages 11-14 to spend time with the computer.
www.girlgamesinc.com

Girltech
Encourages girls' interest in computers, tips for teachers, and links to women and girls in technology.
math.rice.edu/~lanius/club/girls.html

Mentor Net
The National Electronic Industrial Mentoring Network for Women in Engineering and Science pairs women studying these topics to a participating university so they can become a part of

email mentorships.
www.engr.sjsu.edu/~mentornt/

Superkids Software Review of Software for Girls
Teams of parents, teachers, and kids look at software available
for kids.
www.superkids.com/aweb/pages/reviews/girls1/sw_sum1.html

The Backyard Project
For high school girls exploring a career in computer science this
site offers information about jobs, money, interviews, education,
and computers everywhere.
www.backyard.org/edu/

Tomorrow's Women in Science and Technology
Promotes science and math education and career planning for
girls and women.
www.sig.net/~scicomp/twist/twist.html

Women of NASA
Encourages young women to pursue careers in math, science,
and technology this interactive project showcases outstanding
women in these fields.
quest.arc.nasa.gov/women/intro.html

MATHEMATICS AND SCIENCE RESOURCES

Because so many girls have heard and internalized stereotypes
about their math and science abilities, it is important to encourage
young girls to take mathematics and science through all four years
of high school so that as many career options will be open to them
as possible. I have included an extensive listing of mathematics and
science resources to help in this journey. I believe that these resources will help open up possibilities for girls as they gain confidence and experience with mathematics and science.

Annotated Resources

Downie, D., Slesnick, T., & kerr Stenmark, J. (1981) *Math for girls and other problem solvers.* Berkeley, CA: Equals, Lawrence Hall of Science.
This book presents a variety of activities that make mathematics fun and challenging. Topics explored include logic strategies and patterns, creative thinking, estimation, observation, spatial visualization, and careers.

Erickson, T. (1989). *Get it together.* Palo Alto, CA: Dale Seymour Publications.
Erickson, T. (1996) *United we solve.* Oakland, CA: eeps media.
These two books specifically outline activities for groups using manipulatives ranging from pattern blocks to *M&M's* and toothpicks. Problems have a wide range of topics and levels of difficulty, but all have the same format—six clue cards which together provide the information needed to solve the problem. Everyone in a group must work together because each member has different information needed for the solution.

Math for girls: The book with the number to get girls to love and excel in math! (1989). Peachtree City, GA: Gallopade Publishing Group.
Stories, puzzles, games and problems make math enjoyable, and the variety of topics included in the book, such as parties, music, tennis, pizza, and friends) are designed to appeal to girls.
Phone: (707) 631-4222

Research and Planning Center, University of Nevada. *Addventures for girls: Building math confidence: Elementary school.* Newton, MA: WEEA Publishing Center.
Research and Planning Center, University of Nevada. *Addventures for girls: Building math confidence: Junior high teacher's guide.* Newton, MA: WEEA Publishing Center.
These books combine teacher development with strategies that

work in teaching mathematics to girls. They include chapters on computer equity issues which give a list of questions for schools and/or teachers to assess the computer learning climate for girls and discuss strategies for making computer education more accessible and appealing to girls.

Skolnick, J., Langbort, C., & Day, L. (1986). *How to encourage girls in math & science: Strategies for parents and educators.* Reading, MA: Addison-Wesley Publishing.
This book focuses on ways to help girls acquire the skills and confidence they need to pursue a full range of interests in mathematics and science. It includes strategies and activities for developing spatial visualization, working with numbers, logical reasoning, and scientific investigation.

Steiner, R. (1997). *Spaces: Solving problems of access to careers in engineering and science.* Palo Alto, CA: Dale Seymour Publications.
The activities in *Spaces* are designed to stimulate students' curiosity and interest in doing mathematics. The classroom-tested lessons develop problem-solving skills and logical reasoning, build familiarity with mechanical tools, strengthen spatial visualization skills, and teach the importance of mathematics for opening occupational doors.

Other Teaching Resources

Burns, M. (1976). *The book of think (Or how to solve a problem twice your size).* Boston: Little, Brown, & Co.

Burns, M. (1982). *Math for smarty pants.* Boston: Little, Brown, & Co.

Campbell, P. B. (1992). *Nothing can stop us now: Designing effective programs for girls in math, science, and engineering.* Newton, MA: Women's Educational Equity Act.

Campbell, P. B. (1992). *Working together, making changes: Working in and out of schools to encourage girls in science and math.* Newton, MA: Women's Educational Equity Act.

Campbell, P. B. (1992). *Working together, making changes: Working in and out of schools to encourage girls in science and math.* Newton, MA: Women's Educational Equity Act.

Damarin, S. (1990). **Teaching mathematics: a feminist perspective.** In T. J. Cooney & C. R. Hirsch (Eds.), *Teaching and learning mathematics in the 1990s.* (pp. 144-158). Reston, VA: National Council of Teachers of Mathematics.

Eddins, S. & House, P. (1994). **Flexible pathways: Guiding the development of talented students.** In C. A. Thornton & N. S. Bley (Eds.) *Windows of opportunity: Mathematics for students with special needs.* Reston, VA: The National Council of Teachers of Mathematics.

Erickson, T. (1986). *Off & running: The computer offline activities book.* Berkeley, CA: Equals, Lawrence Hall of Science.

Fennema, E., & Leder, G. C. (1990). *Mathematics and gender.* New York: Teachers College Press.

Hanson, K. (1992). *Teaching mathematics effectively and equitably to females.* Newton, MA: WEEA Publishing Center/Center for Equity and Cultural Diversity.

Leder, G.C. (1993). **Mathematics and gender.** In D. A. Grouws (Ed.) *Handbook of research on mathematics teaching and learning.* (pp. 597-622). Reston, VA: The National Council of Teachers of Mathematics.

National Council of Teachers of Mathematics. (1989). *Curriculum and evaluation standards for school mathematics.* Reston, VA: The National Council of Teachers of Mathematics.

National Council of Teachers of Mathematics. (1992). *Data analysis and statistics across the curriculum.* Reston, VA: The National Council of Teachers of Mathematics.

National Council of Teachers of Mathematics. (1991). *Professional standards for teaching mathematics.* Reston, VA: The National Council of Teachers of Mathematics.

Perl, T. (1978). *Math equals.* Menlo Park, CA: Addison-Wesley.

Sanders, J., Koch, J., & Urso, J. (1997). *Gender equity right from the start: Instructional activities for teacher educators in mathematics, science, and technology.* Hillsdale, NJ: Lawrence Erlbaum Association.

Secada, W. G., Fennema, E., & Adajian, L. B. (1995). *New directions for equity in mathematics education.* New York: Cambridge University Press.

Stenmark, J. K., Thompson, V., & Cossey, R. (1986). *Family math.* Berkeley, CA: Lawrence Hall of Science, University of California.

Wilson, M. (Ed.), (1992). *Options for girls: A door to the future. An anthology on science and math education.* Austin, TX: Pro-Ed.

Programs/Projects

Equals

Targeted at teachers and community leaders, this project provides training and curriculum materials that promote female participation and success in mathematics courses and math-based careers. Its "Family Math and Science Programs" link home and school to spur enthusiasm for math and science.

Equals, Lawrence Hall of Science, University of California at Berkeley, Berkeley, CA 94720
Phone: (510) 642-1823   *Fax: (510) 643-5757*

Expanding Your Horizons

This project provides teachers with strategies that assist them in increasing the participation, retention and advancement of girls and women in mathematics, science, and technology.

Exploring Your Horizons, Math/Science Network, 2727 College Avenue, Berkeley, CA 94705
Phone: (510) 430-2222

Operation Smart

This research-based program provides hands-on experiences and exploration of careers in math, science and technology.

Operation, Girls Incorporated, 30 E. 33rd Street, New York, NY 10016
Phone: (212) 689-3700
www.girlsinc.org/programs.html

The Program for Women and Girls

The National Science Foundation offers model and experimental projects to support girls in science, engineering, and mathematics.
The Program for Women and Girls, Division of Human Resources Department, 4201 Wilson Blvd., Arlington, VA 22230
Phone: (703) 306-1637

Science-By-Mail

A one-of-a-kind program, *Science-By-Mail* guides children through inquiry and exploration and helps develop a positive understanding of the process of science. They make their own observations, conduct hands-on activities, ask questions, and communicate with their peers and pen pals.
Science-By-Mail, Museum of Science, Science Park, Boston, MA 02114-1099
Phone: (800) 729-3300
www.mos.org/mos/sbm/sciencemail.html   sbm@mos.org

Space Camp

Programs for grades 4-12 include simulated astronaut training, emphasis on space shuttle operations, and mission training.
Space Camp. U.S. Space & Rocket Center, One Tranquility Base, Huntsville, AL 35805
Phone: 800-63SPACE
www.spacecamp.com

Resources on Notable Women in Mathematics and Science

Cooney, M. (1996). *Celebrating women in mathematics and science*. Reston, VA: National Council of Teachers of Mathematics.

Featuring 22 biographies of notable female mathematicians and scientists, this book shows how their determination, creativity, and intellectual passion helped them excel in their fields. Appropriate for middle and high school levels, the text supplies many references for history of mathematics courses and is filled with excellent illustrations similar to woodcuts.

Edeen, S., Edeen, J., & Slachman, V. (1990). *Portraits for classroom bulletin boards: Women mathematicians.* Palo Alto, CA: Dale Seymour Publications.

Teachers can use this set of black-line drawings (8" x 11") of 15 pioneering mathematicians with accompanying one-page biographies for quick bulletin boards or student handouts. The set is also available with a hypercard program for student exploration or classroom presentation.

McGrayne, S. B. (1993). *Nobel prize women in science: Their lives, struggles and momentous discoveries.* New York, NY: Carol Publishing Co.

The stories of fourteen women, most of whom are far from familiar, who have changed the face of science for all time, are told in this volume. Their lives and work make compelling reading along with the events and conditions that they had to overcome.

National Women's History Project. (1996). *Telling our stories: Women in science* [CD-ROM]. Windsor, CA: National Women's History Project.

Interviews, personal photos, interactive experiments, multimedia field trips, and more tell the compelling stories of eight women scientists and their work are told through. A text and photo database highlights an additional 130 women scientists. For PC Windows or Macintosh.

Perl, T. (1993). *Women and numbers: Lives of women mathematicians plus discovery activities.* San Carlos, CA: World Wide Publishing/Tetra.

Biographies of 13 outstanding mathematicians from the 19th and 20th centuries examine where and how these women's interests in mathematics originated and their accomplishments in their chosen fields. It also includes enjoyable activities based on each woman's contributions to mathematics.

Showell, E. H., & Amram, F. M.B. (1995). *From indian corn to outer space: women invent in America.* Cobblestone Publishing Co.

Fascinating portraits of female inventors reveal their struggles for recognition in this decidedly male area of accomplishment.

Stille, D. R. (1997). *Extraordinary women of medicine.* New York, NY: Children's Press.

Biographical sketches of mainly American women highlight their contributions in the field of medicine during the 19th and 20th centuries. Also in the series are *Extraordinary Women Scientists* and *Extraordinary Young People.*

Veglahn, N. (1992). *Women scientists.* Windsor, CA: National Women's History Project.

This book features biographical sketches of eleven women whose accomplishments have won them recognition in their field. Included are Annie Jump Cannon, Margaret Mead, Alice Hamilton, Barbara McClintock, Rachel Carson, Rosalyn Yalow, Gerty Cori, and others.

Warren, R. L., & Thompson, Mary H. (1995, 1996). *The scientist within you : Women scientists from seven continents, biographies and activities.* Eugene, OR: ACI Publishing.

Warren, R. L., & Thompson, Mary H. (1995). *The scientist within you¨: Experiments and biographies of distinguished women in science.* Eugene, OR: ACI Publishing.

In these two volumes international female scientists take the stage. Each chapter features the work and biography of a scientist, along with a lesson plan including a related experiment, worksheets, and bibliography to make the subject area come alive for students.

Mathematics and Science Organizations

Advocates for Women in Science, Engineering and Math
P.O. Box 91000
Portland, OR 97291-1000
Phone: (503) 690-1261
www.awsem.com/

American Association of University Women
1111 16th Street NW
Washington, DC 20036-4873
Phone: (202) 785-7700
www.aauw.org/

Association for Women in Mathematics
4114 Computer and Space Building
University of Maryland
College Park, MD 20741-2461
Phone: (301) 405-7892

Association for Women in Science
1522 K St. N.W., Suite 820
Washington, DC 20005
Phone: (202) 408-0742

Junior Engineering Technical Society (JET)
1420 King Street, Suite 405
Alexandria, VA 22314
Phone: (703) 548-5387

Linkages Program
American Association for the Advancement of Science
1333 H Street, NW
Washington, DC 20005
Phone: (202) 326-6400

MATH COUNTS
1420 King Street
Alexandria, VA 22314-2794
Phone: (703) 684-2828

Multiply Your Options
Karen Sherrick
PIMMS (Project to Increase Mastery of
Mathematics and Science)
Wesleyan University
Middletown, CT 06457

National Academy of Sciences
NRC, Committee on Women in Science and Engineering
2101 Constitution Ave. N.W.
Washington, DC 20418
Phone: (202) 334-2000

National Coalition for Women and Girls in Education
National Education Association
1201 16th Street NW
Washington, DC 20036

The Association for Women and Mathematics (AWM)
Room 4414, CSS Building
University of Maryland
College Park, MD 20742.

Women and Mathematics Education
SummerMath
Mount Holyoke College
50 College St.
South Hadley, MA 01075
Phone: (413) 538-2608

References

REFERENCES

American Association of University Women (AAUW). (1991). *Short-changing girls, shortchanging America: A call to action.* Washington, D. C.: The American Association of University Women Educational Foundation.

American Association of University Women (AAUW). (1992). *The AAUW report: How schools shortchange girls.* Washington, DC: The American Association of University Women Educational Foundation.

American Association of University Women (AAUW). (1998). *Separated by sex: A critical look at single-sex education for girls.* Washington, D. C.: The American Association of University Women Educational Foundation.

Achenbach, T. M. (1970). Standardization of a research instrument for identifying associative responding in children. *Developmental Psychology, 2,* 283-291.

Ajzenberg-Selove, F., (1994). *A matter of choices: Memoirs of a female physicist.* Brunswick, N J, Rutgers University Press.

Ambert, A.N., & Figler, C. S. (1992). Puerto Ricans: Historical and cultural perspectives. In A. N. Ambert & M. D. Alvarez (Eds.), *Puerto Rican children on the mainland: Interdisciplinary perspectives* (pp. 17-37). New York: Garland Publishing.

American College Testing Program. (1989). *State and national trend data for students who take the ACT Assessment.* Iowa City: American College Testing Program.

American women: Where we are now. (1997, July). *Ladies Home Journal.* 131-133.

Ames, J. E. (1997). *Mastery: Interviews with 30 remarkable people.* Portland, OR: Rudra Press.

Arnold, K. D. (1995). *Lives of Promise.* San Francisco: Jossey-Bass Publishers.

Arnold, K. D., & Denny, T. (1985). *The lives of academic achievers: The career aspirations of male and female high school valedictorians and salutatorians.* Paper presented at the annual meeting of the American Educational Research Association, Chicago, IL.

Axelrod, T. (1988). Patently successful. *Ms., 16*(10), 44-45.

Bandura, A. (1977). Self-efficacy: Toward a unifying theory of behavioral change. *Psychological Review,* 84, 191-215.

Bandura, A. (1986). *Social foundations of thought and action: A social cognitive theory.* EnglewoodCliffs, NJ: Prentice-Hall.

Bardwick, J. M. (Ed.). (1972). *Readings on the psychology of women.* New York: Harper & Row.

Bateson, M. C. (1990). *Composing a life.* New York: Plume, The Penguin Group.

Beard, G.M. (1874). *Legal responsibility in old age.* New York: Russell Sage Foundation.

Beck, M., Kantrowski, B., & Beachy, L. (1990, July 16). Trading places. *Newsweek,* 48-54.

Becker, D. F., & Forsyth, R. A. (1990). *Gender differences in grades 3 through 12: A longitudinal analysis.* Paper presented at the meeting of the American Educational Research Association, Boston, MA.

Belenky, M. F., Clinchy, B. M., Goldberger, N. R., & Tarule, J. M. (1986). *Women's ways of knowing.* New York: Basic Books.

Bell, L. A. (1989). Something's wrong here and it's not me: Challenging the dilemmas that block girls' success. *Journal for the Education of the Gifted, 12*(2), 118-130.

Benbow, C. P., & Stanley, J. C. (1980). Sex differences in mathematical ability: Fact or artifact? *Science, 210,* 1262-1264.

Blaubergs, M.S. (1980) Sex-role stereotyping and gifted girls' experience and education. *Roeper Review, 2*(3), 13-15.

Block, J. H. (1982). *Sex role identity and ego development.* San Francisco: Jossey-Bass.

Boyer, E. L. (1987). *College: The undergraduate experience in America.* New York: Harper & Row.

Brandon, P., Newton, B., & Hammond, O. (1987). Children's mathematics achievement in Hawaii: Sex differences favoring girls. *American Educational Research Journal, 24*(3), 437-461.

Brandwein, P. F., & Passow, A. H. (Eds.). (1988). *Gifted young in science: Potential through performance.* Washington, DC: National Science Teachers Association.

Brophy, J., & Good, T.L. (1974). *Teacher-student relationships: Causes and consequences.* New York: Holt, Rinehart, & Winston

Buerk, D., & Gibson, H. (1994). Students' metaphors for mathematics: Gathering, interpreting, implications. *WME Newsletter, 16*(2), 2-8.

Buescher, T. M., Olszewski, P., & Higham, S. J. (1987). *Influences on strategies adolescents use to cope with their own recognized talents.* (Report No. EC 200 755). Paper presented at the biennial meeting of the Society for Research in Child Development, Baltimore, MD.

Byrnes, J. R., & Takahira, S. (1993). Explaining gender differences on SAT-math items. *Developmental Psychology, 29,* 805-811.

Callahan, C. M. (1979). The gifted and talented woman. In A. H. Passow (Ed.), *The gifted and talented* (pp. 401-423). Chicago: National Society for the Study of Education.

Callahan, C. M., Cunningham, C. M., & Plucker, J. A. (1994). Foundations for the future: The socio-emotional development of gifted, adolescent women. *Roeper Review, 17,* 99-105.

Campbell, J. R., Connolly, C., Lacattiva, C., & Pizzo, J. (1985). *Math/science gender gap: Influence of parents on gifted Asian and Caucasian children.* Paper presented at the annual meeting of the American Educational Research Association, Chicago, IL.

Campbell, K. L., & Evans, L. (1993, November 12). *Gender issues and the math/science curricula: Effects on females.* Presentation to the Mid-South Educational Research Association, New Orleans, LA.

Campbell, P. (1992). *Nothing can stop us now: Designing effective programs for girls in math, science, and engineering.* Newton, MA: Women's Educational Equity Act.

Casserly, P. L. (1975). *An assessment of factors affecting female participation in advanced placement programs in mathematics, chemistry, and physics.* Report of National Science Foundation (Grant GY-11325). Princeton, NJ: Educational Testing Service.

Celsi, T. (1992). *The fourth little pig.* Austin, TX: Raintree Steck-Vaughn Publishers.

Chamberlain, M. K. (Ed.). (1988). *Women in academe: Progress and prospects.* New York: Russell Sage Foundation.

Chipman, S. (1988). Far too sexy a topic. *Educational Researcher, 17*(3), 46-49.

Chipman, S. F., Brush, L., & Wilson, D. (Eds.) (1985). *Women and mathematics: Balancing the equation.* New York: Erlbaum Associates.

Clance, P. R., & Imes, S. A. (1978). The imposter phenomenon in high achieving women: Dynamics and therapeutic intervention. *Psychotherapy: Theory, research, and practice, 15*, 241-245.

Clance, P. R. (1985). The imposter phenomenon. *New Woman, 15*(7), 40-43.

Clark, B. (1992). *Growing up gifted.* New York: Merrill.

Cole, J. (1979). *Fair science: Women in the scientific community.* New York: The Free Press.

Cole, J., & Zuckerman, H. (1987). Marriage, motherhood, and research performance in science. *Scientific American, 256*(2), 119-125.

Cole, K. C. (1994, March). Science discovers women. *Lears.* 56-61, 82-83.

Coleman, J. (1961). *The adolescent society.* New York: Free Press.

Comas-Diaz, L. (1989). Culturally relevant issues and treatment implications for Hispanics. In D. R. Koslow & E. P. Salett (Eds.), *Crossing cultures in mental health* (pp. 31-48). Washington, DC: International Counseling Center.

Cooley, D., Chauvin, J., & Karnes, F. (1984). Gifted females: A comparison of attitudes by male and female teachers. *Roeper Review, 6,* 164-167.

Cordeiro, P. A. (1991). *An ethnography of high achieving at-risk Hispanic youths at two urban high schools: Implications for administrators.* Paper presented at the Annual Meeting of the American Educational Research Association, Chicago, IL.

Cramer, R. H. (1989). Attitudes of gifted boys and girls towards math: A qualitative study. *Roeper Review, 11,* 128-133.

Crocker, A. C. (1987). Underachieving, gifted, working class boys: Are they wrongly labelled underachieving? *Educational Studies, 13*(2), 169-178.

Crombie, G., Bouffard-Bouchard, T., & Schneider, B. H. (1992). Gifted programs: Gender differences in referral and enrollment. *Gifted Child Quarterly, 36*(4), 213-214.

Csikszentmihalyi, M. (1997). *Creativity.* New York: Harper Perennial.

Dabrowski, K. (1967). *Personality-shaping through positive disintegration.* Boston: Little Brown.

Damarin, S. K. (1990). Teaching mathematics: A feminist perspective. In T. J. Conney and C. R. Hiersch (Eds.), *Teaching and learning mathematics in the 1990's.* (pp. 144-158). Reston, VA: National Council of Teachers of Mathematics.

Dash, J. (1988). *A life of one's own.* New York: Paragon House Publishers.

Davis, J. A. (1964). *Great aspirations: The school plans of America's college seniors.* Chicago: Aldine.

Debold, E., Wilson, M., & Malave, I. (1993). *Mother daughter revolution.* Redding, MA: Addison Wesley Longman.

Dembart, L. (1984, March 7). Science: Social and cultural factors limit women's job opportunities. *Los Angeles Times*, p. 2.

Dickens, M. N. (1990). *Parental influences on the mathematics self-concept of high achieving adolescent girls.* Unpublished doctoral dissertation, University of Virginia, Charlottesville.

Dobrzynski, J. H. (1997, October 12). Anonymous gifts, so women artists won't be. *New York Times*, p. 1, 14.

Dolny, C. (1985). University of Toronto schools' gifted students' career and family plans. *Roeper Review, 7*(3), 160-162.

Dowling, C. (1981, March 22). The Cinderella syndrome. *The New York Times Magazine*, 47-50, 54-56.

Dreyden, J. I., & Gallagher, S. A. (1989). The effects of time and direction changes on the SAT performance of academically talented adolescents. *Journal for the Education of the Gifted, 12*(3), 187-204.

Dweck, C. S. (1986). Motivation processes affecting learning. *American Psychologist, 41,* 1040-1048.

Eccles, J. S. (1984). Sex differences in mathematics participation. In M. Steinkamp & M. Maehr (Eds.), *Women in Science.* Greenwich, CT: JAI Press.

Eccles, J. S. (1985). Why doesn't Jane run? Sex differences in education and occupational patterns. In F. D. Horowitz & M. O'Brien (Eds.), *The gifted and talented: Developmental perspectives.* (pp. 251-295). Washington, D C: American Psychological Association.

Eccles, J. S. (1987a). *Understanding motivation: Achievement beliefs, gender roles and changing educational environments.* Paper presented at the annual meeting of the American Psychological Association, New York, NY.

Eccles, J. S. (1987b). Gender roles and women's achievement-related decisions. *Psychology of Women Quarterly, 11*(2), 135-172.

Eccles, J. S., & Blumfield, P. (1985). Classroom experiences and student gender: Are there differences and do they matter? In L. C. Wilkinson & C. B. Marret (Eds.), *Gender influences in classroom interaction* (pp. 79-114). Orlando, FL: Academic Press.

Eccles, J. S., Midgley, C., & Adler, T. F. (1984). Grade-related changes in the school environment: Effects on achievement motivation. In J. Nicholls (Ed.), *Advances in motivation and achievement* (Vol. 3, pp. 283-331). Greenwich, CT: JAI Press.

Educational Testing Service. (1996). *1996 college-bound seniors: A profile of SAT program test takers.* Princeton, NJ: Educational Testing Service.

Ehrlich, V. (1982). *Gifted children: A guide for parents and teachers.* Englewood Cliffs, NJ: Prentice-Hall.

Epstein, G. (1997, December). Low ceiling: How women are held back by sexism at work and child-rearing duties at home. *Barron's,* 35-36

EQUALS. (1986). *Family Math.* Berkeley, CA: Lawrence Hall of Science, University of California.

EQUALS. (1989). *Family Science.* Berkeley, CA: Lawrence Hall of Science, University of California.

Erkut, S. (1983, February). Exploring sex differences in expectancy, attribution, and academic achievement. *Sex Roles, 9,* 217-231.

Etzkowitz, H., Kemelgor, C., Neuschatz, M., Uzzi, B., & Alonzo, J. (1994). The paradox of critical mass for women in science. *Science, 266,* 51-54.

Falicov, C. J. (1982). Mexican families. In M. McGoldrick, J. K. Pearce, & J. Giordano (Eds.), *Ethnicity and family therapy* (pp. 134-163). New York: The Guilford Press.

Feingold, A. (1988). Cognitive gender differences are disappearing. *American Psychologist, 43*(2), 95-103.

Feldhusen, J. F., & Willard-Holt, C. (1993). Gender differences in classroom interaction and career aspirations of gifted students. *Contemporary Education Psychology, 18,* 355-362.

Fennema, E. (1974). Mathematics learning and the sexes: A review. *Journal for Research in Mathematics Education, 5,* 126-139.

Fennema, E. (1990). Teachers' beliefs and gender differences in mathematics. In E. Fennema & G. Leder (Eds.), *Mathematics and gender* (pp. 1-9). New York: Teachers College Press.

Fennema, E., & Leder, G. (Eds.). (1990). *Mathematics and gender.* New York: Teachers College Press.

Fennema, E., Peterson, P. L., Carpenter, T. P., & Lubinski, C. A. (1990). Teachers' attributions and beliefs about girls, boys, and mathematics. *Educational Studies in Mathematics, 21,* 55-69.

Fennema, E., & Sherman, J. (1977). Sex related differences in mathematics achievement spatial visualization and affective factors. *American Educational Research Journal, 14,* 51-71.

Fernandez, R. (1989). *Five cities high school dropout study: Characteristics of hispanic high school students.* Washington, D.C.: ASPIRA Association Inc.

Figler, C. S. (1979). *Puerto Rican families: Their migration and assimilation.* Unpublished manuscript, University of Massachusetts, Boston.

Fitzgerald, L. F., & Crites, J. O. (1980). Toward a career psychology of women: What do we know? What do we need to know? *Journal of Counseling Psychology, 27,* 44-42.

Foley, P. (1986). *The dual role of experience of artist mothers.* Unpublished dissertation, Northwestern University, Chicago.

Ford, D. Y. (1992a). The American achievement ideology as perceived by urban African-American students. *Urban Education, 27*(2), 196-211.

Ford, D. Y. (1992b). Determinants of underachievement as perceived by gifted, above-average, and average black students. *Roeper Review, 14*(3), 130-136.

Fordham, S. (1988). Racelessness as a factor in black students' school success: Pragmatic strategy or pyrrhic victory? *Harvard Educational Review, 58*(1), 54-84.

Fordham, S., & Ogbu, J. U. (1986). Black students' school success: Coping with the "burden of 'acting white'." *Urban Review, 18*(3), 176-206.

Fowler, M. L. (1991). Gifted adolescent girls' science beliefs and strategies on a mechanical design task. *Dissertation Abstracts International, 52*(4), 1279-A.

Fox, L. H. (1977). Sex differences: Implications for program planning for the academically gifted. In J. C. Stanley, W. C. George, & C. H. Solano (Eds.), *The gifted and the creative: A fifty year perspective* (pp. 113-138). Baltimore, MD: Johns Hopkins University Press.

Fredrickson, R. H. (1979). Preparing gifted and talented students for the world of work. *Journal of Counseling and Development, 64*, 556-557.

Fredrickson, R. H. (1986). The multipotential as vocational decision-makers. In R.H. Fredrickson & J. W. M. Rothney (Eds.), *Recognizing and assisting multipotential youth*. Columbus, OH: Charles E. Merrill.

Friedan, B. (1993). *The Fountain of age.* New York: Simon & Schuster.

Gabor, A. (1995). *Einstein's wife: Work and marriage in the lives of five great twenty-first century women.* New York: Viking/Penguin.

Gallagher, S. A. (1996). A new look (again) at gifted girls and mathematics achievement. *The Journal of Secondary Gifted Education,11*(4), 459-475.

Gallagher, A., & DeLisi, R. (1994). Gender differences in Scholastic Aptitude Test-Mathematics problem solving among high-ability students. *Journal of Educational Psychology, 86* (2), 204-211.

Gandara, P. (1995). *Over the ivy walls.* Albany, NY: State University of New York Press.

Gavin, M. K. (1996). The development of math talent: Influences on students at a women's college. *The Journal of Secondary Gifted Education, II*(4), 476-485.

Gavin, M. K. (1997) *A gender study of students with high mathematics ability: Personological, educational, and parental variables related to the intent to pursue quantitative fields of study,* Unpublished doctoral dissertation, University of Connecticut, Storrs.

Gilligan, C. (1982). *In a different voice: Psychological theory and women's development.* Cambridge, MA: Harvard University Press.

Gilman, C. P. (1891). *Women and economics.* New York: Source Book Press.

Girl Scouts of the U.S.A. (1991). Girl Scouts: Its role in the lives of women of distinction. New York: Girl Scouts of the U.S.A.

Girl Scouts of the U.S.A. (1997). Girls, families and communities grow through scouting. New York: Girl Scouts of the U.S.A.

Glaser, R. D., & Thorpe, J. S. (1986, January). Unethical intimacy: A survey of sexual contact and advances between psychology educators and female graduate students. *American Psychologist, 40,* 43-51.

Gold, A. R., Brush, L. R., & Sprotzer, E. R. (1980). Developmental changes in self-perceptions of intelligence and self-confidence. *Psychology of Women Quarterly 5,* 670-680.

Good, T. L. & Brophy, J. E. (1973). *Looking in classrooms.* New York: Harper & Row.

Goodwin, D. K. (1997). *Wait till next year: A memoir.* New York: Simon & Schuster.

Grady, J. (1987). *Trends in the selection of science, mathematics, or engineering as major fields of study among top scoring SAT takers.* Princeton, NJ: Educational Testing Service.

Grant, L. (1988, July-August). The gender climate of medical schools: Perspectives of women and men students. *Journal of the American Medical Women's Association, 43,* 109-110, 115-119.

Grau, P. N. (1985). Counseling the gifted girl. *Gifted Child Today, 38*, 8-11.

Hailey, E. F. (1978). *A woman of independent means.* New York: Avon Books.

Hales, D. (1988, May). The female brain. *Ladies' Home Journal, 128*, 173-184.

Hall, R., & Sandler, B. (1982). *The classroom climate: A chilly one for women?* Washington, DC: Project on the Status and Education of Women, Association of American Colleges.

Hallinan, M. T., & Sorenson, A. B. (1987). Ability grouping and sex differences in mathematics achievement. *Sociology of Education, 60*, 63-72.

Halpern, D. (1989). The disappearance of cognitive gender differences: What you see depends on where you look. *American Psychologist, 44*, 1156-1158.

Hamachek, D. E. (1978). Psychodynamics of normal and neurotic perfectionism. *Psychology, 15*, 27-33.

Handley, H. M., & Morse, L. W. (1984). Two-year study relating adolescents' self-concept and gender role perceptions to achievement attitudes toward science. *Journal of Research in Science Teaching, 21*(6), 599-607.

Hanson, K. (1992). *Teaching mathematics effectively and equitably to females.* Newton, MA: WEEA Publishing Center/Center for Equity and Cultural Diverstiy.

Hany, E. A. (1994). The development of basic cognitive components of technical creativity: A longitudinal comparison of children and youth with high and average intelligence. In R. F. Subotnik & K. D. Arnold (Eds.), *Beyond Terman: Contemporary longitudinal studies of giftedness and talent* (pp. 115-154). Norwood, NJ: Ablex.

Harris, J. R. (1998). *The nurture assumption: Why children turn out the way they do.* New York: The Free Press

Hartmann, H. I. (1981). The family as the locus of gender, class, and political struggle: The example of housework. *Journal of Women in Culture and Society, 6*(3), 366-394.

Heilbrun, C. G. (1988). *Writing a woman's life.* New York: W.W. Norton & Co., Inc.

Heilbrun, C. G. (1997). *The last gift of time: Life beyond sixty.* New York: The Dial Press.

Heilman, M. E. & Stopeck, M. H. (1985a). Being attractive, advantage or disadvantage? Performance-based evaluations and recommended personnel actions as a function of appearance, sex and job type. *Organizational Behavior and Human Decision Processes, 35*(2), 202-215.

Heilman, M. E. & Stopeck, M. H. (1985b). Attractiveness and corporate success: Different causal attributions for males and females. *Journal of Applied Psychology, 70*(2), 379-388.

Henry, J., & Manning, G. (1998). Gender-based intervention making computer science appealing to girls in high school. Unpublished master's inquiry project, University of Connecticut, Storrs.

Hernandez Garduño, E. L. (1997). *Effects of teaching problem solving through cooperative learning methods on student mathematics achievement, attitudes toward mathematics, mathematics self-efficacy, and metacognition.* Unpublished doctoral dissertation, University of Connecticut, Storrs.

Hess, R. D., Holloway, S. D., Dickson, W. P., & Price, G. G. (1984). Maternal variables as predictors of children's school readiness and later achievement in vocabulary and mathematics in sixth grade. *Child Development, 55*, 1902-1912.

Hill, S. T. (1992). *Undergraduate origins of recent science and engineering doctorate recipients.* Washington, DC: National Science Foundation.

Hine, C. Y. (1991) *The home environment of gifted Puerto Rican children: Family factors which support high achievement.* Unpublished doctoral dissertation, University of Connecticut, Storrs.

Hochschild, A. (with Machung, A.). (1989). *The second shift: Working parents and the revolution at home.* New York: Viking/Penguin.

Hoffman, L. (1972). Early childhood experiences of women's achievement motive. *Journal of Social Issues, 28,* 129-155.

Holland, D. C., & Eisenhart, M.A. (1990). *Educated in romance: Women, achievement and college culture.* Chicago: University of Chicago Press.

Hollinger, C. L. (1991). Career choices for gifted adolescents: Overcoming stereotypes. In M. Bireley & J. Genshaft (Eds.), *Understanding the gifted adolescent: Educational, developmental and multicultural issues* (pp. 201-214). New York: Teachers College Press.

Hollinger, C. L., & Fleming, E. S. (1984). Internal barriers to the realization of potential correlates and interrelationships among gifted and talented female adolescents. *Gifted Child Quarterly, 28,* 135-139.

Hollinger, C. L., & Fleming, E. S. (1988). Gifted and talented young women: Antecedents and correlates of life satisfaction. *Gifted Child Quarterly, 32*(2), 254-260.

Horner, M. (1972). Toward an understanding of achievement related conflicts in women. *Journal of Social Issues, 28,* 157-176.

Horner, M. S. (1970). Femininity and successful achievement: A basic inconsistency. In J. Bardwick (Ed.), *Feminine personality and conflict.* Belmont, CA: Brooks/Cole.

Hyde, J. S., & Fennema, E. (1990). *Gender differences in mathematics performance and affect: Results of two meta-analyses.* Paper presented at the meeting of the American Educational Research Association, Boston, MA.

Ianni, F. A. J. (1989). Providing a structure for adolescent development. *Phi Delta Kappan, 70,* 673-682.

Isaac, T. & Shafer, S. (1989). *Sex equity in sports leadership: Implementing the game plan.* Lexington, KY: Eastern Kentucky University.

Jepsen, D. A. (1979). Helping gifted adolescents with career exploration. In N. Colangelo & R.T. Zaffrann (Eds.), *New voices in counseling the gifted* (pp.277-283). Dubuque, IA: Kendall/Hunt.

Jones, M. G. (1989). Gender issues in teacher education. *Journal of Teacher Education, 40,* 33-38.

Jones, M. G., & Wheatly, J. (1990). Gender differences in teacher-student interactions in science classrooms. *Journal of Research in Science Teaching, 27*(9), 861-874.

Josefowitz, N. (1980). *Paths to power.* New York: Addison Wesley Publishing Company.

Just how the sexes differ. (1981, May 18). *Newsweek,* 72-83.

Kahle, J. B. (1985). Retention of girls in science: Case studies of secondary teachers. In J. B. Kahle (Ed.), *Women and science: A report from the field* (pp. 49-76). Philadelphia: Palmer Press.

Kane, J. (1985, September). Star wars: How men are coping with female success. *Ms.,* 52-56.

ker Conway, J. (1989). *The road from Coorain.* New York: Knopf.

ker Conway, J. (1994). *True North.* New York: Knopf.

Kerr, B. A. (1981). Career education strategies for the gifted. *Journal of Career Education, 7,* 318-324.

Kerr, B. A. (1985). *Smart girls, gifted women.* Columbus, OH: Ohio Psychology Publishing Company.

Kerr, B., Colangelo, N., & Gaeth, J. (1988). Gifted adolescents' attitudes toward their giftedness. *Gifted Child Quarterly, 32*(2), 245-247.

Kerry, T. (1981). *Teaching bright pupils in mixed ability classes.* London: Macmillan.

Kimball, M. M. (1989). A new perspective on women's math achievement. *Psychological Bulletin, 105,* 198-214.

Kindergarten awards. (1994, December 5). *Wall Street Journal,* p. 7.

Kirschenbaum, R. J. (1980). Combating sexism in the preschool environment. *Roeper Review, 2,* 31-33.

Kirschenbaum, R. J. & Reis, S. M. (1997). Conflicts in creativity: Talented female artists. *Creativity Research Journal, 10*(2&3), pp. 251-263.

Kissane, B. V. (1986). Selection of mathematically talented students. *Educational Studies in Mathematics, 17,* 221-241.

Kitano, M. K. (1997). Gifted Asian American women. *Journal for the Education of the Gifted, 21*(1), 3-37.

Kitano, M. K. (1998). Gifted latina women. *Journal for the Education of the Gifted, 21*(2), pp. 131-159.

Kline, B. E., & Short, E. B. (1991). Changes in emotional resilience: Gifted adolescent females. *Roeper Review, 13,* 118-121.

Koehler, M. S. (1990). Classrooms, teachers, & gender differences in mathematics. In E. Fennema & G. C. Leder (Eds.), *Mathematics and gender,* (pp. 128-148). New York: Teachers College Press.

Kolloff, P. B. (1996). The development of math talent: Influences on students at a women's college. *Journal of Secondary Gifted Education, 7*(4), 476-485.

Kramer, L. R. (1985). *Social interaction and perceptions of ability: A study of gifted adolescent females.* Paper presented at the annual meeting of the American Educational Research Association. Chicago, IL.

Kramer, L. R. (1991). The social construction of ability perceptions: An ethnographic study of gifted adolescent girls. *Journal of Early Adolescence, 11*(3), 340-362.

Kramer, P. & Lehman, S. (1990). Mismeasuring women: A critique research on computer ability and avoidance. *Signs: Journal of Women in Culture and Society, 16*(1), 158-172.

Krupnick, C. G. (1984). *Sex differences in college teachers' classroom talk.* Unpublished doctoral dissertation, Harvard University, Cambridge, MA.

Krupnick, C. G. (1992). Unlearning gender roles. In K. Winston & M. J. Bane, (Eds.), *Gender and Public Policy: Cases and Comment.* Boulder, CO: Westview Press.

Kuebli, J. & Fivush, R. (1992). Gender differences in parent-child conversations about past emotions. *Sex Roles, 27*(11), 683-98.

Lashaway-Bokina, N. (1996). *Gifted, but gone: High ability, Mexican-American, female dropouts.* Unpublished doctoral dissertation, University of Connecticut, Storrs.

Lauria, A. (1964). Respeto, relajo and interpersonal relations in Puerto Rico. *Anthropological Quarterly, 37,* 53-67.

Leamer, L. (1994). *The Kennedy women.* New York: Villard Books.

Leder, G. C. (1990). Gender differences in mathematics: An overview. In E. Fennema & G. C. Leder (Eds.), *Mathematics and gender* (pp. 10-25). New York: Teachers College Press.

Lee, V. E. (1997). Gender equity and the organization of schools. In *Gender, equity, and schooling: Policy and practice* (p. 152). New York: Garland Publishing.

Lee, V., & Bryk, A. (1986). Effects of single sex secondary schools on student achievement and attitudes. *Journal of Educational Psychology, 78,* 381-395.

Lee, V. E., & Marks, H. M. (1990). Sustained effects of the single-sex secondary school experience on attitudes, behaviors and values in college. *Journal of Educational Psychology, 82*(3), 588.

Lee, V. E., & Marks, H. M. (1992). Who goes where? Choice of single-sex and coeducational independent secondary schools. *Sociology of Education 65*(3), 226-253.

Lee, V. E., Marks, H. M., & Byrd, T. (1994). Sexism in single-sex and coeducational independent secondary school classrooms. *Sociology of Education, 67*(2), 92-120.

Lehman, H. C. (1953). *Age and achievement.* Princeton, NJ: Princeton University Press.

Leppien, J. H. (1995). *The paradox of academic achievement in high ability, African American, female students in an urban elementary school.* Unpublished doctoral dissertation, University of Connecticut, Storrs.

Lerner, G. (1986). *The creation of patriarchy.* New York: Oxford University Press.

Lerner, G. (1993). *The creation of feminist consciousness.* New York: Oxford University Press.

Leroux, J. A. (1988). Voices from the classroom: Academic and social self-concepts of gifted adolescents. *Journal for the Education of the Gifted,* 11(3), 3-18.

Leroux, J. A., & Ho, C. (1994). Success and mathematically gifted female students: The challenge continues. *Feminist Teacher, 7*(2), 42-48.

Lewin, T. (1989, November 14). Ailing parent: Women's burden grows. *New York Times,* p. B1.12.

Linn, M., & Hyde, J. S. (1989). Gender, mathematics, and science. *Educational Researcher, 18*(8), 17-27.

Linn, M. C., & Kessle, C. (1995). Participation in mathematics courses and careers: Climate, grades, and entrance examination scores. Paper presented at the annual meeting of the American Education Research association, San Francisco, CA.

Linn, M., & Peterson, A. (1986). A meta-analysis of gender differences in spatial ability: Implications for mathematics and science achievement. In J. Hyde, & M. Linn (Eds.), *The psychology of gender: Advances through meta-analysis* (pp. 67-101). Baltimore, MD: Johns Hopkins.

Ludwig, M. M. (1996, July/August). Women in the olympics: A sport psychology perspective. *Coaching Women's Basketball,* 30-32.

Lummis, M. & Stevenson, H. W. (1990). Gender differences in beliefs and achievement: A cross cultural study. *Developmental Psychology, 26*(2), 254-263.

Maccoby, E. E., & Jacklin, C. N. (1974). *The psychology of sex differences.* Stanford, CA: Stanford University Press.

Mann, J. (1994). *The difference: Growing up female in America.* New York: Warner, 1994.

Mark, J. (1992, June). Beyond equal access: Gender equity in learning with computers. *Women's Educational Equity Act Publishing Center Digest,* 1-8.

Marsh, H. (1989). Effects of attending single-sex and co-educational high schools on achievement, attitudes, behaviors, and sex differences. *Journal of Educational Psychology, 81*(1), 78, 80.

Marshall, B.C. (1981). A career decision making pattern of gifted and talented adolescents: Implications for career education. *Journal of Career Education, 7,* 305-310.

Martin, D. C., & Murchie, E. B. (1992). *In search of gender free paradigms for computer science education.* (ERIC Document Reproduction Service No. ED 349 941)

Matyas, M. L., & Dix, L. S. (Eds.). (1992). Science and engineering programs: On target for women? Washington, DC: National Academy Press.

Mboya, M. M. (1986). Black adolescents: A descriptive study of their self-concepts and academic achievement. *Adolescence,* 21(83), 689-696.

McGillicuddy-De Lisi, A. V. (1985). The relationship between parental beliefs and children's cognitive level. In R. Sigel (Ed.), *Parental belief systems* (pp. 7-24). Hillsdale, NJ: Erlbaum.

McGrayne, A. B. (1993). *Nobel prize women in science.* New York: Birch Lane Press.

McLoughlin, M., Shryer, T. L., Goode, E., & McAuliffe, K. (1988, August 8). Men vs. women. *US News and World Report,* pp. 48-57.

Media (1998, January 19). Something to do until 'Titanic II' comes out. *Newsweek,* p. 6.

Mee, C. S. (1995, March). Middle school voices on gender identity. *Women's educational equity act publishing center digest,* 1-2, 5-6.

Meece, J. L., Blumenfeld, P. C., & Hoyle, R. H. (1988). Students' goal orientations and cognitive engagement in classroom activities. *Journal of Educational Psychology, 80,* 514-523.

Miller, J. B. (1976). *Toward a new psychology of women.* Boston: Beacon Press.

Munsch, R. (1980). *The paper bag princess.* Toronto: Annick Press, Ltd.

National Council of Teachers of Mathematics. (1989). *Curriculum and education standards for school mathematics.* Reston, VA: National Council of Teachers of Mathematics.

National Council of Teachers of Mathematics. (1992). *Data analysis and statistics across the curriculum.* Reston, VA: National Council of Teachers of Mathematics.

National Research Council. (1989). *Everybody counts: A report to the nation on the future of mathematics education.* Washington, DC: National Academy Press.

National Science Foundation. (1996, September). *Women, minorities, and persons with disabilities in science and engineering.* Arlington, VA: National Science Foundation.

Nelson, C, & Watson, J. A. (1991). The computer gender gap: Children's attitudes, performance, and socialization. *Journal of Education Technology Systems, 19*(4), 343-5-353.

Noble, K. D. (1987). The delimma of the gifted woman. *Psychology of Women Quarterly, 11,* 367-378.

Noble, K. D. (1989). Counseling gifted women: Becoming the heroes of our own stories. *Journal for the Education of the Gifted, 12*(2), 131-141.

Ochse, R. (1991). Why there were relatively few eminent women creators. *Journal of Creative Behavior, 25*(4), 334-343.

Ogbu, J. U. (1981). School ethnography: A multilevel approach. *Anthropology and Education Quarterly, 12*(1), 3-29.

Ogbu, J. U. (1985). Research currents: Cultural-ecological influences on minority school learning. *Language Arts, 62*(8), 860-868.

Ogbu, J. U. (1987). Variability in minority school performance: A problem in search of an explanation. *Anthropology and Education Quarterly, 18*(4), 312-334.

Ogbu, J. U. (1991). Immigrant and involuntary minorities in comparative perspective. In M. A. Gibson & J. U. Ogbu (Eds.), *Minority status and schooling: A comparative study of immigrant and involuntary minorities* (pp. 3-33). New York: Garland Publishing.

Olshen, S., & Matthews, D. (1987). The disappearance of giftedness in girls: An intervention strategy. *Roeper Review, 9*, 251-254.

Olszewiski-Kubilius, P., Kulieke, M. J., Shaw, B., Willis, G. B., & Krasney, N. (1990). Predictors of achievement in mathematics for gifted males and females. *Gifted Child Quarterly, 34*, 64-71.

O'Shea, M. M. (1998). *Characteristics of high ability women who achieve in the 95th percentile on the quantitative section of the scholastic achievement test.* Unpublished doctoral dissertation, University of Connecticut, Storrs.

Ost, O. M.. (1998). Teacher-parent interactions: An effective school-community environment. *Educational-Forum, 52*(2), 165-176.

Paley, V. G. (1984). *Boys and girls.* Chicago: The University of Chicago Press.

Pallas, A. M., & Alexander, K. L. (1983). Sex differences in quantitative SAT performance: New evidence on the differential coursework hypothesis. *American Educational Research Journal, 20*, 165-182

Parsons, J. E., Adler, T. F., & Kaczala, C. (1982). Socialization of achievement attitudes and beliefs: Parental influences. *Child Development, 53*, 310-321.

Perleth, C., & Heller, K. A. (1994). The Munich longitudinal study of giftedness. In R. F. Subotnik & K. K. Arnold (Eds.), *Beyond Terman: Contemporary longitudinal studies of giftedness and talent* (pp. 77-114). Norwood, NJ: Ablex

Perrine, J. (1989). Gifted underachievers. *North Carolina Association for Gifted and Talented Quarterly Journal, 2*(2), 39-44.

Perrone, P. A., & Van Den Heuvel, D. (1981). Career development of the gifted. *Journal of Career Education, 7,* 299-304.

Peters, P. (1990). TAG student defends program against critic [Letter to the editor]. *The Register Citizen,* p. 10.

Peterson, P. L., & Fenneman, E. (1985). Effective teaching, student enjoyment in classroom activities, and sex-related differences in learning mathematics. *Journal for Research in Mathematics Education, 13,* 66-335.

Peterson, C. C., & Peterson, J. L. (1973). Preference for sex of offspring as a measure of change in sex attitudes. *Psychology, 10*(2), 3-5.

Phillips, D. A. (1987). Socialization of perceived academic competence among highly competent children. *Child Development, 58,* 1308-1320.

Piechowski, M.. M. (1986). The concept of developmental potential. *Roeper Review, 8,* 190-197.

Pipher, M. (1994). *Reviving Ophelia: Saving the selves of adolescent girls.* New York: Ballantine Books.

Pirto, J. (1991). Why are there so few? (Creative women: visual artists, mathematicians, musicians). *Roeper Review, 13*(3), 142-147.

Pintrich, P. R., & Blumenfeld, P. C. (1985). Classroom experience and children's self-perceptions of ability, effort, and conduct. *Journal of Educational Psychology, 77,* 646-657.

Pogash, C. (1992, April). The brains behind 'Backlash.' *Working Woman, 17,* 64-68.

Pollard, D. S. (1989). Against the odds: A profile of academic achievers from the urban underclass. *Journal of Negro Education, 58*(3), 297-308.

Pomerleau, A., Bolduc, D., & Malcuit,C. (1990). Pink or blue: Environmental gender stereotypes in the first two years of life. *Sex Roles: A Journal of Research, 22*(5-6), 359-367.

Portner, J. (1997, October 15). Studies illuminate far-reaching ramifications of abuse of girls. *Education Week*, 12.

Ransome, W. (1993). *What every girl in school needs to know.* Concord, MA: National Coalition of Girls' Schools.

Rayman, P., & Brett, B. (1995, July/August). Women science majors. *The Journal of Higher Education, 66*, 388-414.

Read, C. R. (1991). Gender distribution in programs for the gifted. *Roeper Review, 13*, 188-193.

Reinen, J. I., & Plomp, T. (1994). *Gender and computer use: Another area of inequity?* (ERIC Document Reproduction Service No. ED 376 174)

Reis, S. M. (1995). Talent ignored, talent diverted: The cultural context underlying giftedness in females. *Gifted Child Quarterly, 39*(3), 162-170.

Reis, S. M. (1996). Older women's reflections on eminence: Obstacles and opportunities. In K. D. Arnold, K. D. Noble & R. F. Subotnik (Eds.), *Remarkable women: Perspectives on female talent development* (pp. 149-168). Cresskill, NJ: Hampton Press, Inc.

Reis, S. M., & Callahan, C. M. (1989). Gifted females: They've come a long way—or have they? *Journal for the Education of the Gifted, 12*(2), 99-117.

Reis, S. M., Callahan, C. M., & Goldsmith, D. (1996). Attitudes of adolescent gifted girls and boys toward education, achievement, and the future. In K. D. Arnold, K. D. Noble., & R. F. Subotnik (Eds.), *Remarkable women: Perspectives on female talent development* (pp. 209-224). Cresskill, NJ: Hampton Press, Inc.

Reis, S. M., & Diaz, E. (in press). Economically disadvantaged urban female students who achieve in schools. *The Urban Review.*

Reis, S. M., Hébert, T. P., Diaz, E. I., Maxfield, L. R., & Ratley, M. E. (1995). *Case studies of talented students who achieve and underachieve in an urban high school.* Manuscript in preparation.

Reis, S. M. & Kettle, K. (1994). *Project Parity Evaluation.* Unpublished evaluation report, Neag Center for Gifted Education and Talent Development.

Renzulli, J. S. (1977). *The enrichment triad model: A guide for developing defensible programs for the gifted and talented.* Mansfield Center, CT: Creative Learning Press.

Renzulli, J. S. (1978). *What makes giftedness?* Moravia, NY: Chronicle Guidance Publications, Inc.

Renzulli, J. S. (1986). The three ring conception of giftedness: A developmental model for creative productivity. In R. J. Sternberg & J. E. Davidson (Eds.), *Conceptions of giftedness* (pp. 53-92). Cambridge, MA: Cambridge University Press.

Renzulli, J. S. (1994). *Schools for talent development: A practical plan for total school improvement.* Mansfield, CT: Creative Learning Press.

Renzulli, J. S. (1997), *Interest-A-Lyzer.* Mansfield Center, CT: Creative Learning Press, Inc.

Renzulli, J. S., & Reis, S.M. (1991, Winter). The reform movement and the quiet crisis in gifted education. *Gifted Child Quarterly, 35*(1), 26-35.

Renzulli, J. S., & Reis, S. M. (1997), *The Schoolwide Enrichment Model.* Mansfield Center, CT: Creative Learning Press, Inc.

Rhenigold, H. L., & Cook, K. V. (1975). The content of boy's and girl's rooms as an index of parent behavior. *Child Development, 46,* 459-463.

Riordan, C. (1985). Public and catholic schooling: The effects of gender context policy. *American journal of education, 5,* 533.

Riordan, C. (1990). *Girls and boys in school: Together or separate?* New York: Teachers College Press.

Rizza, Mary. (1997), *Exploring successful learning with talented female adolescents.* Unpublished doctoral dissertation, University of Connecticut, Storrs.

Roberts, T. (1991). Gender and the influence of evaluations on self-assessments in achievement settings. *Psychological Bulletin, 109*(2), 297-308.

Roberts, T., & Nolen-Hoeksema, S. (1994). Gender comparisons in responsiveness to others' evaluations in achievement settings. *Psychology of Women Quarterly, 18,* 221-240.

Rodenstein, J. M., & Glickhauf-Hughes, C. (1979). Career and lifestyle determinants of gifted women. In N. Colangelo & R. T. Zaffran (Eds.), *New voices in counseling the gifted.* Dubuque, Iowa: Kendall/ Hunt.

Rodenstein, J. M., Pfleger, L., & Colangelo, N. (1977). Career development of gifted women. *The Gifted Child Quarterly, 21,* 340-347.

Roessner, B. A. (1998, May 17). The genesis of women. *The Hartford Courant,* p. B5

Rogers, P. (1990). Thoughts on power and pedagogy. In L. Burton (Ed.), *Gender and mathematics: An international perspective* (pp.38-46). London: Cassell.

Rosser, P. (1989). *Sex bias in college admissions tests: Why women lose out.* Cambridge, MA: National Center for Fair and Open Testing.

Rossi-Becker, J. (1994, April). *Research on gender and mathematics perspectives and new directions.* Paper presented at the meeting of the American Educational Research Association, New Orleans, LA.

Rubin, L. J., & Borgers, S. B. (1990). Sexual harassment in universities during the 1980s. *Sex Roles, 23*(7-8), 397-411.

Rubin, J. Z., Provenzano, F. J., & Luria, Z. (1974). The eye of the beholder: Parent's view on sex of newborns. *American Journal of Orthopsychiatry, 44,* 512-519.

Ruiz, R. (1989). Considerations in the education of gifted Hispanic students. In C. J. Maker & S. W. Schiever (Eds.), *Critical issues in gifted education: Defensible programs for cultural and ethnic minorities* (pp. 60-65). Austin, TX: Pro-Ed.

Runco, M. A. (1991). *Divergent thinking.* Norwood, NJ: Ablex.

Rutter, M. (1987). Psychosocial resilience and protective mechanisms. *American Journal of Orthopsychiatry, 37,* 317-331.

Sadker, M., & Sadker, D. (1985). Sexism in the schoolroom of the 80's. *Psychology Today, 19*(3), 54-57.

Sadker, M., & Sadker, D. (1994). *Failing at fairness: How America's schools cheat girls.* New York: Charles Scribner's Sons.

Sanborn, M. P. (1979). Career development: Problems of gifted and talented students. In N. Colangelo & R. T. Zaffrann (Eds.), *New voices in counseling the gifted* (pp.284-300). Dubuque, IA: Kendall/Hunt.

Sanders, J. S. (1986). *The neuter computer: Computers for girls and boys.* New York: Neal-Schuman Publishers.

Sanders, J. S. (1994). *Bibliography on gender equity in mathematics, science, and technology: Resources for classroom teachers.* New York: Gender Equity Program, Center for Advanced Study in Education, CUNY Graduate Center.

Sassen, G. (1980). Success anxiety in women: A constructivist interpretation of its source and its significance. *Harvard Education Review, 50*(1), 13-24.

Saying day care is bad for moms and families, church closes center. (1997, April 4). *The Chronicle,* p. 7.

Schmitz, C. C., & Galbraith, J. (1985). *Managing the social and emotional needs of the gifted.* Minneapolis, MN: Free Spirit Publishing.

Schmurak, C. B. (1996, April). *Following the girls: A longitudinal study of girls attitudes and aspirations at single sex and coeduation high schools.* Paper presented at the meeting of the American Educational Research Association, New York, NY.

Schrecker, E. W. (Ed.) (1998, March/April) Doing better: Annual report on the economic status of the profession, 1997-1998. *Academe, 84*(2).

Schroer, A. C. P., & Dorn, F. J. (1986). Enhancing the career and personal development of gifted college students. *Journal of Counseling and Development, 64,* 567-571.

Schubert, J. G. et al. (1984). *Ideas for equitable computer learning.* Palo Alto, CA: American Institutes for Research in Behavioral Sciences.

Schuler, P. A. (1997). *Characteristics and perceptions of perfectionism in gifted adolescents in a rural school environment.* Unpublished doctoral dissertation, University of Connecticut, Storrs.

Schunk, D. H. (1984). Sequential attributional feedback and children's achievement behaviors. *Journal of Educational Psychology, 75,* 511-518.

Schwartz, W. (1987). *Teaching science and mathematics to at risk students.* (ERIC Document Reproduction Service No. ED 289 948)

Schwartz, L. A., & Markham, W. T. (1985). Sex stereotyping in children's toy advertisements. *Sex Roles, 12*(1-2), 157-170.

Schwartz, L. L. (1980). Advocacy for the neglected gifted: Females. *Gifted Child Quarterly, 24,* 113-117.

Sheffield, L. J. (1994). *The development of gifted and talented mathematics students and the national council of teachers of mathematics standards.* Storrs, CT: The National Research Center on the Gifted and Talented.

Shepardson, D., & Pizzini, E. (1992). Gender bias in female elementary teachers' perceptions of the scientific ability of students. *Science Education, 76*(2), 147-153.

Shucard, S. B. (1991). Attributions and self-evaluations by gifted children under success-failure conditions and individualistic-competitive goal structures. *Dissertation Abstracts International, 52*(2), 483-A.

Siegle, D., & Reis, S. M. (1998). Gender differences in teacher and student perceptions of student ability and effort. *Gifted Child Quarterly, 42*(1), 39-47.

Silverman, L. K. (Ed.). (1993). *Counseling the gifted and talented.* Denver, CO: Love.

Simonton, D. K. (1978). The eminent genius in history: The critical role of creative development. *Gifted Child Quarterly, 22*(2), 187-195.

Singer, E. (1984). Reflections on sexual differences in creative productivity. *Journal of Contemporary Psychotherapy, 14*(2), 158-170.

Sloane, K. D. & Sosniak, L.A. (1985). The development of accomplished sculptors. In B. Bloom (Ed.), *The development of talent in young people* (pp. 90-138). New York: Ballantine

Steppe-Jones, C. (1986). Enhancing the intellectual potential of the minority gifted: A shared responsibility. *Negro Educational Review, 37*(3-4), 127-129.

Sternberg, R. J. (1986). A triarchic theory of intellectual giftedness. In R. J. Sternberg & J. E. Davidson (Eds.), *Conceptions of giftedness* (pp. 233-243). Cambridge, MA: Cambridge University Press.

Sternberg, R. J., & Lubart, T. I. (1995). *Defying the crowd.* New York: The Free Press.

Stevenson, H. W., & Newman, R. S. (1986). Long-term prediction of achievement in mathematics and reading. *Child Development, 57,* 646-659.

Subotnik, R. (1988). The motivation to experiment: A study of gifted adolescents' attitudes toward scientific research. *Journal for the Education of the Gifted, 11*(3), 19-35.

Subotnik, R., & Strauss, S. M. (1995). Gender differences in classroom participation and achievement. *The Journal of Secondary Gifted Education, 6*, 77-85.

Tannen, D. (1990). *You just don't understand.* New York: Ballantine Books.

Tidball, M. E. (1973, Spring). Perspective on academic women and affirmative action. *Educational Record, 54,* 130-135.

Tobin, K. G. & Garnett, P. J. (1987). Gender related differences in science activities. *Science Education, 71,* 91-103.

Torrance, E. P. (1997). *Manifesto for children.* Unpublished manuscript, University of Georgia, Athens.

Tyler, A. (1995). *Ladder of Years.* New York: Alfred Knopf.

United Nations Economic Commission for Europe. (1994). *Report of the high-level regional preparatory meeting for the fourth World Conference on Women* (GE.94-25379). New York: United Nations.

United Nations Economic Commission for Europe. (1994). *Report of the high-level regional preparatory meeting for the fourth World Conference on Women: Addendum* (GE.94-25382). New York: United Nations.

United Nations Economic Commission for Europe. (1994). *Report of the high-level regional preparatory meeting for the fourth World Conference on Women: Preambular Declaration* (GE.94-25385). New York: United Nations.

U. S. Bureau of the Census. (1995). *Current population reports.* Washington, DC: . S. Bureau of the Census.

Teenage wasteland? (1995, October 23). *U.S. News and World Report, 119 (16)*, 84-87.

Vernon-Gerstenfeld, S. (1989). Serendipity? Are there gender differences in the adoption of computers? A case study. *Sex Roles,* 161-173.

Vollmer, F. (1986). Why do men have higher expectancy than women? *Sex Roles, 14* 351-362.

Volman, M. (1997). Gender-related effects of computer and information literacy education. *Journal of Curriculum Studies,* 315-328.

Walberg, H. J., & Stariha, W. (1992). Productive human capital: Learning, creativity and eminence. *Creativity Research Journal, 5,* 323-340.

Walker, B., Reis, S., & Leonard, J. (1992, Fall). A developmental investigation of the lives of gifted women. *Gifted Child Quarterly, 36*(4), 201-206.

Webb, N. M. (1984). Sex differences in interaction and achievement in cooperative small groups. *Journal of Educational Psychology, 76,* 33-44.

Webb, N. M., & Kenderski, C. M. (1985). Mathematics small group interactions among high ability learners: Gender differences in small group interaction and achievement in high- and low-achieving classes. In L. C. Wilkinson & C. B. Marrett (Eds.), *Gender influences in classroom interaction* (pp. 209-236). New York: Academic Press.

Weiner, B. (1986). *An attributional theory of motivation and emotion.* New York: Springer-Verlag.

Wells, M. R. (1985, May/June). Gifted females: An overview for parents, teachers and counselors. *Gifted Child Today,* 43-46.

Werner, E. E. (1984). Research in review: Resilient children. *Young Children, 40*(1), 68-72.

Whittaker, C. E. (1997). Title IX twenty-five years later, women's basketball feels its impact. *Coaching Women's Basketball, 10-13.*

Women at thirtysomething. (1991, Fall). *OERI Bulletin,* p. 8.

Yee, D. & Eccles, J. (1988). Parent perceptions and attributions for children's math achievement. *Sex Roles, 19*(5-6), 317-334.

Yong, F. L. (1992). Mathematics and science attitudes of African-American middle grade students identified as gifted: Gender and grade differences. *Roeper Review, 14*(3), 136-140.

Zaldivar, R. A. (1997, November 30). In retirement, women face gender gap. Knight-Ridder Newspapers. *The Hartford Courant,* p. 1, 10.

Index

Index

J

K

Z

8686